THE STORY OF GARDENING

The Story of GARDENING

Martin Hoyles

JOURNEYMAN PRESS
LONDON • CONCORD, MASS

First published 1991 by Journeyman Press
345 Archway Road, London N6 5AA
and 141 Old Bedford Road,
Concord, MA 01742, USA

British Library Cataloguing in Publication Data
Hoyles, Martin
    The Story of Gardening.
    1. History of English gardens
    I. Title
    635.0941

    ISBN 1–85172–028–6

Library of Congress Cataloging in Publication Data
Hoyles, Martin
    The Story of Gardening / Martin Hoyles.
        p. cm.
    Includes bibliographical references.
    ISBN 1–85172–028–6

    1. Gardening–England–History. 2. Gardening–Political aspects-
    -England –History. I. Title.
    SB451.36.G7H69 1990
    635'.0942–dc20   90-31867
                                                                CIP

Designed by Ray Addicott in Stone Serif
Typeset by Stanford Desktop Publishing Services, Milton Keynes
Printed in Great Britain

Contents

INTRODUCTION 1

1. THE MEANING OF GARDENING 7

2. ENCLOSURE AND THE DIVISION OF LABOUR 23

3. MEDIEVAL, ARAB AND AZTEC GARDENING 54

4. JOSEPH BANKS AND AUSTRALIA 79

5. ROBERT FORTUNE IN CHINA 96

6. JOSEPH HOOKER AND KEW GARDENS 110

7. GARDEN CEMETERIES 130

8. PUBLIC PARKS 144

9. POLLUTION, GLASS AND BEDDING-OUT 169

10. WOMEN AND GARDENING 187

11. MODERN GARDENING 213

12. POLITICS, LANGUAGE AND EDUCATION 235

13. UTOPIA 262

AFTERWORD 290

BIBLIOGRAPHY 293

ACKNOWLEDGEMENTS 301

INDEX 303

In memory of my mother
Marjorie Moss

Introduction

It comes as a shock to put the words *politics* and *gardening* together. Usually they are seen as two completely separate spheres. What can gardening have to do with politics? Are they not polar opposites? Gardening is surely an escape from politics and the garden is a refuge from harsh political realities. People of all political persuasions are interested in gardening, and talking about plants and flowers can unite political opponents.

This book is a challenge to the view that gardening has nothing to do with politics, using the word politics in its widest sense to mean theories and practices based on power relations between people. To develop the argument it is necessary to look at the history of gardening and consider certain key themes.

Enclosure

The word 'garden' comes from the Old English 'geard', meaning a fence or enclosure, and from 'garth', meaning a yard or a piece of enclosed ground. *The Oxford Dictionary of English Etymology* gives the meaning of garden as 'enclosed cultivated ground' and *The Shorter Oxford English Dictionary* as 'an enclosed piece of ground devoted to the cultivation of flowers, fruit, or vegetables'. Enclosure is essential to gardening, and this raises fundamental questions, such as who is doing the enclosing, who owns the land, and who is being kept out.

John Clare, the Northamptonshire poet, recognised this issue. He was a cow-herd as a boy and then an under-gardener, and he witnessed the enclosures of the early nineteenth century:

> *Enclosure came and trampled on the grave*
> *Of Labour's rights and left the poor a slave.*

John Clare (1792–1864), gardener and poet,
by William Hilton, 1820.

The Division of Labour

This is a history of gardening, not gardens, so that the work involved in making a garden is not forgotten. Production is as important as consumption, and the division of labour in gardening needs analysis. So too does the gardener's pay. In 1838 in the London area the wage paid to a gardener was twelve shillings a week, less than that of a bricklayer's labourer, street-cleaner or dustman. The same low wage was paid in the royal gardens and also by the Horticultural Society at Chiswick.

English gardening cannot be viewed in isolation. Many Scottish gardeners, for example, have had a great influence on it. One in particular, John Claudius Loudon, stands out in the first half of the nineteenth century, and his writings figure largely in these pages. Neither can English gardening history ever ignore the impact on gardening style at the end of the nineteenth century of the Irishman William Robinson. Equally, no garden history book which I have read discusses the famous Welsh garden in Llangollen belonging to the Irish ladies Eleanor Butler and Sarah Ponsonby.

Colonialism

Gardening in England was affected by Roman and Norman invasions. It was also influenced by Arab gardening, particularly from Spain. European contact with Aztec culture led to further exchanges of plants and horticultural knowledge. This has to be seen, however, against the backdrop of colonialism. European invasions of Asia, Africa and the Americas, accompanied by virulent racism, set the scene for economic botany. This is the exploitation of plants for economic gain and it is closely connected with the development of gardening. This can be seen by looking closely at the activities of people such as Joseph Banks exploring Australia, Robert Fortune collecting plants in China, and Joseph Hooker developing Kew Gardens for the British Empire.

Today this uneven relationship, between Europe and South America for example, still persists. Some 40,000 women working in the Colombian flower industry suffer from rheumatism, eczema, damaged embryos, miscarriages, leukaemia, bronchitis, asthma, epilepsy and cancer, because of the pesticides which are used. Carnations, roses and chrysanthemums are exported from Colombia to Europe, particularly to Aalsmeer, just south of Amsterdam, which is the site of the most important flower market in the world. Eleven million flowers are sold there each day, representing a value of over 1,000 million dollars a year. But as one of the Colombian women put it: 'We die because of the flowers.'

The Industrial Revolution

Gardens are enclosed parts of the countryside, but they have often been developed in towns. They are a link between town and country. After the industrial revolution, the loss of contact with the countryside was felt acutely. Pressure from both the working class and middle class led to the movement for public parks and gardens, and to the idea of the garden cemetery. The smoke and dirt of the cities was often so poisonous as to make gardening virtually impossible, and this issue of environmental pollution is still with us.

Eleanour Sinclair Rohde (1881–1950), gardener and author of many gardening books, including The Story of the Garden *published in 1932, reprinted in 1989. She also became President of the Society of Women Journalists.*

Sexism

Sexism is not a topic dealt with in most gardening history books, yet it is clearly of major concern when over half the population seldom have access to power in gardening activities and are so often confined to weeding. Eleanour Rohde in 1932 commented on how few gardening books had been written by women, and added:

> Yet the care of the garden had always been considered the province of the lady of the house and at least since early medieval days women had been employed as gardeners, though apparently never for anything of greater importance than weeding and watering.

Access and Education

Today gardening is the most popular outdoor leisure activity in England. It provides recreation and creative activities for millions, but there is still a problem of access to gardens and gardening. There is a tension between those who have a garden and those who have not. If there were another Great Fire of London, not everyone would have the advantage of a garden which Samuel Pepys had in 1666. He dug a pit in his garden and there he buried, among other things, his wine and his 'parmazan cheese'.

There is also a split between the public and private spheres of gardening and a division between amateur and professional. Many gardeners feel overawed by the academic disciplines associated with gardening, and there is clearly a need to bridge the linguistic gap between them. It is worth asking too what place horticulture could have in our education system.

The Politics of Gardening

It would be strange if such a fundamental human activity as gardening did not have a connection with politics. Why then is it so seldom acknowledged? Gardening is often seen as a 'natural' occupation, just as capitalism and patriarchy are assumed to be 'natural' conditions which cannot be changed. It is part of a particular political ideology.

Many of the common assumptions in English gardening history reflect this ideology. Why, for instance, is medieval gardening so often looked down on? Why are the influences of Arab and Aztec gardening seldom recognised? Why is the Commonwealth period thought to be so barren? How can people be so proud of the English landscape garden once they know of the exploitation and eviction that was involved in its making? How can the plant hunters all be presented as such noble creatures?

Given the recent growth of the history of popular culture, it is surprising that English historians have not looked more closely at gardening. This book is intended to begin to fill that gap. It is aimed at those who are interested in history and politics, but also at the millions of gardeners who want to think more about the social implications of gardening and to find ways in which their pleasure in gardening can be enjoyed by all.

1

The Meaning of Gardening

How can you be content to be in the World like Tulips in a
Garden, to make a fine shew and be good for nothing?
Mary Astell, *A Serious Proposal to the Ladies* (1694)

Ah, yet, ere I descend to th' Grave
May I a small House, and large Garden have!
Abraham Cowley (1618–67) 'The Wish'

Behind every beautiful flower is a death.

Flowers grow beautiful while women wither away.
Women working in the Colombian flower industry, from the film
Love, Women, and Flowers (1987)

I would say that gardens are non-political.
Ray Desmond (1987) (author of *Bibliography of British Gardens*)

I get away from the Commons during the summer and the
spring and I go down to Kew Gardens two or three times
and walk down Rhododendron Valley ... You're walking in
the park and you're enjoying it and looking at the beautiful
magnolia trees and then you suddenly realise that it's
going to be Prime Minister's Question Time and you're
number three and you've got a bit of a chance and so
you've got to sharpen it up and be topical at the same
time. Dennis Skinner MP 'Desert Island Discs', 7 January 1990

One of the richest aspects of gardening history is that of meaning and association, the ideology of gardening, the ways in which connotations of gardening change and poets and others write about it. People use gardens and gardening for many different ends. Cottage gardens, suburban gardens and landscape gardens serve different functions and the work in them means different things to the gardener. Allotments and public parks have their specific histories in which people struggle over their meaning and their use. Cemeteries can change their use and become public gardens. Rare plants become common and other plants are threatened with extinction. New flowers are imported or created. Attitudes to nature range from seeing it as sinful and disorderly to appreciating its goodness and beauty. There is a kaleidoscope of cultural meanings attached to gardening.

THE COUNTRY AND THE CITY

A garden, representing the countryside as opposed to the city, has often been seen as a place where one can escape from the corruption of urban politics. The image occurs in Roman authors, such as Quintilian who contrasts urban greed with rural innocence, and Juvenal who compares city dangers with the tranquillity of the countryside.

In *The Garden and the City* Maynard Mack shows how this idea became part of our mythology in the seventeenth century:

> Garden imagery and garden situations, in poems of all genres by poets of all persuasions – Jonson, Herrick, Herbert, Waller, Denham, Cowley, Vaughan, Marvell, Milton, to mention only a few – had been made the vehicle for some of the deepest feelings of the age and some of its shrewdest comments on the human condition. Moreover the relevant classical texts, all those passages in the Roman writers glorifying the retired life – its simplicity, frugality, self-reliance, and independence – had been so often culled, so often translated, paraphrased, and imitated that they had become part of the mind of England, and indeed of Europe.

One of those poets, Abraham Cowley (1618–67), who had been in exile with the court in France, wrote a long poem called 'The Garden' in which he praises the 'cool retreat' of the country garden as opposed to the 'immoderate heat' of the town with its 'dirt and smoke'. In another poem, 'The Wish', he writes of wanting to escape from 'this great hive, the city' with its 'crowd, and buzz, and murmurings'. His only problem then would be that others might follow suit:

> I should have then this only fear,
> Lest men, when they my pleasures see,
> Should hither throng to live like me,
> And so make a city here.

8

Raymond Williams argues in *The Country and the City* that this pastoral idyll came to be seen by some in the late seventeenth and early eighteenth centuries as a 'description and thence an idealisation of actual English country life and its social and economic relations'. But it was a mystification of real social relations. The split between urban and rural was a diversion from analysing the system of economic oppression which united them both: 'It was precisely at this point that the "town and country" fiction served: to promote superficial comparison and to prevent real ones.'

In China there is also a tradition of seeing gardening as an alternative to politics. The poet T'ao Ch'ien is portrayed in an eighteenth-century painting walking in the garden of a small country cottage. An enthusiast for chrysanthemums, which originated from China, he was once offered a high government post, but turned it down in order to cultivate his flowers and write poetry. Another example is the garden in Soochow which is called the 'Garden of the Unsuccessful Politician'. The politician concerned was Wang Chin Tsz who said, 'I have built this garden as a memorial to my failure in politics.' After the Chinese Revolution the last Chinese Emperor, who had collaborated with the Japanese, was set to work as a gardener.

An article in *The Gardener's Weekly Magazine* of April 1860 echoes the idea of gardening being incompatible with public affairs. The author claims that gardening comes naturally to the infant who is no sooner walking than planting a flower, and also to the school-boy with his little plot: 'In manhood our attention is generally demanded by more active and imperious duties; but as age obliges us to retire from public business, the love of gardening returns to soothe our declining years.' The present-day allotment is also seen, by Crouch and Ward, as a form of escape, 'representing for many a haven where can be found solace in the midst of a more sophisticated, but ultimately alien, world'.

Cultivating One's Garden

The most famous expression in European culture of gardening meaning retirement or retreat comes from Voltaire's *Candide*, written in 1758. Gardening is synonymous with a withdrawal from the hurly-burly of life, for after all the calamities of his life Candide retires to the country to cultivate his garden. Dr Pangloss, Candide's tutor, describes the violent deaths of many kings and politicians, and the conclusion to be drawn from this is spelt out by an old man sitting at his door, under an arbour of orange trees, in the Turkish countryside. He is unaware of the latest political news from Constantinople and is not interested in finding out: 'I suppose it's true that those who enter politics sometimes come to a miserable end, and deserve it; but I never bother myself about what happens in Constantinople. I send my garden stuff to be sold there, and that's enough for me.'

Voltaire himself had a garden called 'Les Délices' which was the most famous of those laid out in the English style in Switzerland. Rousseau, like Voltaire, was also keen on gardening and advocated a return to nature. In *Émile* he argues that education can best take place in the countryside with plenty of practical activity. As a young man he had become interested in gardening while staying at the house of Madame de Warens in Chambéry. Later in *Julie, ou la Nouvelle Héloïse* he describes his ideal garden as one consisting of meadows, streams, glades and flowers. The Marquis de Girardin, admirer and patron of Rousseau, had a garden built in similar romantic style at Ermenonville, outside Paris, where Rousseau's tomb was later placed on a small island in the lake. Throughout this picturesque landscape garden Latin sayings and quotations from Voltaire and Rousseau were displayed, evoking the requisite moods.

In *The Decameron* by Boccaccio, a group of wealthy young people retire to a country estate outside Florence to escape the Black Death of 1348. A 'delectable garden and meadows lay all around' and the whole house was 'adorned with seasonable flowers of every description'. There they told their tales and 'sauntered through gardens, conversing, weaving garlands and singing songs of love'. Similarly Charles II took refuge at Sion House, with its famous old Tudor garden, during the Plague in 1665.

THE LADIES OF LLANGOLLEN

In Britain the eighteenth-century fascination with retirement, which had been inspired by Rousseau, found one of its most famous practical expressions in the lives of the Ladies of Llangollen. In 1778, after one abortive attempt, two aristocratic Irish women, Eleanor Butler and Sarah Ponsonby, succeeded in eloping to Wales, Sarah to escape marriage and Eleanor to avoid being sent to a convent. They were aged 39 and 23 respectively and were to live together in Llangollen, in a cottage which they christened 'Plas Newydd', for 50 years. Their lesbian relationship caused something of a scandal, but their background and connections, as well as their conservative politics, helped them to survive.

With the assistance of a series of gardeners they created a garden on their four-acre plot which became famous as early as 1782. In 1785 they had a request from Queen Charlotte to send her a plan of the cottage and garden.

The cottage of the ladies of Llangollen, c.1815.

Their romantic garden was offset by their hard-headed policy as employers. They kept sacking their gardeners, either for being drunk or for being Methodists, presumably not both at the same time. One of their early employees provides a further indication of the difficult working conditions. He was required to sleep on the premises every night of the week except Saturday, when he was allowed off to walk the twelve miles to Wrexham to spend the night with his wife and six children. The gardener's pay was also very low. In 1800 the gardener was being paid sixpence a week *less* than twelve years earlier, despite the huge rise in the cost of living caused by the war with France.

According to Elizabeth Mavor in *The Ladies of Llangollen,*

11

Eleanor and Sarah planned a garden 'which was to be useful as it was beautiful', containing 'a fowl yard, a stable, dairy, potager, melon and mushroom beds, vines, while they were already raising roses and holly bushes from seeds they had collected'. They laid out asparagus beds and planted peach trees and flower borders. The garden had winding gravel paths and separate fruit, vegetable and flower enclosures. Behind the cottage a lawn sloped away to a shrubbery.

In 1788 one of their gardeners, Moses Jones, who was later discharged for 'repeated and outrageous Drunkeness', planted a thicket of 'Lilaks, Laburnums, Seringas, White Broom, Weeping Willow, Apple trees, poplar ...'. Sarah's day-book for 1789 lists 44 different kinds of roses in the garden, including 'Maiden's Blush', 'Rosa Mundi', 'Rose d'Amour' and Provence roses. Their friend Anna Seward recorded that not a 'single weed' could be found in the garden. At the age of 80, Eleanor wrote in her diary that she was still working in the garden 'employed in planting hollies'.

Their gardening was in the picturesque style, developed by William Gilpin, Uvedale Price and Richard Payne Knight at the end of the eighteenth century. The library at Plas Newydd contained all the works of Gilpin and two copies of Price's book *The Picturesque*. William Shenstone, the poet, had also recommended this kind of gardening in an essay entitled 'Unconnected Thoughts on Gardening', published in 1764, and he put it into practice on his estate at the Leasowes, on the borders of Shropshire and Worcestershire. The style was a variation of the landscape garden, but instead of the broad sweep of lawn, lake and trees, it involved a variety of scenes, contrasts of colour and texture, light and shade, evoking different emotions.

Eleanor and Sarah had Gothic garden seats installed and a summerhouse built above a rushing stream, furnished with a library of carefully selected books. They became interested in wild gardening, rented more land and had rustic bridges constructed across the brook. Cascades and pools were created and ferns and mosses grown. As at Ermenonville, appropriate Latin quotations were fixed to the trees. In *The Second Sex* Simone de Beauvoir claims that the two women 'were able to create a peaceful Eden apart from the ordinary world'. But sometimes the retreat seemed far from peaceful as there was a constant stream of visitors, including many famous figures of the day, such as Wordsworth, Sheridan, Josiah Wedgwood, Walter Scott, Humphrey Davy and the Duke of Wellington.

GARDENING IN PRISON

The idea of gardening as consolation is used not only by those who can afford a garden retreat, but also by the poor and the imprisoned. Particularly in the nineteenth century, when enclosure and unemployment forced people in their hundreds of thousands into the industrial towns and cities to work in factories, many felt the loss of contact with gardens. It seemed 'natural' to be in touch with plants and to have a right to grow flowers, as John Loudon expressed it in his *Encyclopaedia of Gardening* in 1822:

> The laborious journeyman-mechanic, whose residence, in large cities, is often in the air, rather than on the earth, decorates his garret-window with a garden of pots. The debtor deprived of personal liberty, and the pauper in the work house, divested of all property in external things, and without any fixed object on which to place their affections, sometimes resort to this symbol of territorial appropriation and enjoyment. So natural it is for all to fancy they have an inherent right in the soil.

Charles Dickens makes a similar point in the address which he gave to the Gardeners' Benevolent Institution on 14 June 1852: 'The poor man in crowded cities gardens still in jugs and basins and bottles; in factories and workshops people garden; and even the prisoner is found gardening in his lonely cell, after years and years of solitary confinement.'

In prison making a garden is a sign of hope and freedom. In 1662 when John Lambert, the parliamentary general, was tried and condemned to death, he was sent for a short while to Guernsey, where he continued his botanising and gardening. British civilians, interned in Germany during the First World War, cultivated gardens in their prison camp at Ruhleben, on the outskirts of Berlin. They even became affiliated to the Royal Horticultural Society which sent them seeds and bulbs. Rosa Luxemburg, the Polish revolutionary socialist who was also imprisoned during the First World War, made a garden in her prison yard and managed as well to continue her studies in botany and geology. As a child she had shown her fascination for flowers by staying up all night to watch a rose open.

Leigh Hunt, poet and journalist, made a garden when he was

imprisoned for seditious libel in 1813. He had written an article in his paper, the *Examiner*, calling the Prince Regent, the future King George IV,

> a violator of his word, a libertine over head and ears in disgrace, a despiser of domestic ties, the companion of gamblers and demireps, a man who has just closed half a century without one single claim on the gratitude of his country, or the respect of posterity!

For that he was sentenced to two years in prison and a fine of £1,000. He was ill when sent to gaol and was put in a ward in the prison infirmary where he 'papered the walls with a trellis of roses'.

Part of the prison yard he fenced off with 'green palings, adorned it with a trellis, bordered it with a thick bed of earth from a nursery, and even contrived to have a grass-plot'. In his autobiography he goes on:

> The earth I filled with flowers and young trees. There was an apple-tree, from which we managed to get a pudding the second year. As to my flowers, they were allowed to be perfect. Thomas Moore, who came to see me with Lord Byron, told me he had seen no such heart's-ease.

In the autumn he grew 'scarlet runners' up the trellis.

His wife was eventually allowed to live with him in prison, where their eldest daughter was born:

> I was obliged to play the physician myself, the hour having taken us by surprise. But her mother found many unexpected comforts; and during the whole of her confinement, which happened to be in very fine weather, the garden door was set open, and she looked upon trees and flowers.

William Cobbett also maintained his interest in gardening whilst in prison. In 1809 he was sentenced to two years in Newgate Gaol for criminal libel, but carried on running his farm and garden with the help of his eldest son and daughter. In *Advice to Young Men* he describes his enjoyment of flowers in prison:

> We had a *hamper* with a lock and two keys, which came up once a week, or oftener, bringing me fruit and all sorts of country fare ... The hamper brought me plants, bulbs, and the like, that I might see the size of them; and almost every one sent his or her *most beautiful*

14

William Cobbett (1763–1835) author of The English Gardener
engraving by F. Bartalozzi after J.R. Smith.

flowers, the earliest violets, and primroses, and cowslips, and blue-
bells; the earliest twigs of trees; and, in short, every thing that they
thought calculated to delight me.

In 1833 Loudon records in the *Gardener's Magazine* his visit to
the garden of Reading Gaol:

The Governor has a taste not only for gardening, but for natural
history. He has on his lawn or grass plot, a beautiful piece of
rockwork, composed of flints and fragments of mural antiquities. He
has also a variety of plants of the choicest kinds, such as Wistaria,
double furze, Ribes several species, Petunia phoenicia, and numerous
pelargoniums, the whole mixed with fruit trees. Every advantage
was taken of the high brick walls of the gaol for training vines and
fruit trees.

Loudon saw the prisoners watering the plants and observed how neatly they kept the garden. Nevertheless he felt 'the deepest regret at seeing so many persons imprisoned for mere trifles, without any reference to their reformation; which imprisonment, as the gaoler himself remarked, could only have the effect of making them worse.'

GARDENING AND MORALITY

The public gardens created in the nineteenth century were meant to decrease drunkenness and improve manners. A letter to *The Floricultural Cabinet and Florists' Magazine* makes the same point about private gardens for the working class: 'How desirable to induce the working-man to attend to his little plot, and desert the beer-shop and skittle-ground.' A writer in the *Cottage Gardener* in the middle of the century continues the theme: 'There is moral beauty, too, in the cultivated cottage garden. Neatness and attendance bespeak activity, diligence, and care; neglect and untidiness tell of the *beer-house.*'

George Johnson in *A History of English Gardening* makes even greater claims for the moral influence of private gardens in maintaining social order:

> The labourer who possesses and delights in the garden appended to his Cottage is generally among the most decent of his class; he is seldom a frequenter of the ale-house; and there are few among them so senseless as not readily to engage in its cultivation when convinced of the comforts and gain derivable from it. When the lower order of a state are contented, the abettors of anarchy cabal for the destruction of its civil tranquility in vain, for they have to efface the strongest of all earthly associations, home and its hallowed accompaniments, from the attachment of the labourer, before he will assist in tearing them from others, in the struggle to effect which, he has nothing definite to gain, and all those flowers of life to lose.

The Polish botanical explorer Mlokosewitch established a 'teaching garden' at his home where his children could learn the elements of natural history 'as a guarantee of moral purity'. Dickens, in his plans for an Asylum for Fallen Women, sees gardening as a way of reforming prostitutes: 'The cultivation of little gardens, if they be no bigger than graves, is a great resource and a great reward. It has always been found to be productive of good effects wherever it has been tried.' Gilbert White, on the other hand, extols the virtues of natural history for the rich:

> Happy would it be for many more men of fortune if they knew what to do with their time; if they knew how to shun 'The pains and penalties of Idleness', how much dissipation, riot and excess would they escape.

Budding's new lawn mower advertised in 1832.

When the lawn-mower was invented it was advertised in the *Gardener's Magazine* of 1832 as providing 'amusing, useful and healthy exercise'. This is the purpose which Cobbett endorses in *The English Gardener* in 1829:

> Gardening in general is favourable to the well-being of man. As the taste for it decreases in any country, vicious amusements and vicious habits are sure to increase. Gardening is a source of much greater profit than is generally imagined; but, merely as an amusement, or recreation, it is a thing of great value: it is a pursuit not only compatible with, but favourable to, the study of any art or science: it is conducive to health, by means of the irrestible temptation which it offers to early rising; to the stirring abroad upon one's legs; for a man may really ride till he cannot walk, sit till he cannot stand, and lie abed till he cannot get up. It tends to turn the minds of youth from amusements and attachments of a frivolous or vicious nature: it is a taste which is indulged at home: it tends to make home pleasant, and to endear us to the spot on which it is our lot to live.

GARDENING AND POLITICS

Thomas Fairfax, who became Commander-in-Chief of the New Model Army at the age of 33, managed to combine enthusiasm for gardening and for politics. In 1641 he supported the citizens of Manchester petitioning for a university and he had a number of political discussions with Winstanley, despite Winstanley's refusal to remove his hat. He was not unduly worried by the Diggers taking over land to farm communally, but the Leveller revolt was too radical for him and he was instrumental in its suppression at Burford in 1649, ordering the execution of its leaders.

In June 1650 Fairfax resigned as Lord General of the army because he disapproved of Cromwell's plans to invade Scotland, and he retired to his garden at Nunappleton, just south of York. In the same year, the poet Andrew Marvell, who was Milton's secretary and later MP for Hull, joined Fairfax on his estate as tutor to Mary, Fairfax's only child.

Vita Sackville-West called Marvell 'my most delectable poet'. There is a tension in his garden poems between the contemplative life and the life of action. In 'The Garden' he recalls the 'happy

Nunappleton House today.

garden-state' in Eden and compares the 'delicious solitude' of the garden to the 'rude society' outside. But in his poem 'An Horatian Ode upon Cromwell's Return from Ireland' he praises Cromwell's decision to leave his garden and change the course of English history:

> *And, if we would speak true,*
> *Much to the Man is due:*
> *Who, from his private Gardens, where*
> *He liv'd reserved and austere,*
> *As if his highest plot*
> *To plant the Bergamot,*
> *Could by industrious Valour climbe*
> *To ruine the great Work of Time,*
> *And cast the Kingdoms old*
> *Into another Mold.*

In 'Upon Appleton House' Marvell describes Fairfax's garden and its fort-like flower-beds, guarded by sentinel bees, as the general reviews his regimented tulips:

> *See how the flowers, as at parade,*
> *Under their colours stand display'd:*
> *Each regiment in order grows,*
> *That of the tulip, pink and rose.*

The poet expresses regret that Fairfax has now retired to his garden and abandoned the power which may have helped make England a paradise once more:

> *And yet there walks one on the Sod*
> *Who, had it pleased him and God,*
> *Might once have made our Gardens spring*
> *Fresh as his own and flourishing.*

In the same period Ralph Austen saw a close connection between horticulture, Puritanism and politics. In his writing he wants to use his horticultural discoveries to convert the reader to Puritan Christianity. He uses gardening images to portray the revolution which he supports. The mess caused by winter pruning is likened to the violent political changes taking place, promising a good crop the following year. He describes the high yield of small fruit trees to prove that low-born 'mechanic preachers' are the best ministers, and that bulky unproductive trees, representing the religious establishment, should be cut down. Wild trees are lost souls, but cultivated trees in a walled garden are saved. Fruit-growing gives pleasure and profit to the body and the mind. Austen believed horticulture could establish the kingdom of heaven on earth. It would make England 'another Canaan, flowing with Milke and hony'.

John Bunyan, similarly, likens his church to a garden: 'Christians are like the flowers in the garden, that stand and grow where the gardener hath planted them.' They are 'jointly nour-ished and become nourishers of one another'. The flowers vary in 'stature, in quality and colour, and smell, and virtue', but 'where the gardener has set them, there they stand, and quarrel not one with another'.

A contemporary preacher, Paul Hobson, speaks of his church as 'a garden inclosed', compared to the 'confused wilderness' of the Church of England. As Christopher Hill writes of Bunyan in *A Turbulent, Seditious and Fractious People*: 'The beauty of holiness consists not in incense or stained glass or deferential bowing, but in flowers helping one another to grow: and all flowers in the garden are equal.'

'The pursuit of politics from the vantage of retirement' is the way Maynard Mack describes Alexander Pope's use of his garden in Twickenham in the 1730s. Safely outside the ten-mile exclusion zone for Catholics, Pope 'nourished the self-image of retired leisure', but also 'mounted a satirical campaign of some intensity against the court of George Augustus and the ministry of Robert Walpole'. In the same context Mack quotes from Marvell's poem 'Upon Appleton House':

> *How safe, methinks, and strong, behind*
> *These Trees have I incamp'd my Mind;*
> *Where Beauty, aiming at the Heart,*
> *Bends in some Tree its useless Dart;*
> *And where the World no certain Shot*
> *Can make, or me it toucheth not.*
> *But I on it securely play,*
> *And gaul its Horsemen all the Day.*

Vita Sackville-West consoled herself gardening at Sissinghurst during the dark days before and during the Second World War:

> *Yet shall the garden with the state of war*
> *Aptly contrast, a miniature endeavour*
> *To hold the graces and the courtesies*
> *Against a horrid wilderness.*

She had plans to commit suicide if the Germans landed in Kent. Nevertheless she planted for the future, in particular a new pink magnolia which was very slow-growing: 'I do not think we should be put off by such considerations. A hundred years hence someone will come across it growing among the ruins of the tower and will say Someone must have once cared for this place.' Her philosophy was alternatively expressed as: 'Let us plant and be merry, for next autumn we may all be ruined.'

Shortly before her death she wrote a letter to her husband explaining how she saw that her gardening, however futile, was better than demonstrating against nuclear weapons. Pleasure is opposed to politics:

> Meanwhile I go on with my futile little occupation. It sometimes seems rather silly, but as Voltaire wisely remarked, Il faut cultiver notre jardin. It is really better to have created a Jardin which gives pleasure to us as well as to many other people, than for me to go and sit down in Trafalgar Square.

Socialists too have often encouraged this split between pleasure and politics. Politics is seen as a serious, joyless business, while gardening and other forms of pleasure are considered a diversionary escape, or something unattainable. It was to counter this attitude that the slogan 'Bread and Roses' was created by women workers during the 1912 textile strike in Lawrence, Massachusetts. The struggle of these young women, Italian, Polish, Russian and Lithuanian, was commemorated in a song written by James Oppenheimer:

> *As we come marching, marching, unnumbered women dead*
> *Go crying through our singing their ancient cry for bread.*
> *Small art and love and beauty their drudging spirits knew*
> *Yes it is bread we fight for ... but we fight for roses too.*

Why not make a garden *and* sit down in Trafalgar Square?
The strength of socialism is that it recognises where the key

problem lies – in the private ownership of property and the exploitation of labour. This has led to great gardens being created by the poor for the rich, to alienated production for private consumption. The history of the enclosure of land and the division of labour requires a detailed examination.

2

Enclosure and the Division of Labour

The law locks up both man and woman
Who steals a goose from off a common,
But lets the greater felon loose
Who steals the common from the goose.

Anon

England black with industrialism, foul with poverty, irri-
descent with the scum of luxury, was held up to my infant
eyes as the noblest work of God and the aristocracy. I was
exhorted to glory in industrialism and pity such savage
parts as Ceylon and Burma, where you may travel for
years and never come on anything like Wigan and Burnley.
A stainless history of England was produced by the process
of elimination. I was never taught that in the fifteenth
century there was a green and happy England in which the
common labouring man was neither starved nor landless. I
was never taught how this class was betrayed into poverty:
how, after the quick decline caused by the royal debase-
ment of the currency, the landlord and the farmer slowly
bled the labouring classes till they fell weakly into the
hands of the capitalists at the beginning of the nineteenth
century.   Rebecca West, *The Clarion* (1913)

Enclosure like a Buonoparte let not a thing remain,
It levelled every bush and tree and levelled every hill
And hung the moles for traitors, though the brook is running still
It runs a naked stream cold and chill.

John Clare, 'Remembrances' (1832–5)

The forces of production, the state of society, and
consciousness, can and must come into contradiction with
one another, because the division of labour implies the
possibility, nay the fact that intellectual and material

23

activity - enjoyment and labour, production and consump-
tion - devolve on different individuals, and that the only
possibility of their not coming into contradiction lies in the
negation in its turn of the division of labour.

Karl Marx, *The German Ideology* (1846)

Who built Thebes, with its seven gates?
In books we find the names of kings.
Did the kings drag along the lumps of rock?
And Babylon, many times destroyed -
Who rebuilt it so many times?
Where did the builders of glittering Lima live?
On the evening, when the Chinese Wall was finished,
Where did the masons go?

Bertolt Brecht, 'A Worker Questions History' (1935)

The garden is a powerful image in our culture, but it is some-times difficult to separate the myth from the reality. The myth is tied up with religion, a story of the past or a dream of things to come. It is also attached to real gardens which have acquired symbolic importance for representing fabulous wealth and luxury, such as the hanging gardens of Babylon, which were one of the seven wonders of the world, or Kubla Khan's gardens in China. The social relations involved in making such royal gardens are largely ignored, only the finished product remaining in our minds.

The same can be said of eighteenth-century English landscape gardens. It is often claimed that these are the glory of English gardening, the only creation in the visual arts which is peculiarly English, and which has been exported all over the world as 'le jardin anglais'. According to garden history books these gardens were made by William Kent, 'Capability' Brown and Humphrey Repton, but little mention is made of those who undertook the actual physical work. There is a marked division of labour between those who did the mental work of design and those who carried out the manual work of construction. A similar division exists between those who produced the gardens and those who enjoyed them.

Little stress is normally laid on the enormous upheavals in ordinary people's lives which took place in order to make these gardens or parks. Not only was common land enclosed and laws passed to uphold the power of property, but whole communities were sometimes uprooted to make way for the new landscapes.

When Adam delved and Eve span
Who was then the gentleman

This rhetorical question was used as a political slogan in the Peasants' Revolt. Pen and ink drawing by Burne-Jones with lettering by William Morris for the frontispiece to Morris's A Dream of John Ball, 1888.

THE GARDEN OF EDEN AND PARADISE

According to the Bible, life began in a garden and gardening is the oldest profession: 'God planted a garden eastward in Eden; and there he put the man he had formed.' It was 'pleasant to the sight, and good for food'. Adam was the first gardener and had to 'dress it and keep it'. Apart from that, all he had to do was think up names for everything and sleep; though one night he did lose one of his ribs and wake up with a woman. When he finally ate the fruit of the tree of the knowledge of good and evil, his punishment was to be banished from the garden, to be confronted by 'thorns and thistles', and to have to work: 'In the sweat of thy face shalt thou eat bread.' Tending the garden of Eden evidently produced no sweat and there were no weeds.

The story can also be read as an account of the change from a hunting, food-gathering community to a farming society. The former relied on the bounty of nature; the latter demanded more complex social organisation. Settled farming communities eventually led to the development of towns for marketing produce, and to the invention of writing and mathematics for accountancy. Farming also led to the second crucial division of labour, after that between male and female, between those who owned the land or animals and those who had to till the land or look after the animals.

The first division of labour is referred to in the Bible, since God created Eve to be a 'help meet' for Adam. The second division of labour is less apparent, though you could see God as the owner of the garden and Adam as his employee. As we shall see, this division of labour in gardening is often obscured. It was clear to the Aborigines, however, who reinterpreted the story of Eden as being a tale about injustice. They saw God as white, and Adam and Eve as black. The expulsion from Eden explained why the Aborigines had so little and why the white settlers had all the power and the food they needed.

Life also ends in a garden - in paradise, if you are fortunate. The word 'paradise' comes from the old Persian *pairidaeza* which means an enclosed park used for hunting by the king. It eventually came to mean not only the garden of Eden, but also the equivalent in Islam to heaven, as described in the Koran:

> This is the Paradise which the Righteous have been promised. There shall flow in it rivers of unpolluted water and rivers of milk for ever fresh; rivers of delectable wine and rivers of clearest honey. They shall eat therein of every fruit and receive forgiveness from their Lord.

This passage echoes the four rivers in Eden and the original sin of Adam, now atoned. The garden contains trees and fountains, protecting those within its gates from the scorching heat and the biting cold: 'Trees will spread their shade around them and fruits will hang in clusters over them.' A garden divided by four rivers is also depicted in the Vedas, the Hindu holy books; whilst the Aztec heaven was seen as a place to 'revel amidst the rich blossoms and odours of the gardens of paradise'.

ROYAL GARDENS

The kind of garden which in reality corresponded to these visions of paradise required great wealth and an enormous amount of labour to produce. Many of the trees, for example, were imported from other countries. Queen Hatshepsut of Egypt had incense trees brought from Somalia, and Tiglath-Pileser, King of the Assyrians around 1100 BC, records:

> Cedars and box, & allakanu wood have I carried off from the countries I conquered, trees that none of my forefathers have possessed, these trees have I taken, and planted them in mine own country, in the parks of Assyria have I planted them.

In 1495 BC Queen Hatshepsut had incense trees brought to Egypt from Somalia.

27

Often there were elaborate machines for watering the gardens, as in the hanging gardens of Babylon 'built' by Nebuchadnezzar in the sixth century BC. Water was drawn up from the river Euphrates to the top of the gardens and then channelled through conduits. The gardens themselves were made up of a series of huge terraces and galleries built on a hillside, supported by arches up to 170 feet high, with walls 22 feet thick.

Similarly, a century before the Spanish arrived, in the Aztec hanging gardens of Texcotzingo an aqueduct of baked clay was constructed to supply the terraces with water from a distance of eleven miles. Mountains and valleys were levelled to let the water flow under its own power to the gardens, which had been built on the top of a hill. There the water was fed through a system of wells, fountains and canals to irrigate all the plants. A flight of 520 steps led to the top. In Peru the Incas built long irrigation canals and subterranean aqueducts, one of which measured 'between four and five hundred miles'.

When Marco Polo journeyed to China at the end of the thirteenth century he gave an account of Kubla Khan's gardens in what is now Beijing:

> The Great Khan has made an earthwork, that is to say a mound fully 100 paces in height and over a mile in circumference. This mound is covered with a dense growth of trees, all evergreens that never shed their leaves. Whenever the Great Khan hears tell of a particularly fine tree he has it pulled up, roots and all with a quantity of earth, and has it transported to this mound by elephants.

Coleridge writes, in 'Kubla Khan', about one of the Mongol lord's other palace gardens:

> *So twice five miles of fertile ground*
> *With walls and towers were girdled round:*
> *And there were gardens bright with sinuous rills,*
> *Where blossomed many an incense-bearing tree;*
> *And here were forests ancient as the hills,*
> *Enfolding sunny spots of greenery.*

Marco Polo describes it more accurately as an enclosed hunting park:

> A wall encloses and encircles fully sixteen miles of parkland well watered with springs and streams and diversified with lawns. Here

28

the Great Khan keeps game to provide food for the gerfalcons and other falcons which he has here in mew. Often, too, he enters the park with a leopard on the crupper of his horse; when he feels inclined, he lets it go and thus catches a hart or a stag or a roebuck.

Written records also tell us how much these parks cost and how much they were often resented. The vast royal park of the Han emperor Wu Ti (140 BC to 87 BC) at his capital Chang-an, in the west of China, extended for 50 square miles. It aroused so much indignation that he was forced to release the land back for cultivation. In Rome hundreds of people were ousted from their homes to create Nero's gardens which contained vineyards, woodlands stocked with game, a large lake and waterfalls.

These royal hunting parks, like those in medieval or eighteenth-century England, can be seen as attempts to recreate a golden age in which nature provides food freely. In fact, of course, they are based on theft and enclosure, as when William the Conqueror evicted the villagers from their agricultural settlements in the New Forest so that he could use it for hunting. Oliver Rackham in *The History of the Countryside* points out that this was the original meaning of the word 'forest': 'To the medievals a Forest was a place of deer, not a place of trees.'

ROYAL ENCLOSURE

The history of royal enclosure since 1066 reveals the extent of the theft of common land. By the time of the Domesday Book in 1086 about 25 Royal Forests had been established. In 1110 Henry I had one enclosure in Woodstock, Oxfordshire, turned into a zoo. In part of the forest he had a park made which was surrounded by a stone wall. He stocked it with lions, lynxes, leopards, camels and a porcupine sent from Montpellier. During the reign of Henry II (1154–89) more than a quarter of the country was subject to the Forest Law which protected deer. In 1433 Henry VI granted a licence to his uncle Humphrey, Duke of Gloucester, to enclose 200 acres of the common land of Blackheath 'to make a park in Greenwich'. Fallow deer were introduced into the park by Margaret, Henry VI's wife, and deer can still be seen there today in what is called the Wilderness.

A move against a different kind of garden enclosure took place in the fifteenth century. The Wars of the Roses ended in 1485 and in 1487 Henry VII established the Star Chamber administrative court, increasing the power of the throne. He ordered that the protective walls of medieval castles be torn down, so changing the nature of the *Hortus conclusus*, which was an enclosed garden usually containing lawns and arbours, shrubs, flowers and herbs. Pulling down the castle walls destroyed one sort of enclosure, but at the same time made it possible to enclose more of the country-side as part of the garden.

In 1526 Henry VIII took over Hampton Court from Wolsey, after having accused the cardinal of giving him syphilis through his 'perilous and infective breath', and increased the area of the garden, surrounding it with a deer park of 2,000 acres. In *King Henry the Eighth*, Shakespeare has Wolsey describe his fall from office in horticultural terms:

> *Farewell! a long farewell, to all my greatness!*
> *This is the state of man: to-day he puts forth*
> *The tender leaves of hopes; to-morrow blossoms,*
> *And bears his blushing honours thick upon him;*
> *The third day comes a frost, a killing frost;*
> *And, when he thinks, good easy man, full surely*
> *His greatness is a-ripening, nips his root,*
> *And then he falls, as I do.*

Henry VIII's palace at Nonsuch in Surrey, reproduced in John Loudon's Encyclopaedia of Gardening.

A year later the gardens of Henry VIII's palace at Nonsuch in Surrey were created. At the end of the century they are described by Hentzner as 'parks full of deer, delicious gardens, groves ornamented with trellis work'. The kitchen garden, filled with fruit trees, was surrounded by a wall 14 feet high. To make all this the king had enclosed 1,582 acres. In 1538 Henry dissolved Charterhouse, the Carthusian monastery, and from there three loads of bay trees, 91 fruit trees, rosemary and other shrubs, as well as a load of hay, were taken to the king's garden in Chelsea.

Thomas Cromwell copied the king's behaviour. Amongst other things, he took from Charterhouse 'all such bay trees and grafts' as his gardeners found convenient, a bundle of rose trees and twelve loads of timber. He also wanted to extend his garden, and did so without informing his neighbours, whose grounds were being enclosed. John Stow in his *Survey of London* of 1598 describes what happened to his father, who was one of Thomas Cromwell's victims:

> This house being finished and having some reasonable plot of ground left for a garden, hee caused the pales of the gardens adjoining to the north parte thereof, on a sodaine, to bee taken down, twenty-two foote to be measured forth right into the north of everyman's ground, a line there to be drawne, a trench to be cast, a foundation laid, and a high bricke wall to be builded. My father had a garden there, and an house standing close to his south pale; this house they loosed from the ground, and bore upon rollers into my father's garden, twenty-two foot, ere my father heard thereof. No warning was given him, nor other answere, when hee spoke to the surveyor of that worke, but that their mayster, Sir Thomas, commanded them so to doe; no man durst argue the matter, but each man lost his land ...

Richmond Park was enclosed by Charles I as a hunting park in 1637. It amounts to 2,470 acres and still contains herds of fallow and red deer. At the beginning of the eighteenth century Queen Anne enlarged her garden at Kensington House by enclosing 30 acres of Hyde Park. The garden was further extended by Queen Caroline who took another part of the park to bring the garden up to 275 acres.

Such enclosure has always been resisted. Robin Hood and his outlaws opposed the privatisation of the forests. In the sixteenth century the Norfolk rising against the whole system of enclosures took place. Apart from the Peasants' Revolt of 1381, it is seen by

A.L. Morton as the 'most important of all the English peasant wars'. It was led by Robert Kett who in 1549, with an army of 20,000, captured Norwich, the second city of the country. In the uprising the Earl of Surrey's newly enclosed gardens at St Leonard's Priory near Norwich were destroyed.

Attempts by James I to enclose Northwood Common in south London were met with prolonged and successful resistance. It was led by the Lewisham parish priest, Abraham Colfe, and involved tearing down the illegal fences and sending a deputation to the king. Later in the seventeenth century the Diggers argued that the land belonged to the whole people. In 1649 they cultivated common land on St George's Hill in Surrey, attempting to set up a model community.

At the end of the eighteenth century gangs of armed poachers waged a guerrilla war all over England against rival gangs of gentry and their gamekeepers. In the nineteenth century public campaigns were necessary to stop Hampstead Heath and Wimbledon Common from being enclosed for development. In 1905 15,000 people successfully defended Peckham's One Tree Hill in south London from being seized and enclosed to make a golf course. Ben Whitaker also records in *Parks for People* how in July 1969 six 'Hampshire citizens chose to go to prison rather than drop their protest about a proposal to put sixpence on the entrance fee to their local park'.

EIGHTEENTH-CENTURY ENCLOSURE

During the first 30 years of the eighteenth century the great estates were still largely laid out in a formal manner, as can be seen from the pictures of Badminton or Chatsworth, published in 1709. At Badminton the radiating avenues extended for miles, covering a large area of the counties of Wiltshire and Gloucestershire. Roger North visited it in 1680 and describes how the geometry of the house and gardens was not even contained within the Duke of Beaufort's own 15,000 acre estate, but extended to those of his lesser neighbours. North went up to the roof of the house and saw how it was situated

in the centre of an asterisk of glades cut through the woods of all the country round, 4 or 5 in a quarter ... Divers of the gentlemen cut their trees and hedges to humour his vistas; and some planted their hills in his lines for compliment at their own charge.

32

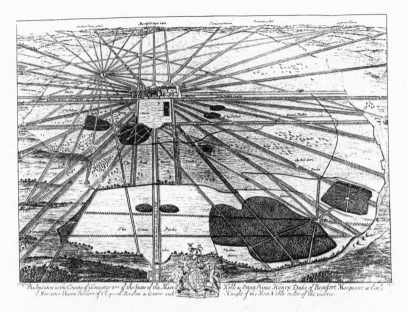

Radiating avenues at Badminton, the Duke of Beaufort's
15,000-acre estate in Gloucestershire, drawn by Leonard
Knyff and engraved by Joannes Kip for their
Britannia Illustrata *of 1709.*

As John Prest comments: 'The whole of a man's possessions could be surveyed from a single point. The exiled aristocracy had spent their time in France and learned their lesson well. The avenue was the policeman's truncheon of topography.'

At Boughton in Northamptonshire, the first Duke of Montagu, who had been ambassador at Versailles, began in 1680 to lay out avenues which stretched for miles in all directions. Later his son even contemplated planting an avenue which would extend in a straight line for 70 miles, all the way to London.

At the beginning of the eighteenth century many deer parks were constructed by the gentry. The word 'lawn' was used throughout the eighteenth century to mean a deer park. Instead of an extent of open space and woodland which could easily be poached, the parks were surrounded by high brick walls and protected by game-keepers.

In the eighteenth century visitors were sometimes allowed to visit the country estates, though they were not always appreciated by the owners. Lord Lyttelton, who owned Hagley in Worcestershire, wrote in 1788:

> Coaches full of travellers of all denominations and troops of holiday neighbours are hourly chasing me from my apartment or, strolling about the environs, keep me a prisoner in it. The Lord of the Place can never call it his during the finest part of the year.

By 1826, however, Prince Pückler-Muskau is commenting on 'the illiberality of the present race of Englishmen, who shut their parks and gardens more closely than we do our sitting rooms'. The public was only allowed a glimpse inside the park:

> Whenever the high road lies through an English park, a part of the wall is replaced by a ha-ha, or a transparent iron fence, that the passer-by may throw a modest and curious glance into the forbidden paradise: but this effort exhausts the stock of liberality usually possessed by an English landowner.

THE BLACK ACT

In 1723 the Black Act became law, introduced by Prime Minister Robert Walpole specifically to protect enclosed property. The Act made poaching, particularly hunting the king's deer, a capital offence if the persons offending were armed and disguised, their faces blacked. One could also be hanged for cutting down trees 'planted in any avenue, or growing in any garden, orchard or plantation'.

In the same year, Earl Cadogan completed the reconstruction of his 1,000 acre Caversham estate. Half of it was given over to gardens, lawns, woods and a deer-park of 240 acres. The terrace in front of the house extended for a quarter of a mile; avenues and vistas were planted; canals and basins stocked with fish; statues, obelisks and urns, valued at £3,987, were placed in the gardens; there was a pheasantry, menagerie, and quail yard. As E.P. Thompson concludes, 'it is improbable that such extensive landscaping could have been carried out without evicting cottagers and without displacing farmers from customary grazing rights'.

One of the most vicious people to use the Black Act to defend his property was Viscount Cobham. Like Cadogan, he had made a fortune out of Marlborough's wars and spent it on the buildings and garden at Stowe. In 1748 two men were caught raiding his

Stowe in Buckinghamshire: a bird's-eye view by Desmadryl of 'Capability' Brown's lay-out.

deer park and sentenced to death. According to oral accounts which were later written down by Rev. Linnell, the wives of the men went to see Cobham at Stowe to beg for their husbands' lives. He was apparently moved by their tears and promised that the men would be returned by a certain day - as they were. Their corpses were brought to the cottage doors on a cart. Cobham celebrated the occasion by placing statues of the two men in his park, a deer across their shoulders.

EVICTION

The concept of emparking, the creation of large landscaped parks, dates from the eighteenth century and as Gillian Darley makes clear: 'Emparking often involved the removal of entire communities and, therefore, their rehousing elsewhere.' Edward Russell, first Lord of the Admiralty and later Lord Orford, began emparking at Chippenham in Cambridgeshire as early as 1696. The park and lake eventually swallowed up half the village High Street and another road which intersected it. Russell had been

35

granted a licence to block these roads in 1702: 'Only two cottages remained isolated, at the furthest point of the park, which by now comprised most of the available land, Russell having bought five-hundred acres from five men and having taken over the common land.'

Robert Walpole certainly evicted people to make his park at Houghton Hall in his ancestral estate in Norfolk. He tore down the old village and built it again outside his park. The church remained isolated in the park where the village had been and the spot is marked by a stone memorial. The 23-acre park was designed by Eyre, an imitator of Bridgeman, and it was one of the first of the new landscape gardens, breaking loose from rigid symmetry and also uniting the garden near the house with the rest of the grounds.

In 1761 Lord Harcourt, at Nuneham Courtenay near Oxford, created the 'deserted village' of Goldsmith's poem. The village street became a path in the park for viewing the valley below. The church was turned into a classical temple and the congregation, still responsible for its upkeep, now had to walk a mile and a half to worship. Cows were provided with a special underground passage so they could pass from field to field without spoiling the view. One old woman, the shepherdess Babs Wyatt, was allowed to stay in her cottage in the middle of the new landscape garden. In the same way William Mason in 1772 suggests in *The English Garden* how the pastoral scene could be enhanced: 'Instead of a fence, the children of some poor but worthy cottagers, prettily disguised as shepherds, might be employed to keep the sheep from straying.'

The work at Milton Abbas in Dorset, carried out between 1773 and 1786, involved the destruction of a small town with its own market, grammar school, almshouses, shops, four inns and a brewery. Joseph Damer MP, later Earl of Dorchester, employed 'Capability' Brown to landscape the new park and also to try to stop the pillaging carried out by local children.

At Kedleston in Derbyshire a group of houses and an inn were demolished and re-erected outside the park. The village of Edensor near Chatsworth House in Derbyshire was destroyed and rebuilt twice, once by Brown in the eighteenth century because the fourth Duke of Devonshire thought it spoilt his view, and again by Paxton in the nineteenth century. The work involved in constructing new parks and gardens was massive, as is clear from Paxton's great rockery at Chatsworth, which was begun in 1842.

Two years later it was reported that 'huge masses of rock are collecting and forming into a rockwork, the like of which has never before been seen. Some of these masses weigh upwards of 370 tons.'

In 1775 Charles Cottrell-Dormer, the owner of Rousham in Oxfordshire, demolished nine houses and used the land to extend his park. Similarly in France, Le Nôtre's design for Fouquet's gardens at Vaux-le-Vicomte involved destroying three hamlets, diverting rivulets and transplanting whole woods. Some 18,000 men were employed in the construction work. At Versailles over 22,000 men and 6,000 horses were used.

It has been estimated by Edward Hyams that

> between 1760 and 1867 England's small class of rich men, using as their instrument Acts of the Parliament which they controlled through a tiny and partly bought and paid for electorate, stole seven million acres of common land, the property and the livelihood of the common people of England.

Marion Shoard arrives at the same figure in her book *This Land is Our Land*, and she explains what it means: 'Seven million acres is more than the total area of the following ten contemporary English counties: Derbyshire, Nottinghamshire, Northampton-shire, Buckinghamshire, Bedfordshire, Hertfordshire, Cambridge, Essex, Norfolk and Suffolk.'

To compensate cottagers for the loss of their land, a whole series of Acts of Parliament were passed to provide them with allotment gardens. These were to be big enough to grow fruit and vegetables to feed their families, but not so big that they could get a living from them and so afford to stop working for a farmer. This is made clear by the *Commercial and Agricultural Magazine* in 1800, which argues that allowing the 'labouring man to acquire a certain portion of land' would reduce the poor-rates:

> since a quarter of an acre of garden-ground will go a great way towards rendering the peasant independent of any assistance. However, in this beneficent intention moderation must be observed, or we may chance to transform the labourer into a petty farmer. When a labourer becomes possessed of more land than he and his family can cultivate in the evenings, the farmer can no longer depend on him for constant work, and the hay-making and harvest must suffer to a degree which would sometimes prove a national inconvenience.

Enclosure of land between 1750 and 1850 involved planting about 200,000 miles of hedges, at least equal to all those planted in the previous 500 years. This required 1,000 million plants, mainly hawthorn. Hedges were big business and made fortunes for several nursery firms.

Resistance to such enclosure was common, but more and more severely punished. In 1731 Thomas Chester was sentenced to death for cutting down some of Mr Blinco's young trees. He had done it because he had 'too much zeal for the publick good', for Blinco had sown acorns in an enclosed area which was 'esteem'd by all people in several adjacent villages to be his Majesties property or highway'. After a petition, drawn up by his mother, had been signed by four clergy, one baronet, seven gentlemen and others, Chester was eventually reprieved and transported instead.

Henry Fielding's account in *The Adventures of Joseph Andrews* is clearly not just fiction:

> 'Jesu!' said the Squire, 'would you commit two persons to bride-well for a twig?'
> 'Yes,' said the Lawyer, 'and with great lenity too; for if we had called it a young tree they would have been both hanged.'

Eighteenth-century Landscape Gardens

The attempt to hide the exploitation and division of labour involved in gardening is most apparent in the second half of the eighteenth century, the heyday of the English landscape garden. At this time 400 families owned a quarter of the cultivated land in the country. This was not the first time, however, that people, along with earth and trees, were moved in order to create new landscapes for country estates. In the sixteenth century, which had also been a period marked by enclosure, Sidney wrote his *Arcadia* in a park which had been made by enclosing a whole village and evicting the tenants.

Goldsmith describes this recurring process in 'The Deserted Village' (1769):

> *the man of wealth and pride*
> *Takes up a space that many poor supplied;*
> *Space for his lake, his park's extended bounds,*
> *Space for his horses, equipage and hounds.*

38

The garden for the few is the grave for the many:

> *Thus fares the land, by luxury betrayed;*
> *In nature's simplest charms at first arrayed;*
> *But verging to decline, its splendours rise,*
> *Its vistas strike, its palaces surprise;*
> *While scourged by famine from the smiling land,*
> *The mournful peasant leads his humble band;*
> *And while he sinks without one arm to save,*
> *The country blooms – a garden, and a grave.*

The vista was an important expression of authority and power, but it was more subtly expressed than through the earlier radiating avenues. It was now to appear more 'natural', like the seventeenth-century landscape paintings of Claude Lorrain and Gaspard Poussin. At Rousham in Oxfordshire in the late 1730s, William Kent got rid of most of Charles Bridgeman's more formal elements. He divided up the grounds with groups of trees to provide varied glimpses of the scenes from different levels, angles and distances. Some of the scenes were still very imposing, as the head gardener John Macclary describes in 1750: 'the most noble view we have from one place in our Gardens, we look into four Countys, and see no less then ten parrish Churches at one time'.

The use of the ha-ha, with its military origin as a means of defence, disguised the division between garden and countryside.

The ha-ha disguised the division between garden and countryside.

This ditch and rampart provoked surprise, hence 'ha-ha' or more phonetically 'a-ha', when approached from the house. Its meaning as a barrier or fortification was, however, more apparent when it was seen from the countryside looking towards the house.

Vistas of lawn, lake and trees could be seen from the house or from other vantage points, but the labour on the land, which created the wealth to construct the vistas, was banished from sight. The most famous landscape designer Lancelot Brown (1715–83), known as 'Capability' Brown because he saw capabilities for improvement in every garden, had the flower, fruit and kitchen gardens hidden behind walled enclosures. The only human being you might see would be a hermit, specially hired to live in the hermitage, and liable to be sacked if he did not live a sufficiently austere life. At Pain's Hill in Surrey, the man employed by Mr Hamilton to sit in his Hermit's Cave gave up the job after only three weeks.

Animals were, however, often allowed to grace the landscape. Horace Walpole, youngest son of Robert Walpole, used an especially small breed of cow in his fields at Strawberry Hill, so that in perspective the grounds would look larger. Horace Walpole wrote an essay 'On Modern Gardening' in 1770 supporting the new landscape style. According to George Johnson in *A History of English Gardening*: 'He very powerfully contributed to abolish the mathematical style of Gardening, being one of the most strenuous advocates of Landscape Gardening.'

Meanwhile off-stage the hard work would go on, often casual labour at the lowest wages, separating production from consumption. The enclosed fields were set out in mathematical grids with straight hedges and straight roads, in contrast to the winding curves of the landscape garden. The former were being organised for efficient capitalist farming, using new mechanical inventions such as Jethro Tull's seed drill, scientific crop rotation, improved sheep and cattle breeding. This was the practical, productive side of the coin. The garden, on the other hand, was the aesthetic side, the composed, yet natural, landscape of 'pleasing prospects' where sensibility could be cultivated.

STEPHEN DUCK

The price of this sensibility was paid by people like Stephen Duck at the beginning of the eighteenth century. He describes himself as for 'many Years a poor Thresher in a Barn, at Charleton in the

County of Wilts, at the Wages of four Shillings and Sixpence per Week' and he strongly challenges the pastoral image of the countryside:

> *No Fountains murmur here, no Lambkins play,*
> *No Linnets warble, and no Fields look gay;*
> *'Tis all a gloomy, melancholy Scene,*
> *Fit only to provoke the Muse's Spleen.*
> *When sooty Pease we thresh, you scarce can know*
> *Our native Colour, as from Work we go:*
> *The Sweat, the Dust, and suffocating Smoke*
> *Make us so much like Ethiopians look.*

He also points accurately to the division between production and consumption:

> *Let those who feast at Ease on dainty Fare*
> *Pity the Reapers, who their Feasts prepare:*
> *For Toils scarce ever ceasing press us now;*
> *Rest never does, but on the Sabbath, show:*
> *And barely that our Masters will allow.*
> *Think what a painful Life we daily lead;*
> *Each morning early rise, go late to Bed;*
> *Nor, when asleep, are we secure from Pain;*
> *We then perform our Labours o'er again.*

Ironically Stephen Duck was later patronised by Queen Caroline and installed as a guide in Merlin's Cave at Richmond. The cave

Merlin's Cave at Richmond, designed by William Kent for Queen Caroline, where Stephen Duck was installed as a guide.

was designed for her with a Gothic archway and thatched roof by the famous garden designer William Kent. Duck then wrote poems about 'blissful Groves' and 'Sylvan Nymphs'. In 1756 he drowned himself in a fit of melancholy.

Stephen Duck was attacked for underestimating the significance of women's labour when he implied that women agricultural workers had 'their wages paid for sitting on the ground'. In 1739 Mary Collier wrote 'The Women's Labour; an Epistle to Mr Stephen Duck' in answer to his poem 'The Thresher's Labour':

> *What you would have of us we do not know:*
> *We oft' take up the Corn that you do mow;*
> *We cut the Peas, and always ready are*
> *In ev'ry Work to take our proper Share;*
> *And from the Time that Harvest doth begin,*
> *Until the Corn be cut and carry'd in,*
> *Our Toil and Labour's daily so extreme,*
> *That we have hardly ever Time to dream.*

She also explains that when finished in the fields, a woman has all the housework to do, as well as looking after husband and children.

In 1783, in 'The Village', George Crabbe reiterated the contrast between the charms of the countryside for the owners and the harsh reality of agricultural labour for the workers:

> *I grant indeed that fields and flocks have charms*
> *For him that grazes or for him that farms;*
> *But when amid such pleasing scenes I trace*
> *The poor laborious natives of the place,*
> *And see the mid-day sun, with fervid ray,*
> *On their bare heads and dewy temples play;*
> *While some, with feebler heads and fainter hearts,*
> *Deplore their fortune, yet sustain their parts:*
> *Then shall I dare these real ills to hide*
> *In tinsel trappings of poetic pride?*

On the big estates in the seventeenth and eighteenth centuries the head gardener was often the only member of the garden staff who was permanent. The others were casual workers, mainly male, though women were employed particularly for weeding.

*Lancelot 'Capability' Brown (1715–83) painted by
Nathaniel Dance, c.1770.*

'CAPABILITY' BROWN

In *The Story of the Garden* Eleanour Sinclair Rohde describes the
'destruction wrought' by 'Capability' Brown:

> What must fill the least imaginative with horror is to think of the
> wanton destruction of fine old gardens, many of them established
> for centuries and full of interesting plants, the cutting down of trees
> and magnificent avenues, the wholesale destruction of orchards and
> so forth, perpetrated by the new school. The people who must have
> suffered most were the gardeners, who had to engage in the work of
> uprooting and cutting down their carefully tended treasures. Why
> our flower-loving nation tolerated such vandalism it is hard to
> understand. So far from making or attempting to improve gardens
> the landscape 'gardeners' destroyed them, substituting fields and
> lawns and 'natural' lakes and streams.

John Loudon records of Brown that 'there was scarcely a
country gentleman who did not on some occasion consult him'.

43

He goes on to say that so rapidly did the face of the country alter that 'in 1772 Sir W. Chambers declared that if the mania was not checked, in a few years more, three trees would not be found in a strait line from the Land's-end to the Tweed.' On one estate Brown planted 100,000 trees. He used mainly elm, oak, beech, lime, Scots fir, plane, larch and the Cedar of Lebanon.

A few years after the Russian Revolution, H. Avray Tipping in 'English Gardens', published by *Country Life*, compares Brown to Lenin:

> Few bands of reformers - hardly, even, the Russian Bolsheviks - have ever acted more ruthlessly or attained their destructive ends more completely than the English 'landscape' gardening school of the eighteenth century, with 'Capability' Brown as their Lenin. Root and branch they destroyed the works of their predecessors so successfully that sparse indeed is the flotsam and jetsam of the survivals.

The story goes that Brown declined a job in Ireland because he 'hadn't finished England yet'.

Smaller gardens, however, were not affected in the same way, as Tipping points out: 'Little gardens were fortunate in that their lack of "capabilities" for landscaping enabled them to escape the destruction of their walls, clipped hedges and straight paths. It was here that garden craft and the love of flowers continued.'

MANUAL LABOUR

As we have seen, the extensive changes in garden design in the eighteenth century required a great deal of manual labour. The landscapes had to be dug and dammed, as well as designed. At Rousham in 1738, the steward William White informed the owner: 'We have been enabled to carry on the work from the river and that upon the slope at the same time. Upwards of seventy hands have been employed in both places.'

Plants had to be transported and planted. In 1708, the Duchess of Marlborough's personal garden at Blenheim required thousands of bulbs, including 4,600 tulips and 18,500 Dutch yellow crocuses. In the next century the Duke of Devonshire bought a huge palm tree from Lady Tankerville. The circumference of its trunk was 8 feet 4 inches and the whole tree and root ball weighed 12 tons. Turnpikes were demolished in order to transport it along the road from Surrey to Derbyshire.

Kenneth Woodbridge, in 'Henry Hoare's Paradise', claims: 'The energy which produced the transformation of the landscape in eighteenth century England was prodigious, comparable, it could be said, to that which had created the great monuments of Gothic art.' He goes on to describe the artists and designers responsible for the transformation of the landscape at Stourhead in Wiltshire, built on Hoare's banking profits. No mention is made of the labourers, except when the designer Henry Flitcroft complains: 'Tis too true that workmen of this age study only their too much profit, rather than to be expert in geometry and mechanicks and the nature of materials.' He also says of some of the building: 'This is but labourers' work.'

As William Morris succinctly puts it in his pamphlet *The Lesser Arts*, published in 1878, though referring only to men:

> You look in your history-books to see who built Westminster Abbey, who built St Sophia at Constantinople, and they tell you Henry III, Justinian the Emperor. Did they? or, rather, men like you and me, handicraftsmen, who have left no names behind them, nothing but their work?

Nineteenth-century photograph of the garden staff at
Chatsworth House in Derbyshire.

Upkeep of the gardens was labour intensive. In 1831 at Chatsworth 22 men were employed in the kitchen garden. In *The Gardener's Magazine* of 1842, Loudon describes how the arboretum at Bicton in Devon was kept in shape:

> Messrs. Veitch and Son having six men constantly employed mowing the grass, and mulching the dug circles round the plants with it as practised in the Derby Arboretum; destroying weeds as soon as they appear; and removing dead leaves, suckers from grafted plants, insects, decayed blossoms, etc.

During the same period the Earl of Harrington employed 90 gardeners at Elvaston Castle, near Derby. When he died in 1851 and it was discovered that he had spent beyond his means, the workforce was cut to eight.

Great care had to be taken to keep everything looking perfect. It would take three men with scythes a whole day to cut an acre of grass. They would be followed by lawn women who gathered up the grass cuttings. In 1721 at Canons Park in Middlesex, home of the Duke of Chandos, the grass was scythed two or three times a week and weeded every day. The lawns were often rolled and, according to the anonymous author of *The Gardener's New Kalendar* of 1758, 'care must be taken that the horses should be without shoes and have their feet covered with woollen mufflers.'

A contemporary of Brown's, Richard Woods, was commissioned to improve over 40 estates between 1758 and 1792. In 1769 at Irnham Hall in Lincolnshire he was confronted by a strike of the workers and expressed his anger about it in a letter to the owner, Lord Arundell:

> I could scarcely in a sheet of paper describe the disposition and behaviour of those unaccountable creatures in human shapes indeed but that is all, for in all other respects are Bruits. The 1st Monday morning after I arrived they all draw'd up in a body, swore they wou'd not unlock a tool unless i would give them 18d. a day, the planting being in hand I was oblig'd to comply being at so great distance from any of my own companeys.

He later sacked the leaders of the strike and sent for some of his own men to take their place.

In the winter, during periods of frost and snow, many gardeners

Frozen-out gardeners, drawn by Foster, from The
Illustrated London News, *21 December, 1850.*

would be laid off. In the nineteenth century groups of them could
be found begging in the streets, holding aloft the tools of their
trade. The precarious nature of the job of gardening was also illustrated in the employment practice at the Chelsea Physic Garden.
In the diary of William Anderson, who was curator in 1815,
dismissals are recorded and the reasons given: 'John Hutchins,
discharged for a dunce', 'Henry Wood, too wise', another man 'for
a blockhead'. Other gardeners were sacked for pilfering, fighting
or getting drunk.

The gardener's working hours could be very unpredictable. At
Fonthill Abbey Mr Beckford had relays of men working night and
day on various projects, as Loudon recalls in 1833:

> When he wished a new walk to be cut in the woods, or any work of
> that kind to be done, he used to say nothing about it in the way of
> preparation, but merely gave orders perhaps late in the afternoon,
> that it should be cleared out and in a perfect state by the following
> morning at the time he came out to take his ride. The whole
> strength of the village was then put in requisition, and employed
> during the night.

GARDENERS' PAY

The job of gardening was so poorly paid and precarious at the beginning of the nineteenth century that gardeners often had to beg or advertise for charity in the gardening press. In 1839 the 'Benevolent Institution for the Relief of Aged and Indigent Gardeners and Their Widows' was formed to deal with such cases.

In his *Gardener's Magazine* (1826–44), Loudon constantly calls for better wages, hours and lodgings for the hired gardener. During this period horticulture suffered an economic recession as Loudon explains: 'Capital employed in the nursery business returns at present less than capital employed in any other trade.' One correspondent to the magazine writes: 'There is no class of servants so ill paid as gardeners, and none, who from their general good conduct, and the long study and attention required to excel in their profession, deserve to be so well paid.'

He goes on to compare an illiterate bricklayer, with wages of between five and seven shillings a day, to a journeyman gardener who, despite having studied geometry, land surveying and botany, received only two shillings and sixpence a day.

In 1841 even head gardeners were paid only about a tenth of a cook's salary and half that of a footman. In 1871 the Public Parks Committee of Manchester advertised for a head gardener for Alexandra Park, offering a salary of £84.4s a year, with a house, coal, gas and water. This was the same salary as that given to the previous gardener, Mr Macmillan, whose widow and children were destitute and who were appealing for help to keep them from the workhouse.

Living conditions for gardeners were often atrocious. John Loudon wrote in 1829: 'There is no class of gentlemen's servants so badly lodged as gardeners generally are.' In his *Encyclopaedia of Gardening* he describes how they lived:

> In one ill-ventilated apartment, with an earthen or brick floor, the whole routine of cooking, cleaning, eating, and sleeping is performed, and young men are rendered familiar with filth and vermin, and lay the foundation of future diseases, by breathing unwholesome air ... How masters can expect any good service from men treated worse than horses, it is difficult to imagine ...

In some parts of the country the bothy system operated, in which families were actually split up and consigned to separate bothies. A bothy is described in an article in the 1860s as 'a house set apart for the men to sit in and cook their victualls, with a sleeping apartment or apartments adjoining. In many cases the bothy is badly kept, and the sleeping apartment dirty and untidy.' The article goes on to say that the system is not necessarily bad for single men, as the men 'prefer it to going into the house for their food', but 'as regards married men, the system is radically wrong'. The bothy was often a shed built on the north wall of the kitchen garden, a dark and damp place to live.

As David Stuart concludes in his book *The Garden Triumphant: A Victorian Legacy*:

> Even going into business saved no more than a few gardeners from poverty, and for all the thousands of peaches, pineapples, bunches of camellias, pots of new and even Guatemalan orchids grown for their employers, for all the auctions and advertisements, for all the moral rectitude and abstinence, innumerable respectable lives must, on ill health or the death of the husband, have ended in destitution, despair or the poor-house.

At the end of the nineteenth century a ten-hour day was normal. A 60-hour week was common, with unpaid Sunday duty, and holidays consisting of three feast days a year. Sometimes half a day was granted to visit a flower show, but the time usually had to be made up.

At the beginning of this century the National Union of Horticultural Workers negotiated wages for its members. In May 1920 *The Horticultural Worker* recorded an agreement with the employers in the Lea Valley District whereby 14–15-year-old workers were to be paid 16 shillings a week, 15–16-year-olds 20 shillings, and so on up to 50 shillings for 20–21-year-olds. Those over 21, 'if efficient in tomatoes and with three years experience of nursery work', could earn 55 shillings. 'Men engaged as cucumber hands so long as cucumbers are grown in the nursery, provided they have three seasons' experience of cucumber growing', were paid 60 shillings. Time and a quarter was paid for over 50 hours work a week in the summer, or for over 48 hours in the winter; time and a half on Sundays and public holidays.

Every famous garden we have heard about has been dug and planted, weeded and pruned, by workers such as these, usually without any protection from a trade union. Theophrastus had slaves to dig his garden in Athens, the Aztec King Nezahualcoyotl (1403–74) had men from the provinces tending his Texcotzingo gardens as a tribute, and medieval monks employed labourers to cultivate their monastery gardens. In Pond Yard, in Hampton Court gardens, Henry VIII had the water supplied for the ponds by 'labourers ladyng of water out of ye Temmes to fyll the ponds in the night tymes', using only 'pots and dishes'.

As Teresa McLean documents in her book *Medieval English Gardens*, casual labour was hired by monasteries to do the 'digging, weeding, planting, felling and trimming of trees, fruit picking, grass cutting, the making and repairing of walls and hedges, ponds and ditches'. At the Abbey of Beaulieu in Hampshire Brother John had overall charge of the kitchen garden which covered several acres. In 1269 he paid workmen 3s 6d to plant beans and leeks in it. His profits were enormous: '20d worth of surplus leek seeds to sell, 28s 6d worth of leeks, 22d worth of onion seeds and 5 quarters 5 bushels of beans which he sold for 18s 9d.' They also grew hemp and cider apples and had enough beehives to produce a surplus of 5 gallons of honey and 2 lbs of wax which Brother John sold in 1270.

Gardeners are still amongst the most exploited workers in the country. According to the National Union of Public Employees, in September 1987 gardeners' wages were between £95.75 and £113.15 a week. The bottom grade was for the basic gardening job in parks and gardens. The top grade was for the 'interpretation of plans, site preparation and construction; soft and hard land-scaping and setting out of pitches, tree-care, and propagation', as well as being in charge of 'resources of a significant nature (such as sports establishments and facilities) together with a consider-able supervisory role (for example allocation of duties, work rotas and training)'.

The New Earnings Survey of April 1987 gives the average gross weekly earnings of male manual workers in Britain. Bottom of the list are general farm workers on £124 and second to bottom gardeners and groundsmen on £132. The average wage for all male manual workers was £185 and the average female manual wage £115. All these figures are based on an overall 1 per cent sample of workers and they include overtime and bonuses. The Trade Union Congress campaign for a minimum wage set the minimum at two thirds that average, or about £124. Many gardeners, therefore, must have been getting less than that proposed minimum.

The Department of Employment does not keep separate statis-tics for the number of gardeners. In its category of agricultural and horticultural workers for March 1988 there were 205,397 men and 71,834 women. The Ministry of Agriculture, Fisheries and Food, however, distinguishes the following, in descending order of pay: foremen, dairy cowmen, all other stockmen, tractor drivers, general farm workers, horticultural workers, females, youths. For the year ending March 1988, the average basic wage for a 40-hour week was £102.44 for horticultural workers, £96.97 for females, and £74.94 for youths. Clearly very little has changed over the centuries in the way gardeners are paid.

Gardeners working in Peel Park, Salford, 1989.

ALIENATION AND THE DIVISION OF LABOUR

In the eighteenth century Lady Luxborough was banished, for alleged infidelities, to her husband's derelict estate at Barrels. She set about creating a garden:

> I have made a garden which I am filling with all the flowering shrubs I can get. I have also made an aviary, and filled it with a variety of singing birds, and am now making a fountain in the middle of it, and a grotto to sit and hear them sing in.

No mention is made of the people who actually did the physical work. She employed a Scottish gardener, but even he would have supervised the work of others.

Joseph Paxton, according to Brent Elliott, 'erected the Great

Exhibition building in Hyde Park'. We know this means that he designed it, but the wording conceals the actual physical labour that was involved. In 1896, the architect Lutyens is said to have 'built' a new house for Gertrude Jekyll in a clearing in a wood at Munstead, and she to have 'made' the 15-acre garden, without mention of those who did most of the manual work. Similarly Tipping writes in 1925 about Ellen Willmott's gardens at Warley Place, near Brentwood in Essex: 'Miss Willmott has worked hard, and with rich result, to make her garden a place of interest and joy from January to December.' No mention of the 86 gardeners she employed.

However, not all gardening work has been alienating. There were always cottage gardens where farm-labourers could grow their own produce. At the end of the eighteenth century florists' clubs were organised all over the country by factory workers and artisans to cultivate flowers. They probably had their origin in sixteenth-century Norwich, connected with its 'worsted manufactures', and spread to London in the seventeenth century. In the middle of the eighteenth century they were attended by people of all classes.

According to Loudon, writing at the beginning of the nineteenth century: 'A florists' society is established in almost every town and village in the northern districts.' Derbyshire miners raised pansies, Lancashire cotton workers auriculas, Sheffield workers polyanthus, colliers of Northumberland and Durham pinks. Norwich was noted for its carnations, Manchester for its gooseberries, and Spitalfields in London was famous especially for its auriculas and tulips. Also at the end of the eighteenth century the Corresponding Societies were set up to discuss radical politics and to campaign for manhood suffrage, annual parliaments and controls over the enclosure movement.

Paisley and Glasgow were famed for their pinks. The most famous pinks were produced by Paisley weavers, who obtained seeds from London between 1785 and 1790. Some of the seedlings showed a pattern of lacing. Through careful selection, these laced forms were propagated and by the early nineteenth century Paisley pinks were being exported to the rest of the country. During this period over 300 new varieties of pink were raised. (The name pink comes from 'pink-eye' meaning a small eye, the Scots word 'pinky' meaning the little finger. Hence, the word for the colour pink comes from the flower, rather than the other way round.)

An anonymous writer of this period writes of the difference between hired labour and free labour in the garden:

> The auricula is to be found in the highest perfection in the gardens of the manufacturing class, who bestow much time and attention on this and a few other flowers, as the tulip and the pink. A fine stage of these plants is scarcely ever to be seen in the gardens of the nobility and gentry, who depend upon the exertions of hired servants, and cannot therefore compete in these nicer operations of gardening with those who tend their flowers themselves, and watch over their progress with paternal solicitude.

In the 1850s some of the best-known tulip varieties were raised by Tom Storer, an engine-driver, who lived near Derby.

The 'exertions of hired servants', as well as the free labour of the working class, need to be acknowledged in any history of gardening. Without their work no gardens would have been created. In the same way we have to look beyond these shores, to see how English gardening has been influenced from abroad.

3

Medieval, Arab and Aztec Gardening

3rd Century BC
Theophrastus inherits Aristotle's botanic garden in Athens.

1533
Oldest university chair of botany in Europe, founded in Padua by the Venetian Republic.

1543
Europe's first botanic garden, established in Pisa by Luca Ghini.

1550
Europe's first museum of natural history, in Bologna.

1621
First botanic garden in England, the Oxford Physic Garden.

1670
First Scottish botanic garden, in Edinburgh.

1673
Chelsea Physic Garden founded by the Society of Apothecaries.

From the time of Theophrastus before the birth of Christ there was little discovery or original thought prior to the seventeenth century.

Dr D.G. Hessayon, *The Armchair Book of the Garden* (1986)

During the Dark Ages, when garden-craft in the greater part of Europe was at its lowest ebb, the Moors in Spain were making gardens, the remains of which are to this day amongst the most remarkable in the world ... The gardens of ancient Mexico were of a splendour comparable only to those of the great civilizations of the East.

Eleanour Sinclair Rohde, *The Story of the Garden* (1932)

Western Europe owes many plants as well as much horti-
cultural technique to the dominion of the Moors in Spain
from AD 711 to 1492. Under the Western Omayyad
Caliphate of Cordova (929–1031) Andalusia was the
highest centre of civilisation in the Euro-mediterranean
region and produced scientific literature in all fields, linked
with the immense Islamic culture in Arabic. Botany,
Agriculture and Horticulture, with the Pharmacopoeia,
formed branches of a subject eagerly pursued by scholars
and by practical collectors and cultivators. Though the
debt of Europe, and of modern civilisation, to Arabic
science is well known, the importance of the Islamic contri-
bution to horticulture has not been sufficiently recognised.

John Harvey, *Gardening Books and Plant Lists of Moorish Spain* (1975)

Just as an examination of class relations, the ownership of land
and the division of labour, is crucial to an understanding of
gardening, so too is a look at international relations, particularly
colonialism. Like the class conflict involved in creating the eighteenth-century landscape gardens, it is a connection that is
usually hidden or mystified.

The origins of plants and their interchange between countries
are often described as a marvellous example of international cooperation and goodwill, benefiting everyone. The plant hunters are
described by Kenneth Lemmon, in *The Golden Age of Plant Hunters*,
as 'men of god', 'courageous adventurers', 'men who must rank
among the greatest of our nation's benefactors'. In *The Quest for
Paradise* Ronald King writes of 'the great succession of plant collectors ... who harvested the wild plants of south-east Asia in the first
half of the twentieth century'. Julia Berrall in *The Garden* calls
Joseph Banks, Robert Fortune and Joseph Hooker 'intrepid and
dedicated plant explorers'. Few questions are normally asked
about the forces behind this activity, its relationship with colonialism and empire, the politics and economics of it all.

A connection can be made, for example, between the Chelsea
Physic Garden and the construction of landscape gardens, by
looking at colonial trade. In 1732 Philip Miller of the Chelsea
Physic Garden sent a packet of cotton seed with a plant collector
to Georgia. From this little packet three quarters of the world's
cotton is descended. Cotton plantations in the southern states of
the USA led to an increased demand for slaves, so boosting the
triangular trade and enabling some of the landscape gardens to be
built with the profits from that trade.

GOSSYPIUM

MONODELPHIA POLYANDRIA

Antilles cotton: an original water colour painted in
Madeira, attributed to Margaret Meen.

It is also interesting to note, that as well as taking English garden plants to America, the settlers also introduced a large number of weeds which were previously unknown in the country. John Josselyn, in his *New Englands Rarities Discovered* of 1672, lists these as couch-grass, shepherd's purse, dandelion, groundsel, sow-thistle, mullein, knot-grass and comfrey.

In the seventeenth century the most famous plant collectors were the Tradescants, father and son. Gladys Taylor, in her book *Old London Gardens*, writes: 'One of the most honourable names in the history of gardening is that of the Tradescants.' But their 'honourable' travels were closely connected with war and colonialism. The elder John Tradescant botanised whilst on diplomatic and military missions. In 1618 he was on a mission to Russia which was taking government money to the Tsar to help him in the war against Poland. Two years later he was collecting plants in Algeria, sailing with the navy who were fighting the Barbary pirates who disrupted British trade. In 1627 he went on the Duke of Buckingham's disastrous expedition to try to relieve the Huguenot stronghold of La Rochelle. A rare acknowledgement of Tradescant's military adventures comes in *Gardens of Delight* by Miles and John Hadfield, where they call him 'a superior form of pirate'.

The Tradescant Garden in the churchyard of
St Mary-at-Lambeth, Lambeth Palace Road, where the
Tradescants are buried. The church now houses the
Museum of Garden History.

Tradescant's son, also called John, collected plants in Virginia and helped settle the colony, under the system known as 'head-rights'. To stimulate emigration and settlement the Virginia Company had decreed that any person paying his own fare to Virginia should be granted 50 acres, with a further 50 acres for each additional person he transported. Tradescant went with

Bertram Hobert who, by paying for the transportation of 13 people, became entitled to 650 acres of land. This involved moving the Indians off the land, just as villagers in England were evicted and deprived of common land in the enclosure movement. The Indians resisted but were gradually pushed further and further west by the settlers.

The influence of colonialism and racism in gardening history is clear when one considers the activities of the Spanish *conquistadores*, the way in which the influence of Arab horticulture has been neglected, the plant hunters of the eighteenth and nineteenth centuries, the role of Kew Gardens in the British Empire, or the very language of gardening. In all the gardening magazines, books and television programmes I have ever seen, there has only been one reference to black gardeners – in the remarkably detailed and sensitive book by David Crouch and Colin Ward, *The Allotment: Its Landscape and Culture*, published in 1988. In it the authors discuss the contribution made to gardening culture on our allotments by people originating from the West Indies, India and Pakistan.

English gardening history often excludes the international scene, even though it has always been influential. Often too the legacy of the Middle Ages is ignored, as if the history of gardening only really began in the sixteenth or seventeenth century. It is the result of an attitude which sees our past as 'primitive', just as it sees foreigners in the same way. This chapter attempts to counter this view by looking at the influence of Arab and Aztec horticulture and by recording our medieval gardening heritage.

MEDIEVAL GARDENING

The list of dates at the beginning of this chapter is misleading in a way which reflects assumptions about our 'primitive' past. The gap between classical times and the Renaissance suggests that nothing of note happened in between. It has often been claimed, for example, that pleasure gardening did not exist in medieval England. Richard Gorer in *The Flower Garden in England* claims that 'the monastery garden, although it might contain many plants that we now grow for their flowers, was purely functional. Plants were grown either for food or for their medicinal virtues.' Miles Hadfield also, in his influential book *A History of British Gardening*, writes: 'It seems not improbable that gardening as an

58

art and the aesthetic appreciation of flowers scarcely existed until the late fifteenth or early sixteenth centuries.'

On the contrary, medieval England was full of 'beautiful flower gardens', as Teresa McLean documents in *Medieval English Gardens*. In 970 Brithnod, the Abbot of Ely, had gardens and orchards planted around the church. According to his chronicler, they were stocked with shrubs and fruit trees 'in regular and beautiful order', adding much to the 'beauty of the place'. At the Benedictine nunnery of Wherwell in the thirteenth century the Abbess Euphemia had vineyards and a shrub and flower garden created 'in places that were formerly useless and barren, and which now became both serviceable and pleasant'. Flowers were regularly used to decorate medieval churches on feast days and to make garlands for religious processions. In 1405 when Roger de Walden was installed as bishop at St Paul's Cathedral, both he and the canons were decked with garlands of red roses.

Medieval gardeners.

John Harvey, in *Medieval Gardens*, also attacks the myth that there was no gardening for pleasure in the Middle Ages. He provides a wealth of evidence to the contrary, mainly describing royal and monastic gardens of the period:

There is ample proof that ornamental gardening flourished in England as well as in north-western Europe, from the late eleventh century if not earlier; that it was based on a keen delight in the appearance of plants and their perfumes, and also in the sight and sound of running water. Trees were planted, not only for timber or for fruit, but as decorative adjuncts to houses; the therapeutic value of their shade was recognised, and walking under trees, or where their beauty could be appreciated, was an accepted recreation and also a factor in convalescence.

At the end of the twelfth century Alexander Neckham, Abbot of Cirencester, writes in his *De Naturis Rerum*:

The garden should be adorned with roses and lilies, the turnsole or heliotrope, violets, and mandrake, there you should have parsley, cost, fennel, southernwood, coriander, sage, savery, hysop, mint, rue, ditanny, smallage, pellitory, lettuce, garden cress, and peonies. There should also be beds planted with onions, leeks, garlic, pumpkins, and shallots. The cucumber, the poppy, the daffodil, and brank-ursine ought to be in a good garden. There should also be pottage herbs, such as beets, herb mercury, orach, sorrel, and mallows.

The first English gardening book, written by Jon Gardener some time in the fourteenth century, gives recommendations for sowing, planting, pruning and grafting. It also refers to plants grown for decorative as well as medicinal use. The author lists 97 plants, including many flowers for the pleasure garden, for example cowslip, foxglove, gentian, periwinkle, primrose, daffodil, daisy, iris, hollyhock, lavender, lily, peony, violet and rose. Eleanour Sinclair Rohde, in *The Old English Gardening Books* published in 1924, confirms this: 'As the well-known lists testify, our ancestors' gardens in the Middle Ages were filled with the beauty of roses, lilies, violets, lavender, foxgloves, irises, holly-hocks, thyme, honeysuckle, periwinkle, and many others too numerous to mention.'

Monasteries often had several different kinds of garden. In the ninth century in the Benedictine monastery of St Gall in Switzerland, a plan was drawn up showing an ideal monastery of the time and its gardens. Next to the infirmary is a quadrangular physic garden, planted with roses and lilies which the plan calls 'herbs both beautiful and health-giving', and with sage, rosemary and other 'kitchen herbs'. On the other side of the infirmary is the cemetery, planted with rows of fruit and blossom trees in 'ordered regularity'. Next to the cemetery is a garden with 18 parallel beds planted with vegetables, herbs and flowers; for example onions, garlic, leeks, shallots, parsley, chervil, coriander, dill and poppies. At each end of the church is a semi-circular portico planted as a garden and labelled 'paradise'. The Arabs had built these paradises in Sicily and from there they were taken by the Normans to northern and western Europe.

The garden of Eden as a medieval flowery mead, by J.P. Bergomensis, 1510.

There were also gardens in castles, palaces and manor houses. Some consisted of flowery meads, either walled or left open, as described by Chaucer in his translation of the *Roman de la Rose*:

> *There sprang the violet all new,*
> *And fresh periwinkle, rich of hue,*
> *And flowers yellow, white and red;*
> *Such plenty grew there never in mead.*

In 'The Franklin's Tale' he adds:

> *This garden full of leaves and flowers;*
> *And craft of man's hand so curiously*
> *Arrayed had this garden, truly,*
> *That never was there garden of such prys*
> *But if it were the very paradise.*
> *The odour of flowers and the fresh sight*
> *Would have made any heart for to light ...*
> *So full was it of beauty with pleasance ...*

Town Gardens

There were also town gardens. In the twelfth and thirteenth centuries between 400 and 500 new towns were created and many rural settlements were raised to borough status. London was by far the biggest town and after the fire of 1135 many of the wealthiest people had their houses rebuilt in stone. Attached to them were large gardens and vineyards. Holborn in particular was the most magnificent of London's garden suburbs with huge gardens reaching down to the river where there were rows of trees. Alexander Neckham, travelling through London on his way to Paris in 1178, describes Holborn as full of houses and pretty gardens.

Public gardens also existed, for they are mentioned in William FitzStephen's 'Description of London', a prologue to his life of Becket, written at the end of the twelfth century. He describes the wells to the north of London, particularly Holywell, Clerkenwell and Clement's Well which were the most famous. Around the wells were public gardens with walks shaded by trees where students and young people went out from the city on summer evenings to take the air. The trees planted for shade and recreation were elm, oak, ash and willow. Spa gardens next to London's wells were to be further developed in the eighteenth century. FitzStephen also refers to the private suburban gardens in London: 'Everywhere without the Houses of the Suburbs, the Citizens have Gardens and Orchards planted with trees, large, beautiful, and one joining to another.'

In the thirteenth century the Tower of London was a garden centre as well as a royal residence, and the slopes of Tower Hill were terraced with vines and fruit trees. Tower Hill was also the site of some of the earliest English market gardens, producing fruit for the London market, though there is an earlier reference in the Domesday Book to market gardens in Fulham. In 1372 the City Corporation took action against the Tower Hill gardeners over the refuse they had allowed to pile up there.

In the fourteenth century the Earl of Lincoln's garden in Holborn was immense. It stretched to the river, surrounded by a wooden fence and divided into flower, fruit and vegetable gardens. The Earl sent to the continent for new apple and pear cuttings and employed an expert gardener to graft and look after them. Besides fruit and vegetables, he sold 'little plants', which implies he was running a commercial nursery garden, and roses.

In Holborn too was the famous garden of the Bishops of Ely. In the fourteenth century a vineyard, orchard and kitchen garden were added. In 1483, on Friday 13 June, according to Holinshed, the Duke of Gloucester, later to become Richard III, referred to the strawberries in this garden. In Shakespeare's play, Gloucester says:

> My Lord of Ely, when I was last in Holborn,
> I saw good strawberries in your garden there;
> I do beseech you, send for some of them.

Also in the fourteenth century Henry Daniel, a distinguished scholar and botanist, wrote a herbal, as well as translating medical treatises. He was a keen gardener and kept a private botanic garden in Stepney with 252 species of plants, more than any monastery would have contained.

Arab Gardening

Even more neglected than the medieval period in England is the influence of Arab horticulture of the time. Henry Daniel refers to a 'Christian man that mickle had learned among the Saracens', and John Harvey points out in *Medieval Gardens* that it was

under the influence of Arabic civilization that the era of modern science began during the Middle Ages. Whereas western Christian learning remained under the dead hand of verbal authority, direct observation and experiment inspired learned men of Islam from the frontiers of India to the Atlantic coast of Morocco.

In the ninth century a research institute was set up in Baghdad from which an immense literature of Arabic translations, mainly from Greek and Indian languages, was to influence horticulture in places as far apart as Spain and Turkey. The whole of the *Materia Medica* by Dioscorides, for example, was translated. By the tenth century Cordova had become the main centre of botanical studies. In 1031 Muslim Spain broke up into succession states, the most important being Seville and Toledo. The sultans of both states maintained important palace gardens and both became genuine botanical gardens. The one at Toledo was created by Ibn Wafid (999–1075), and carried on after his death by his colleague Ibn Bassal who was a great botanist and plant collector.

Ibn Bassal wrote a handbook on agriculture and gardening

which was both scientific and practical. In it he discusses water supply, soils, manures, choice of ground and its preparation. He describes methods of planting, pruning and grafting trees, sowing seeds, different classes of vegetables, herbs, aromatic flowering plants and bulbs. He ends by providing some topical tips, such as how to deal with slugs:

> Form your beds, strew on them an inch of ashes from the Public Baths, then lay on your manure and sow the seed; thus the animal mentioned, on leaving the earth in search of the plants, will meet with the ashes and retire confounded.

Ibn Bassal travelled widely and collected plants from Sicily, Egypt, Saudi Arabia, Iran. During the century between 1080 and 1180 the variety of cultivated plants grown in Andalusia doubled, partly through these new introductions, but also through bringing native plants into cultivation. In his *Encyclopaedia of Gardening* Loudon recognises this horticultural knowledge of the 'Arabs of Spain': 'Ebn-Alwan has left us a list of plants in the garden of Seville, in the eleventh century, which are more numerous than those which were cultivated by the Greeks and Romans.'

INFLUENCE OF MOORISH SPAIN

It was this Arab horticulture, particularly from Moorish Spain, which influenced medieval British gardens. Adelard of Bath stayed in Spain around 1120 and brought back Arabic science. He was particularly interested in discovering how grafting worked. Daniel de Morley studied at Toledo and returned to England about 1185 'with a precious multitude of books'. Another source of information was the medical school at Montpellier in southern France, founded by Arab and Jewish physicians from Spain in the twelfth century. Montpellier was under Spanish influence for the next two centuries and in 1593 the first French botanic garden was founded there.

There was an expanding seed trade within Britain in the thirteenth century and plants and seeds were also brought in from abroad, particularly by monks and nuns. Jews too, such as the physician Solomon, who maintained the first recorded medicinal herb-garden in Norwich, were in a good position to obtain seeds and plants from abroad, particularly from Spain where Jewish physicians were highly regarded. Eleanor of Castile, Edward I's first queen, employed gardeners from Aragon to work on her garden at King's Langley in Hertfordshire. Aragon was then an integrated country of Muslims, Christians and Jews which had at its disposal the accumulated knowledge of both East and West, and also a tradition of advanced horticulture centred on Valencia.

George Johnson in *A History of English Gardening*, published in 1829, shows how the 'Crusades to the Holy Land' and 'wild expeditions to the continent' contributed to the art of gardening in this country:

> So true is the observation that good is often the offspring of evil; for our foreign wars introduced us to the Horticulture of France, who excelled us in the practical parts of the Art; to the disposition of the Pleasure Grounds of the Easterns, which were magnificent; and to the numerous new plants of which previously we had been ignorant.

He also demonstrates how Philip II's suppression of revolt in the Netherlands had a similar effect:

> The taste for flowers, we have seen in a previous section, was prevalent in this country at a very early period; a great increase of information as to their cultivation, as well as new varieties, were introduced by the Flemish Worstead Manufacturers, who were driven over to Norwich during the persecutions in their country, by Philip the II and by the Duke of Alva in 1567. They brought over with them Gilliflowers, Provence Roses, and Carnations.

Huguenot refugees also started flower societies and set up a number of market gardens such as those at Battersea and Bermondsey.

TURKEY AND PERSIA

In the sixteenth century the first major wave of exotic plants came to the west from the Ottoman Empire. The plants brought from Turkey and placed on the European market were not found in the wild, but were cultivated species which had been improved by centuries of culture, grafting or hybridisation. They were the result of Muslim gardening over a long period and included species of hyacinth, narcissus, lily, iris, tulip, anemone, carnation, hollyhock, jasmine, peony, crocus, poppy and primrose.

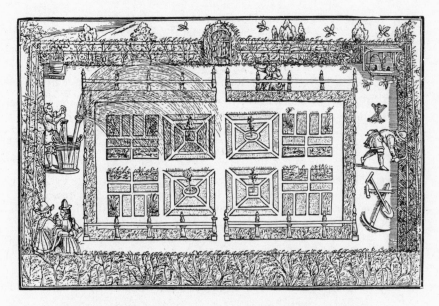

A Tudor garden as 'the natural development of the medieval garden' and showing 'the influence of the traditional garden of the ancient East'. Entitled 'The maner of watering with a Pumpe in a Tubbe', it comes from Thomas Hyll's The Gardeners Labyrinth, *first published in 1577.*

In 1453 the Turks captured Constantinople. Kristovoulos, in his contemporary account *History of Mehmed the Conqueror*, recounts how they 'planted gardens with trees bearing all sorts of fruit for the delectation and happiness and use of many'. About 1465 the pleasure grounds round the Topkapi Palace were completed:

> Around the palace were constructed very large and lovely gardens abounding in various sorts of plants and trees, producing beautiful fruit. And there were abundant supplies of water flowing every-where, cold and clear and drinkable, and conspicuous and beautiful groves and meadows.

The French botanist Deleuze comments on this period: 'When the Turks, by the taking of Constantinople, had given stability to their empire, they devoted themselves particularly to the culture of flowers.' Loudon quotes Belon, in 1558, speaking with admiration of the gardens he saw: 'There are no people who delight more to ornament themselves with beautiful flowers, nor who praise them more, than the Turks.'

Eleanour Rohde points to the continuing medieval tradition as well as the influence of Persia on English gardens:

> The 'garden enclosed' of Elizabethan and Stuart days was the natural development of the medieval garden, and in it we see also the influence of the traditional garden of the ancient East. Although lacking the rivulets of water flowing in shallow tiled canals which were one of the most entrancing features of Persian gardens, there is much in the Tudor garden suggestive of the mystic beauty of the old Persian garden. The similarity between the gardens of the Great Mughals and Tudor gardens is remarkable. In both we find the formal rectangular beds, the pleached alleys, the fountains, and 'proper knots'. In early Tudor times the characteristic features of medieval gardens appear almost unchanged.

Just as the debt of classical Greek culture to Africa is rarely acknowledged, so the contribution of Arab culture to western horticulture is often ignored. Even more brutally suppressed has been the Aztec contribution to our gardening heritage.

AZTEC GARDENING

In 1519 Cortes and his conquistadores entered the Aztec capital Tenochtitlan, now Mexico City. In *Discovery and Conquest of Mexico* his chronicler Bernal Diaz del Castillo later described what he saw:

> When I beheld the scenes around me, I thought within myself that this was the garden of the world! Gardens so wonderful to see and walk in, I was never tired of looking at the diversity of trees, and noting the scent which each one had, and the paths full of roses and flowers, and the ponds of fresh water ... And of all these wonders that I then beheld, today all is overthrown and lost, nothing is standing.

It was not only the gardens which were destroyed by the *conquistadores*, but also a developing botanical science. The knowledge was appropriated and stored away by the King of Spain.

The Spanish invaders, on their journey from the coast to the capital, were continually astonished at the flowers of Mexico, used for decoration, greeting, and religious festivals. In his *History of the*

Conquest of Mexico, written in 1843 but largely based on the eye-witness account of Diaz, William Prescott records the Spaniards' entry into the city of Cempoalla:

> The women, as well as men, mingled fearlessly among the soldiers, bearing bunches and wreaths of flowers, with which they decorated the neck of the general's charger, and hung a chaplet of roses about his helmet. Flowers were the delight of this people.

'Bunches and wreaths of flowers' given as a greeting.

An Aztec florist displays his wares.

In Tlascala men and women gave 'bunches and wreaths of roses' to the Spanish soldiers and 'the houses were hung with festoons of flowers, and arches of verdant boughs, intertwined with roses and honeysuckle, were thrown across the streets'. The people of Cholula 'showed the same delicate taste for flowers as the other tribes of the plateau, decorating their persons with them, and tossing garlands and bunches among the soldiers'.

The market in Tenochtitlan amazed Diaz:

There were amongst us soldiers who had been in many parts of the world, – in Constantinople and in Rome, and through all Italy, – and who said that a market-place so large, so well ordered and regulated, and so filled with people, they had never seen.

Aztec gardeners transplanting seedlings.
(Aztec drawings from Historia General de Nueva España.*)*

Fruiterers and florists sold their wares alongside all the other products of the country and every stall was decorated with flowers. Prescott describes some shops or booths 'tenanted by apothecaries, well provided with drugs, roots, and different medicinal preparations'.

Royal Gardens and Botanical Gardens

The most remarkable Aztec garden was the tropical one at Huaxtepec. In a letter to Charles V, Cortes calls this royal garden 'the most beautiful and the most delightful which had ever been beheld'. It was over six miles in circumference with many exotic and aromatic shrubs planted in symmetrical order, a variety of fountains and streams, tanks stocked with fish and aquatic birds, and at intervals pavilions and statues. Plants were imported from throughout the region, including the subject kingdom of Cuetlaxtlan. Envoys were sent to its capital in Vera Cruz to bring back cacao and magnolia trees, the vanilla orchid and other tropical plants, along with native gardeners to plant and care for them. Montezuma even declared war to get hold of a particularly rare tree in the possession of an Oaxacan lord. He had sent ambassadors with gifts to purchase it, but when his offer was rejected, he sent an army instead which soon returned with the tree and many human captives too.

In this respect the Aztec royal gardens were little different from royal gardens throughout the world, but they also inspired the development of botanical gardens and the classification of plants.

Tobacco plant (Nicotiana tabacum) *from the second part of Monardes' book, published in 1571.*

In the gardens of Tenochtitlan and Huaxtepec an organised group of physicians carried out systematic experiments with herbal remedies. Cortes was so impressed by how quickly his wounds had been healed by his Indian allies that he asked the Spanish Crown that no European doctors be allowed to come to the country because they could not match the skill of native physicians.

Spanish doctors adopted many herbs, under their Mexican names, into their own list of herbal remedies. In 1552 two Aztecs produced an illustrated manuscript herbal. They were Martin de la Cruz, described as an 'Indian physician who is not theoretically learned, but is taught only by experience', and Juanues Badianus, who translated the work into Latin.

The Spaniard Nicolas Monardes also wrote about the botany of the new world, his books being published in 1569 and 1571. Monardes acknowledges the advanced medical knowledge that had been revealed: 'And as there is discovered newe regions, newe kyngdomes, and newe Provinces, by our Spanyardes, thei have brought unto us newe Medicines and newe Remedies.' He also includes one of the earliest pictures of tobacco to appear in print. The work was translated into English by John Frampton as *The Three Books* or *Joyfull newes out of the newe founde worlde* and Frampton indicates the close connection between England and Spain by commenting: 'the afore saied Medicines ... are now by Marchauntes and others brought out of the West Indias into Spaine, and from Spain hether into Englande, by suche as dooeth daiely trafficke thether'.

The systematic collections of the Aztecs and their understanding of plants were more extensive and advanced than any to be found in Europe at the time. It is even possible that the botanic gardens established in Europe in the sixteenth century – Pisa, Padua, Leyden, Montpellier, Breslau, Heidelberg – were based on earlier Aztec models. Prescott says the Aztec nurseries were 'more extensive than any then existing in the Old World' and he concludes: 'It is not improbable that they suggested the idea of those "gardens of plants" which were introduced into Europe not many years after the Conquest.'

At Iztapalapan, a few miles from the capital, the famous gardens covered an immense tract of land. They were

> laid out in regular squares, and the paths intersecting them were bordered with trellises, supporting creepers and aromatic shrubs that loaded the air with their perfumes. The gardens were stocked with fruit-trees, imported from distant places, and with the gaudy family of flowers which belonged to the Mexican flora, scientifically arranged, and growing luxuriant in the equable temperature of the table-land. The natural dryness of the atmosphere was counteracted by means of aqueducts and canals that carried water into all parts of the grounds.

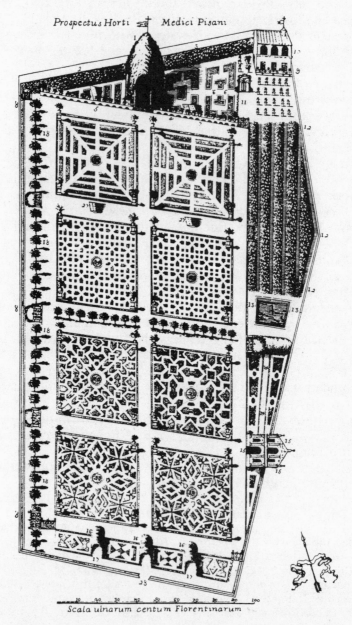

Plan of the Botanic Garden in Pisa, drawn when it was moved to its present site in 1593.

The gardens at Huaxtepec were even more extensive

embellished with trees, shrubs, and plants, native and exotic, some selected for their beauty and fragrance, others for their medicinal properties. They were scientifically arranged; and the whole establishment displayed a degree of horticultural taste and knowledge of which it would not have been easy to find a counterpart, at that day, in the more civilized communities of Europe.

Medicinal plants from these gardens were later used in a great hospital built nearby after the Conquest.

In 1529 a Franciscan friar, Bernardino de Sahugun, came to Mexico from Spain and made a famous study of Aztec culture, *Historia General de Nueva España*. Materials were compiled by Aztec scholars, then translated into Spanish, and numerous illustrations were commissioned showing Aztec gardening activities such as transplanting seedlings, gathering flowers, and making floral designs, necklaces, wreaths and bouquets. The eventual manuscript was repeatedly rewritten between 1558 and 1569, but was not published until 1829.

In 1570 the naturalist Francisco Hernandez was sent by Philip II to study the resources of the new colony. He spent seven years drawing and describing the plants which he saw, particularly at Huaxtepec, and returned with 16 folio volumes ready for publication. The king had them bound and placed in his library. A century later this 'Inventory of the Medicinal Resources of New Spain', still unpublished, was destroyed by fire. Copies of some parts of the manuscript, however, had been smuggled into Italy, probably by the Papal Delegation to Spain, and were eventually published in 1651. A Spanish law, dating from 1566, required all books containing information about Spain's colonies to be licensed for publication by the Council of Indies, which existed for the sole purpose of preventing any such publication. They never issued a licence of any kind to any work.

This tight control of botanical knowledge was extended to anyone putting forward new theories. A Jew named Garcia de Orta, who was nominally a Christian, had to leave Spain and go to India to expound his botanical theory, in which he argued the Arabist position against the Hellenist one. The Arabists accepted the teachings of the classical authors only as they had been corrected and amplified by the medieval Arab physicians. The Hellenists regarded the Greeks, such as the physician Galen, as the

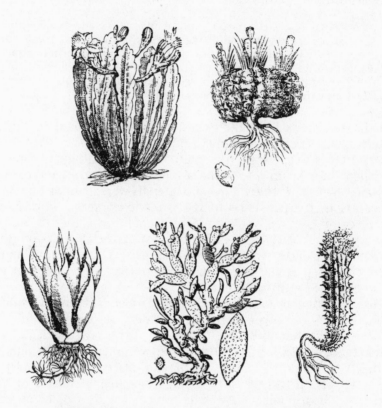

Drawings of cacti by Francisco Hernandez for his Inventory of the Medicinal Resources of New Spain, *written between 1570 and 1577.*

sole authorities on botany. De Orta's book was published in Goa in 1563, one of the first European books to be printed in India. As he says, 'Even I, when in Spain, did not dare to say anything against Galen or against the Greeks'.

Gardens of the Aztec Commoners

Just as English cottage gardens existed alongside the great landscape gardens, so the Aztec commoners made gardens as remarkable as those of the nobility. In the language of Nahuas there were two words for a garden. *Xochitecpancalli* referred to a large pleasure ground, and *xochichinancalli* meant a small garden. Prescott refers to the 'trim gardens and orchards that lined both sides of the road' leading to Cempoalla, and in the Valley of Mexico 'stretching far away at their feet, were seen noble forests of oak, sycamore, and cedar, and beyond, yellow fields of maize and the towering maguey, intermingled with orchards and blooming gardens'. He describes the houses of the nobles in Tenochtitlan as having flat roofs protected by parapets: 'Sometimes these roofs resembled parterres of flowers, so thickly were they covered with them, but more frequently these were cultivated in broad terraced gardens, laid out between the edifices.'

There were also *chinampas*, or floating gardens. Prescott calls them 'fairy islands of flowers', 'wandering islands of verdure, teeming with flowers and vegetables, and moving like rafts over the water'. They were rectangular, up to 300 feet long, made of willow and marsh plant roots, and covered with fertile mud from the lakes and canals. Some floated freely, 'moving like some enchanted island over the water', others were anchored to the ground. Each produced about seven crops a year. Some of the *chinampas* were firm enough to sustain small fruit trees and even a hut for the gardener – like a floating allotment.

Plants from Mexico

Through careful selection and plant breeding Aztec farmers discovered and cultivated hundreds of varieties of our present-day crops, such as maize, tomatoes, marrows, pumpkins, beans, peppers, cacao, vanilla, cotton and tobacco. Cacao was so important that bags of it were used as currency, along with tin coins and quills of gold dust. The word chocolate comes from the Nahuatl word *choco-atl*, meaning 'bitter water', as it was made into a drink. A kind of foaming chocolate mousse, flavoured with vanilla and other spices, was Montezuma's favourite food.

Of the flowers, one of the most famous to come out of Mexico was the African marigold, so called because it was first taken to Africa and then on to Europe. Sunflowers and dahlias also come from this region. The wild dahlia grew up to 30 feet high. The Aztecs made water pipes out of the stems, and from the root a sweet extract was used for medicinal purposes. Hybrids of these plants were eventually grown in the Royal Gardens of Madrid in

The continent of America (bottom right) represented by a cactus.

1789 by the curator Abbé Cavanilles. He named the plant after his Swedish assistant, the botanist Andreas Dahl. In England the flowers were bred by florists and by 1830 there were over 1,500 named varieties.

The cactus also originates from Mexico. The name Tenochtitlan means 'a cactus on a stone'. At the front of Parkinson's *Theatrum Botanicum* of 1640 the four continents are represented and the cactus is used to symbolise the Americas. One form of cactus is the prickly pear which is a species of opuntia. Alice Hopf describes the uses to which it was put:

> Many edible opuntias were cultivated by the pre-Columbian peoples for diverse purposes. Besides food and drink, the plants supplied them with fibre for rope, woolly hair for textiles, spines for fish hooks and knitting needles, and a variety of medicinal compounds. Some flowers produce a heart stimulant and some roots have proven efficacious against dysentery. Plasters made from powdered roots are still used by some Indians to set bones, and the stems of some species are used as a poultice on various swellings and on the breasts of nursing mothers whose milk supply has dwindled. Tea made from the stems of other species is commonly used as a wash to cure headaches, ease eye troubles and to dispel insomnia.

Cactus provided nourishment for the coccus insect, which when dried was made into cochineal. This scarlet dye formed one of the staple tributes to the crown from various districts, despite the claim by some historians that the Spanish taught the Mexicans how to use it.

In the same way the agave and maguey plants had many uses: the leaves were made into paper or into thatch for houses, the juices were fermented to make pulque and tequila, the fibres made thread and ropes, the thorns were used as pins and needles, and the roots cooked as food. As Prescott remarks: 'The agave, in short, was meat, drink, clothing, and writing-materials for the Aztec!'

Plants from Mexico continued to be brought to England. In the 1830s Mexican flowers began to be recommended for bedding-out. According to Andrew Murray, writing in the *Gardeners' Chronicle* of 1862, the origins of the bedding system came from 'the vast flowering prairies of Mexico': 'It was the Nemophilas, the Coreopsides, the Eschscholtzias of these plains that first formed the glowing beds' of English gardens.

Loudon comments on the use of Mexican plants in cottage gardens. Visiting Derby in 1839 he is pleased to see the marked improvement in the construction of the roadside cottages, including

> the greater display of fine flowers in the front gardens, both of new and old cottages. There is hardly one of these gardens that does not contain some of the fine plants sent home by Douglas and Drummond, or plants of Mexico and South America.

Later in the century there was an attempt to create a Mexican landscape of cacti at Eythrope in Buckinghamshire, and in 1882 a proposal was published to build a garden house based on the Mexican ruins at Chichen Itza. The roof was to be covered with subtropical plants in imitation of the temple discovered in the Mexican rain forest.

This brief account of the influence of Aztec and Arab horticulture illustrates the need to avoid an insular approach to English gardening history. The dates at the beginning of the chapter have to be looked at again in the light of what the Moors achieved in Spain and what the Aztecs created in Mexico. By the seventeenth century the English had overtaken the Spanish as the leading imperial power in the world. In the next two centuries colonies in Australia, China and India, for example, played a large part in the development of economic botany and were to change the face of English gardening.

4

Joseph Banks and Australia

The humble Lichen was one of the ingredients in the dye of imperial purple, for which Tyre and Sidon were famous; and the search for it brought Phoenician commerce to the Irish shores in the days of Ptolemy.

Anon, *The Language of Flowers* (c.1880)

Another World was search'd, through Oceans new, To find the Marvel of Peru.

Andrew Marvell (1621–78) 'The Mower against Gardens'

Many flowers have become so familiar, that it is hard to picture a garden without them, yet numbers of plants now to be seen almost everywhere had not been brought to our shores one hundred years ago. To bring about such changes many men have been at work, in every department, each contributing something towards the progress of gardening. There have been practical gardeners and nurserymen, great botanists and men of knowledge and daring, whose lives have been risked in the cause of science, and to whose courage and perseverance we owe so many of the treasures of a modern garden.

Alicia Amherst, *A History of Gardening in England* (1895)

On Banks's mind a vision of these lands, grown rich and prosperous because peopled by men of his own race, was indelible.   Hector Cameron, *Sir Joseph Banks* (1952)

The new landscape gardens of the eighteenth century reflected the Whig ascendancy, a period of relatively stable rule after the previous century's revolutionary times. They mirrored the wish of the ruling class to present their authority as natural, not

79

won by force. This has helped support the powerful myth of England as a place free from revolution, unlike France. Instead England is seen as a steadily evolving society, growing and maturing like a plant or a landscape, the seventeenth century all forgotten.

The life of Joseph Banks, in the way in which it is usually presented, contributes to this myth and also to the idea of independent scientific advance. It is clear, however, that Banks's botanical and horticultural activities were not disinterested, but inextricably linked to English colonial commerce.

Joseph Banks was one of the key figures in gardening and botanical science at the end of the eighteenth century. A friend of King George III and President of the Royal Society for over 40 years, he was also the founding father of Kew Gardens. Both his plant hunting round the world and his work at Kew are tied up with the development of colonialism.

THE LIFE OF JOSEPH BANKS

Joseph Banks was born in 1743 and had the distinction of going to both Harrow, from the age of nine to 13, and Eton. At neither place did he learn any botany, so while at Eton he decided to pay local herb-women to teach him. These were women 'employed in culling simples to supply the Druggists and Apothecaries shops'. They taught him the names of plants and where and when they could be found. He paid them sixpence for every specimen they brought him. At this time he also read his mother's copy of Gerard's *Herball*.

In 1760 he went to Oxford where there was a professor of botany called Humphry Sibthorp, but unfortunately for Banks this was a typical Oxford professor of the day, who did no teaching. In his 35 years as a professor he apparently delivered only one lecture. Banks had to import a teacher from Cambridge instead.

During his first year at Oxford his father died, so on reaching the age of 21 he inherited Revesby Abbey and the accompanying estate in Lincolnshire, thus becoming an immensely wealthy landowner.

He became particularly involved in enclosing and draining the nearby fen-lands. This led to the creation of many casual labourers out of those who lost their rights to the land. The land was then used for grazing sheep, and Banks was also interested in improving their breeding to produce better wool. To this end in 1787 he arranged to smuggle some merino sheep out of Spain, via Portugal where they spent the winter, despite the opposition of the Spanish government. This was done in consultation with the King of England who also profited from the sale of these sheep. By the beginning of the nineteenth century there were more sheep, and better sheep, in Lincolnshire than in any other county in England. The same breed of sheep was eventually introduced into Australia, where Banks was also to be so instrumental in introducing human settlements. The number of sheep in Australia finally rose to 160 million.

Revesby Abbey in Lincolnshire: ancestral home of Joseph Banks.

It was estimated that half of the Banks estate brought in rents of £5,721, from 268 tenants. From the 62 farms in the manor of Revesby, constituting 3,401 acres, the rent amounted to £1,397. It is not surprising that he could afford the £10,000, worth about £500,000 today, needed to finance Captain Cook's round the world voyage which was to last three years; nor that he was considered by Sir Everard Home in 1822 to have been 'the greatest Patron of Science in Europe'.

In 1766 Banks had been plant collecting in Newfoundland and Labrador, and later in 1772 he was to go on an expedition to Iceland. But his most famous journey was with Captain Cook to Australia.

In 1767 the Royal Society wrote to King George III, claiming

> that the passage of the Planet Venus over the Disc of the Sun, which
> will happen on the 3rd of June in the year 1769, is a Phaenomenon
> that must, if the same be accurately observed in proper places,
> contribute greatly to the improvement of astronomy on which
> Navigation so much depends. That several of the great Powers in
> Europe, particularly the French, Spaniards, Danes and Swedes, are
> making the proper dispositions for the Observation thereof.

This was to be the spur to the Australian voyage. When the
Endeavour set sail in August 1768, Joseph Banks was 25. The
announcement of the ship's departure gave Gilbert White, the
naturalist, 'some odd sensations, a kind of mixture of pleasure and
pain at the same time', as he recorded in a letter written in
October of that year:

> When I reflect on the youth and affluence of this enterprizing
> gentleman I am filled with wonder to see how conspicuously the
> contempt of dangers, and the love of excelling in his favourite
> studies stand forth in his character. And yet though I admire his
> resolution, which scorns to stoop to any difficulties; I cannot divest
> myself of some degree of solicitude for his person. The circumnavi-
> gation of the globe is an undertaking that must shock the
> constitution of a person inured to a sea-faring life from his child-
> hood; and how much more that of a landman!

Banks left behind his betrothed, Harriet Blosset, whom he
rejected on his return. He had already been a Fellow of the Royal
Society for two years and found no difficulty joining the expedition, for he was self-financing and also a close friend of Lord
Sandwich, First Lord of the Admiralty. In fact, at the time it was
seen very much as Banks's voyage, rather than Captain Cook's. He
took with him nine personal assistants: Dr Solander and another
Swedish naturalist; three artists and botanical draughtsmen, two
servants from Revesby, and two black servants.

As a letter sent by John Ellis FRS to Linnaeus, the famous
Swedish naturalist who invented the modern system of plant classification, recounts:

No people ever went to sea better fitted out for the purpose of natural history, nor more elegantly. They have got a fine library of natural history; they have all sorts of machines for catching and preserving insects; all kinds of nets, trawls, drags and hooks for coral fishing; they have even a curious contrivance of a telescope by which, put under water, you can see the bottom at a great depth, where it is clear. They have many cases of bottles with ground stoppers, of several sizes, to preserve animals in spirits. They have the several sorts of salts to surround the seeds, and wax, both bees' wax and that of Myrica.

In the same letter Ellis explains the purpose of the voyage:

I must now inform you that Joseph Banks, Esq., a gentleman of £6,000 per annum estate, has prevailed on your pupil Dr Solander to accompany him in the ship that carries the English astronomer to the new discovered country (the Society Islands) in the South Sea ... where they are to collect all the natural curiosities of the place and, after the astronomers have finished their observations on the transit of Venus, they are to proceed under the direction of Mr Banks, by order of the Lords of the Admiralty, on further discoveries.

This concise list of aims should probably be reversed in order of priority. Just as Darwin's work as a naturalist with the *Beagle* was secondary to the main aim of charting the coasts of South America for navigational purposes connected with trade and war, so it was with this expedition. Similarly sixteenth-century naturalists, such as William Turner, Thomas Penney, Thomas Moffet and John Gerarde, had collected information during the overseas voyages of Drake, Cavendish and Frobisher.

Secret orders from the Admiralty instructed Cook to sail southwards in search of 'a continent or land of great extent'. It was considered vital to find it before the French or Spanish. In his journal, Cook reveals the secret orders:

I was therefore ordered to proceed directly to Otaheite and, after the astronomical observations should be completed, to prosecute the design of making discoveries in the South Pacific Ocean by proceeding to the south as far as the latitude of 40 degrees; then if I found no land, to proceed to the west between 40 and 35 degrees till I fell in with New Zealand, which I was to explore and thence to return to England by such route as I should think proper.

The other investigations too could hardly be seen as purely

related to natural history. Cook was ordered:

> You are also to be careful to observe the nature of the soil and the products thereof, the beasts and fowls that inhabit or frequent it; the fish that are to be found in the rivers or upon the coast, and in what plenty, and in case you find any mines, minerals or valuable stones, you are to bring home specimens of each, as also such specimens of the seeds of trees, of fruits and grains as you may be able to collect, and transmit them to our Secretary that we may cause proper examination and experiments to be made of them. You are likewise to observe the genius, temper, disposition and number of the Natives.

On the first leg of the journey, they stopped at Rio de Janeiro, but the Brazilian authorities would not let the plant hunters go ashore, and a guard was put on board the ship by the Viceroy. As usual in the history of plant hunting, such a measure was not sufficient to stop these brave explorers. They frequently stole out of the cabin window at night, let themselves down into a boat by a rope and rowed off to the shore where they landed and made several excursions inland. They also bribed the sailors, who were allowed ashore for provisions, to collect plants and smuggle them back on board. Banks listed 316 different plants collected in this manner.

Two months later they landed in Tierra del Fuego, the southern part of Argentina, and set off on an expedition in the mountains to look for alpine plants. They were caught in a snowstorm and had to spend the night in the open. In *Flowers in History* Peter Coats writes that Solander 'literally nearly died of cold', but he makes no mention of the fact that Banks's two black servants did freeze to death, the first of many casualties on the voyage. Banks describes the experience of the blizzard as 'terrible', but he still managed to collect 125 plants which he calls 'truly the most extraordinary I can imagine ... to speak of them botanically, probably no botanist has ever enjoyed more pleasure in the contemplation of his favourite pursuit than did Dr Solander and I among these plants'.

Three months were then spent on Tahiti and when the transit of Venus had been observed, they sailed south to search for the 'great continent'. Before leaving, Banks decided to take home with him Tupia, one of the chief priests, whose son had been taken to France the previous year and presented in Paris as an example of Rousseau's noble savage. Banks writes: 'I do not know why I may not keep him as a curiosity, as well as some of my neighbours do lions and tigers.' Tupia was used as an interpreter, particularly when the expedition reached New Zealand.

A number of Maoris were shot dead while the coast of New Zealand was botanised. Banks maintained that of the 400 species of plant which they saw, only a handful had ever before been described by any botanist. He also claims to have proved that the natives were cannibals, with 'their barbarous custom of eating the

A Maori Chief, drawn by Sydney Parkinson.

bodies of such of their enemies as are killed in battle'. At one meeting with Maoris, he says he was given the bone from a human arm 'and to show us that they eat the flesh, they bit and gnaw'd the bone and draw'd it through their mouths and this in such manner as plainly shewed that the flesh to them was a dainty bit'. It must have been this kind of reporting that led George Johnson in 1829 to refer to 'New Zealand savages' in his book *A History of English Gardening.*

Kenneth Lemmon in *The Golden Age of Plant Hunters* (1968) describes the natives variously as 'hostile and troublesome', 'all grotesquely tattoed', 'a war-whooping mob', 'excited gibbering natives', 'a bow and arrow mob of wildly shrieking natives black as the ace of spades', 'miserable natives streaked with red and black', 'a posse of near head-hunting, betel-chewing natives', 'cannibals and thugs'. All this is compared with the 'superhuman efforts and great personal sacrifice' of the plant hunters, the 'intrepid exploits' and 'blood sweat and tears' of these 'courageous adventurers', the 'services of our great botanical collectors, men who must rank among the greatest of our nation's benefactors'.

SETTLEMENT IN AUSTRALIA

On 28 April 1770 these benefactors landed in Australia at Sting Ray Bay, later to be called Botany Bay because of the large number of plants found there. Banks describes the Aborigines he encountered as 'savages, perhaps the most uncivilised in the world'.

Captain Cook and Joseph Banks are said to have 'discovered' Australia, though there is some evidence that the Chinese may have landed in northern Australia in the fifteenth century. In the first half of the sixteenth century Portuguese navigators had sighted the coast and in 1606 the Spaniard Torres sailed through the strait between Australia and New Guinea which still bears his name. Dutch explorers had also charted much of the north and west coast. For centuries Indonesian fishing boats had operated off the coast with the cooperation of the Aborigines. They came mainly from Macassar, 1,200 miles away at the southern end of Celebes, and fished for trepang or sea-slug.

The most important point of all, however, is that Aborigines had lived there for 50,000 years, their history recorded by cave paintings and substantiated by archaeological evidence.

In January 1788 the first white settlement, made up of over 500 convicts, was established by Captain Phillip in Sydney. On the journey 36 had died. The second consignment, arriving in 1790, fared much worse. Of the 983 men who set out, 263 died on board and a further 82 died within six weeks of landing. From the start starvation threatened the settlement. Phillip complained that not only was the stock of agricultural tools completely inadequate, but also no one except his servant knew anything about gardening.

The suggestion that Botany Bay be used for convict settlements had been made by Banks to a Committee of the House of Commons as early as 1779. It became more urgent after the

American War of Independence when convicts could no longer be sent to America. It was also seen by Matra in 1783 as a place of 'asylum to those unfortunate American Loyalists, whom Great Britain is bound by every tie of honour and gratitude to protect and support, where they may repair their broken fortunes and again enjoy their domestic felicity'.

Banks saw the commercial value of cultivating the New Zealand flax, which he had brought home, in Australia,

> the supply of which would be of great consequence to us as a naval power, as our own manufacturers are of the opinion that canvas made of it would be superior in strength and beauty to any canvas made of the European material, and that a cable of the circumference of ten inches would be superior in strength to one of eighteen inches made of the latter. The threads or filaments of the New Zealand plant are formed by nature with the most exquisite delicacy, and may be so minutely divided as to be manufactured into the finest linen.

So closely was Banks involved in the 'discovery' and botanising of Australia that Linnaeus wanted to call the country 'Banksia' after him, just as the various Australian bottle-brush shrubs are called banksias. It was Matthew Flinders, who sailed round the whole country in 1802–3 in an expedition equipped by Banks, who first regularly used the name Australia.

Banks's botanising was inseparable from his interest in imperialism and colonialism. In a letter to the Governor of New South Wales in 1797, he expresses the wish that he could settle there himself: 'I see the future of empires and dominions which cannot be disappointed. Who knows but that England may revive in New South Wales when it has sunk in Europe?'

He organised a scheme to transport bread-fruit on the *Bounty* from Tahiti to the West Indies in order to provide cheap home-grown food for slaves. It was suggested in 1784, in a letter to him from a planter in Jamaica, who said that it would be

> of infinite importance to the West India Islands, in affording a wholesome and pleasant food to our negroes, which would have the great advantage of being raised with infinitely less labour than the plantain, and not subject to danger from excessively strong winds.

Banks was responsible for designing the ship and for appointing David Nelson to be in charge of the floating conservatory. On the

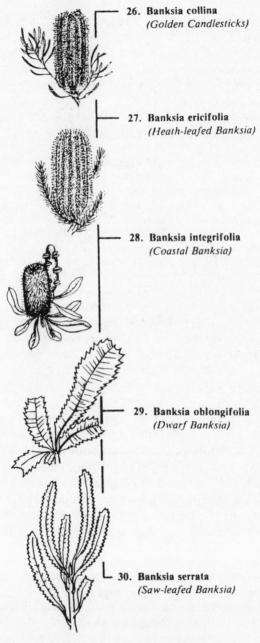

26. **Banksia collina**
    (Golden Candlesticks)

27. **Banksia ericifolia**
    (Heath-leafed Banksia)

28. **Banksia integrifolia**
    (Coastal Banksia)

29. **Banksia oblongifolia**
    (Dwarf Banksia)

30. **Banksia serrata**
    (Saw-leafed Banksia)

Australian Banksias, a source of nectar for the Aborigines who also used the seed cones as hair brushes.

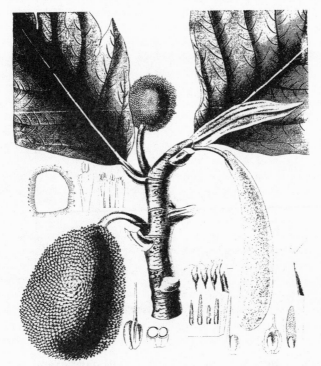

Engraving of bread-fruit (Artocarpus incisa) *from a drawing by*
L. Guilding (1797–1831) from Curtis's Botanical Magazine,
vol. 55, 1828.

design plans, across where the Great Cabin was, had been written
'Garden'. There were complaints that the authority structure of
the ship was being undermined. Whereas David Nelson had
instructions, Captain Bligh had none. The Minister of War, Sir
George Yonge, said 'he supposed Nelson had his own instructions
but the Captain of a ship cannot be expected to take his orders
from a gardener'.

The commercial results of the original voyage on the *Endeavour*
are clearly set out by Banks:

The number of natural productions discovered in this voyage is
incredible; about one thousand species of plants that have not been
at all described by any botanical author; five hundred of fishes; as
many of birds; with insects, sea and land, innumerable. With some
of these very considerable economical purposes may be answered;

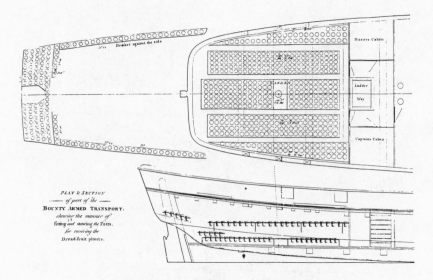

Plan of the Bounty *showing for the first time on a British naval ship the Great Cabin labelled 'Garden' to hold the bread-fruit pots.*

particularly with the fine dye of the Otaheitians, and the plant whereof the New Zealanders make their cloth, of both which we have brought over the feeds.

The material exploitation of Australia, the violence and racism which were evident in this expedition, have left a considerable legacy. As Aboriginal activist Gary Foley says: 'The Aborigines want their land back – the land stolen from their ancestors when the British arrived, 200 years ago.'

Much of the land was taken from the Aborigines simply by hunting them out of the way and by killing as many as possible. In response guerrilla war was waged throughout the country against the British, often successfully, until eventually the Aborigines were defeated by vastly superior numbers and the introduction in the 1870s of the breech-loading repeating rifle. At Toongabbie, west of Sydney, Permulwoy led Aboriginal fighters against the soldiers and settlers until he was finally shot down. His severed and pickled head was sent to Joseph Banks in England.

Back in England Banks was feted. He had an interview with the King, visited Lord Sandwich and had meetings with Sir Joshua

Reynolds, who painted his portrait. Dr Johnson wrote a Latin epigram about the *Endeavour's* goat which had provided the milk 'for the Gentlemen's Coffee'. Banks had brought back 30,000 specimens of plants which could be divided into 3,500 different species. More than half of these were unknown in Europe. Linnaeus's comprehensive plant list at the time, for example, contained only 6,000 species altogether.

Sir Joseph Banks (1743–1820) painted by
Sir Joshua Reynolds, 1772–3.

Of Banks's party of ten, only four survived: Banks, Solander and the two servants from Revesby. Tupia and his servant boy were buried at sea, as was Charles Green the astronomer, and about 30 sailors also died, mainly of fever. The *London Evening Post* of 15 July 1771 reported the return:

Their voyage upon the whole has been as agreeable and successful as they could have expected, except the death of Mr Green who died upon the passage from Batavia. Dr Solander has been a good deal indisposed but it is hoped a few days refreshment will soon establish his health. Captain Cooke and Mr Banks are perfectly well.

THE ROYAL SOCIETY

In 1772 Banks was made Scientific Adviser to the Royal Garden at Kew and in 1778 was elected President of the Royal Society. The Society had become the Royal Society in 1662 and at one of its first meetings in that year had formally considered 'Mr Buckland's proposition to plant potatoes through all parts of England, with the result that all those members of the Society, as have land, should be desired to begin planting this root, and to persuade their friends to do the same.'

The Society, however, had grown out of the English Revolution. Its forerunner had been the Invisible College of 1645–8. The seeds had been sown by the educational reformers Comenius and Hartlib, who in 1641 wanted to found 'a universal college wholly devoted to the advancement of the sciences'. The aim of the Society was an academic revolution:

to improve the knowledge of naturall things, and all useful Arts, Manufactures, Mechanick practises, Engynes and Inventions by Experiments (not meddling with Divinity, Metaphysics, Moralls, Politicks, Grammar, Rhetorick, or Logick). In order to the compiling of a complete system of solid Philosophy for the explicating all Phenomena produced by Nature or Art, and recording a rationall account of the causes of things.

It was this attempt at a rational explanation of the world, like that made by the intellectuals of the French Revolution, which Banks supported, and it enabled him to escape the prevailing Francophobia of the time. In 1801 he was elected to the National Institute of France. He saw the wars with France as disrupting plant-hunting voyages. Only when Napoleon was defeated in 1814 could they safely begin again.

In the same year the Corn Law was passed, prohibiting the import of wheat below a fixed price. It aroused popular indignation which resulted in four successive nights of rioting during which the houses of prominent landowners were attacked, including Banks's house in Soho, as he described:

> I have thank God suffered as little from the miscreants as could have been expected. The windows and doors of my house and the hall-table and chairs was all they destroyed. They dared not enter the house as those inside must have been caught, when the soldiers came, and hanged them as burglars.

Earlier, in 1796, Banks had been instrumental in putting down riots in his native Lincolnshire. The people had literally been up in arms against the pressure on them to join the militia to defend England against a French invasion. Banks was a rationalist, but he was also a member of the ruling class.

KEW GARDENS

In 1772 the King placed Banks in charge of Kew Gardens. He soon turned it into a Botanic Garden which became the centre of world plant exchange, as Cameron points out:

> It was to be the great exchange house of the Empire, where the possibilities of acclimatising plants from one part of the globe to another might be tested and from which material for experimental work in any climate would always be available.

It became the key link in a chain of botanic gardens around the world. Banks also used plants from Kew to carry out international diplomacy. The King asked him to send a collection of plants to the Empress Catherine II of Russia to improve Anglo–Russian relations. In 1795 Banks sent her, initially at his own expense, 226 species which had been cultivated at Kew.

In 1788 Banks presented to the Directors of the East India Company a detailed plan to transfer tea plants from China to India. The Chinese growers were to be induced to take their shrubs, tools and skills to the Botanic Gardens in Calcutta. There they were to teach the Indians who would then be sent off to the 'places ultimately destined for the permanent Establishment of the Manufacture'. The plan was not to be carried out successfully till half a century later, and then finally brought to fruition by Robert Fortune after the Opium War.

93

Banks had long been involved in attempts to explore Africa. In 1788 he presided over the foundation of the Association for Promoting the Discovery of the Inland Districts of Africa, later to be merged with the Royal Geographical Society. He served for many years on its committee, helped finance it and was responsible for Mungo Park's expedition to Africa between 1795 and 1797.

After the establishment of the Australian settlements Banks was in constant correspondence with the early governors of New South Wales and sent them many consignments of plants and seeds. He collaborated with the Governor of Bengal in schemes to transplant there the sago-palm from Malacca and also the Persian date-palm. Many Indian plants, such as the camphor tree and the mango, were sent via Kew to the Botanic Garden in Jamaica, founded in 1775.

In 1803 Banks sent William Kerr to China, which had proved difficult to botanise owing to the travel restrictions placed on foreigners. He told Kerr to 'pay special attention to plants producing fibres and other economic plants that can be acclimatized'. Banks hoped 'England and her colonies will derive solid and substantial benefit' and was also keen to obtain Chinese fruits: 'for our personal gratification I shall be grateful for good varieties of apricots, peaches and plums or cherries, and have no doubt we shall be enabled by observation the gardener will make to cultivate them to advantage'. Kerr also brought back many ornamental plants from the famous Canton gardens, including different kinds of azalea and a wide variety of chrysanthemums. At the time only one variety of chrysanthemum was known in England – Blanchard's variety, 'Old Purple' – sent to Kew from France in 1790.

Banks's botanising is closely connected with the creation of the British Empire. It is also linked with the eighteenth-century change in gardening style. The formal French style in the second half of the seventeenth century, typified by Le Nôtre's gardens at Versailles and copied at Hampton Court and Chatsworth, aimed at controlling nature through geometric patterns. In the eighteenth century the great English landscape gardens, such as Stowe, were created, 'improving' on nature, while restoring the 'natural' look. Shrubberies and rolling parkland took the place of straight avenues and clipped hedges, and new shrubs and trees were wanted for these new gardens. Deleuze, the French historian of botany, even goes so far as to argue that the new style of

The eighteenth-century 'natural' landscape of
Stowe in Buckinghamshire.

gardening arose from the necessity of finding room for the great number of ornamental shrubs and trees imported from America.

Banks was instrumental in organising the introduction of these new plants from abroad. It was calculated by John Loudon that during the reign of George III (1760–1820) nearly 7,000 new plants were introduced into cultivation in England, most of them through the instigation of Banks. He sent out collectors to all corners of the world, for example Francis Masson to South Africa, the West Indies and North America; David Nelson to Australia, South Africa and Timor; A.P. Hove to India; William Kerr to China; Allan Cunningham to Brazil, South Africa, Australia and New Zealand; David Lockhart to the Congo; Archibald Menzies to South America and North America.

Far from being the disinterested activity of men risking their lives 'in the cause of science', as described by Alicia Amherst, this plant hunting was an integral part of English colonialism. The 'treasures' of the modern garden have to be seen in the context of what was done to obtain them and in the light of the ideology of racism which this produced.

5

Robert Fortune in China

*Perhaps the most successful of all adventurous collectors
was Robert Fortune.*

Alicia Amherst, A History of Gardening in England (1895)

*How Fortune shaved his head and wore Chinese costume,
how he smuggled the little camellias (that's what they are)
on board a junk, and how his junk was attacked by pirates
is one of horticulture's hairiest escapades. Fortune was on
a bed of fever when the alarm was raised. He obviously
enjoyed telling the story of his crawling on deck with his
12-bore, waiting for the junks to bump, then firing both
barrels over the gunwale into the pirate crew.*

Hugh Johnson (author of Principles of Gardening), Sunday Times,
19 June 1988

*This tea transfer of 1848–51 is one of the first instances of
a botanic garden (Calcutta) influencing the course of
empire through the organized transfer of a plant of prime
importance in international trade. It antedates and fore-
shadows the activities of Kew Gardens, which had only
recently (1841) become a state institution. The key factors
in successful botanical imperialism were all at hand here,
providing a model for Kew to follow in a few years' time: a
corps of trained botanists supported by the state and ready
to cooperate with the government in removing from a
weaker nation a desirable plant for development on British
soil, under British control.*

Lucile Brockway, Science and Colonial Expansion (1979)

Just as the Spanish colonists exploited native botany in Mexico
for their own purposes, so the British did likewise in China. It
was accompanied by similar invasion, arrogance and deceit. But
just as Cortes is often presented as a brave adventurer, so too are

the intrepid plant hunters. Robert Fortune is a good example and it is particularly revealing to look at his own account of his two journeys to China.

Although Africans had been trading with India and China for centuries, the first Europeans to reach China by boat were the Portuguese in 1516. In 1548 they brought back to Europe the first plant to arrive there by sea from China, the sweet orange, *Citrus sinensis*.

Plants that were brought to Britain from China include the tree peony (*Paeonia moutan*), the common hydrangea (*H. macrophylla*), and the chrysanthemum (*C. sinensis indicum*) which was used to cultivate the florists' chrysanthemums, all arriving at the turn of the eighteenth century. In 1816 the wisteria was introduced (*W. chinensis*), but the real influx began in the middle of the nineteenth century, after the First Opium War of 1839–42.

ECONOMIC EXPLOITATION OF CHINA

From the late seventeenth century the British East India Company had been importing luxury goods from China, such as silk and porcelain, and also tea. At English ports the government collected custom duties of at least £3 million annually on Chinese tea, a sum equal to half the expense of the Royal Navy.

To pay for these imports the company forced China to take the opium grown in Bengal which it sold at auction to intermediaries and on which it collected a transit tax. When the Chinese tried to stop the trade, the British government sent in gunboats to ensure that it continued. So it can be argued that Chinese opium addiction, often used as an example of Chinese decadence, was forced on them to reduce the British trade deficit. As late as 1870 almost half of China's total imports consisted of this drug.

After the war the Treaty of Nanking legalised the trade and opened up China to economic penetration. Hong Kong was annexed and five other ports opened up to British traders. This was particularly important for the sale in China of Lancashire cotton goods which had earlier flooded India, destroying the Indian hand-loom industry.

When discussing the significance of all this for plant collecting, however, many gardening writers ignore the crucial factor of British imperialism. Richard Gorer, for example, in *The Flower Garden in England*, after writing about Robert Fortune's 'visits' and 'trips' to China, adds: 'Japan was even later in giving of its botanical wealth'.

Likewise Littlefield and Schinz, in their book *Visions of Paradise*, describe the situation in the blandest of terms, as if China and Japan willingly offered England their botanical riches:

> Botanists, adventurers, and professional plant hunters were sent out on exploratory trips to Africa, South America, and other distant lands to ship home horticultural treasures. For years, however, only captains of merchant ships and missionaries returning from China and Japan were able to import occasional Oriental plants. But when these two countries finally opened their gates to the West, plant exports surged. England was an eager recipient of that bounty and, because of its temperate climate, proved a particularly hospitable ground for a huge number of foreign species.

Robert Fortune, whom Anne Scott-James calls one of 'our most distinguished collectors', arrived in China in the wake of the Opium War: 'When the news of the peace with China first reached England, in the autumn of 1842, I obtained the appointment of Botanical Collector to the Horticultural Society of London, and proceeded to China in that capacity early in the spring of the following year.' He succinctly sums up the situation in the most northerly of the five treaty ports, Shanghai:

> Taking into consideration its proximity to the large towns of Hangchow, Souchow, and the ancient capital of Nanking; the large native trade; the convenience of inland transit by means of rivers and canals; the fact that teas can be brought here more readily than to Canton; and, lastly, viewing this place as an immense mart for our cotton manufacturers, – there can be no doubt that in a few years it will not only rival Canton, but become a place of far greater importance.

Later he refers back to this prediction:

> When these remarks were written the war had just been brought to a satisfactory termination, and the treaty of Nanking had been wrung from the Chinese. The first merchant-ship had entered the river, one or two English merchants had arrived, and we were living in wretched Chinese houses, eating with chop-sticks, half starved with cold, and sometimes drenched in bed with rain. A great change has taken place since those days. I now find myself (September, 1848), after having been in England for nearly three years, once more in a China boat sailing up the Shanghae river towards the city. The first

object which met my view as I approached the town was a forest of masts, not of junks only, which had been so striking on former occasions, but of goodly foreign ships, chiefly from England and the United States of America. There were now twenty-six large vessels at anchor here, many of which had come loaded with the produce of our manufacturing districts, and were returning filled with silks and teas.

'Anemone on the Tombs' from Robert Fortune's
Three Years' Wanderings in the Northern Provinces of China, *1847: 'When I first discovered the* Anemone Japonica *it was in full flower among the graves of the natives, which are round the ramparts of Shanghae; it blooms in November when other flowers have gone by, and is a most appropriate ornament to the last resting-places of the dead.'*

THE LIFE OF ROBERT FORTUNE

Fortune was a Scot, born in 1812 near Kelloe, Berwickshire. In 1839 he went to the Royal Botanic Garden in Edinburgh to train as a gardener under William McNab. Three years later he joined the staff of the Royal Horticultural Society in London and almost immediately was sent to China as a collector.

In 1847 his book on China was published entitled *Three Years' Wanderings in the Northern Provinces of China.* He went to northern China because already 'the south of China had been ransacked by former botanists'. His aim was to bring back ornamental plants, particularly hardy ones, but he was also told by the Royal Horticultural Society to look for certain peaches, oranges, and the plants that produced tea and rice-paper. Fortune was responsible for first introducing into this country forsythia (*Forsythia viridissima*), winter jasmine (*Jasminum nudiflorum*), *Skimmia japonica*, *Mahonia japonica*, and many other plants including the Japanese anemone (*Anemone japonica*) which he found growing in Chinese graveyards.

'The White Japan Anemone in the Wild Garden' from William Robinson's The Wild Garden, 1870.

It was still forbidden to travel into the interior of China, so he disguised himself as a Chinaman: 'I was, of course, travelling in the Chinese costume; my head was shaved, I had a splendid wig and tail, of which some Chinaman in former days had doubtless been extremely vain; and upon the whole I believe I made a pretty fair Chinaman.'

This is particularly ironic when one hears his description of the Chinese as full of 'cunning and deceit'! He calls them 'lawless', 'conceited', 'lazy', 'stupid', despite his claim that he is 'far from having any prejudices against the Chinese people'.

100

Fortune writes: 'A great proportion of the northern Chinese seem to be in a sleepy or dreaming state, from which it is difficult to awake them.' Nevertheless he thinks they are more 'civil and obliging' than the 'haughty and insolent southerners'. It is reminiscent of my old stamp album's description of China as 'a large country in eastern Asia, which boasts the oldest civilisation in the world, and but for her people being slow in thought and backward it is certain that she could be a far greater power than she is today'. The album was published just before the Chinese Revolution in 1949.

ECONOMIC BOTANY

It is clear from his book that Fortune's interests, and those of the Horticultural Society, were not simply gardening, but extended to the wider field of economic botany. In 1834 a few tea plants had already been taken to the Botanic Garden in Calcutta, but they failed to survive transplanting. The previous year a Dutchman called Jacobson had taken Chinese planters and seven million seeds to Java to start tea cultivation there. By 1836, however, tea plantation in the Himalayas had started, and Fortune was determined to make it as successful as the Chinese industry by 'procuring a large supply of young plants from the province of Cheking, where it evidently grows most luxuriantly'.

He poses the following questions:

> Have we the same variety of the tea plant in India which produces the best teas of China? – Has India the advantage of cheap labour, as we are informed it has? – Is the soil and modes of management and manufacture the same in both countries? If these questions can be answered in the affirmative, we may confidently look forward to the same results in the end.

His conclusion sounds philanthropic, but he fails to mention the profits that would accrue to the East India Company:

> The advantages which would result from the successful cultivation of the tea plants in India are immense. The vast population of our empire in the East would have a cheap and harmless beverage produced amongst themselves, and thousands of families would find a healthy and profitable employment in the cultivation and manufacture of tea. These results are altogether independent of the benefit which would be conferred upon our population at home.

He also came across the finest silk produced in China and thought it might be the result of using a different variety of mulberry tree to feed the worms:

> If the plant should prove a different species or variety from that which is cultivated in the south of Europe, it may be a matter of some importance to introduce it to the plantations of Italy, as Chinese silk is much heavier in the thread than the Italian, and is used in the manufacture of those fabrics requiring lustre and firmness.

He gives a full description of how the silk is produced and seems surprised that the Chinese thought he was going to rob them of their silkworms.

Most of the ornamental plants Fortune obtained were from mandarin gardens or from nursery gardens. He often had great difficulty finding the gardens and gaining access. In Shanghai he asked for assistance from Her Majesty's Consul, Captain Balfour, to help overcome the Chinese reticence.

The whole expedition cost the Horticultural Society just over £1,800. But the value of Fortune's collections can be indicated by referring to one example. On a trip to the Philippines he was looking for the orchid, *Phaloenopsis amabilis*, which was still very rare in England. He offered to buy one for a dollar, which he considered to be a large sum of money. A few years earlier the Duke of Devonshire had bought the first plant in England for 100 guineas, indicating the kind of profit which Fortune could make out of these plants.

After nearly three years in China Fortune had his collections packed in Shanghai and he left for Hong Kong and then England:

> As I went down the river, I could not but look around me with pride and satisfaction; for in this part of the country I had found the finest plants in my collections. It is only the patient botanical collector, the object of whose unintermitted labour is the introduction of the more valuable trees and shrubs of other countries into his own, who can appreciate what I then felt.

In Hong Kong he divided his collection, sending eight glazed cases of living plants to England. He kept duplicates of them all and took 18 glazed cases with him, 'filled with the most beautiful plants of northern China', on his journey back to London. The voyage took four and a half months and he concludes the book:

The plants arrived in excellent order, and were immediately conveyed to the garden of the Horticultural Society at Chiswick. Already, many of those which I first imported have found their way to the principal gardens in Europe; and at the present time (October 20 1846) the *Anemone japonica* is in full bloom in the garden of the Society at Chiswick, as luxuriant and beautiful as it ever grew on the graves of the Chinese, near the ramparts of Shanghae.

PLANT HUNTING

Two years later Fortune was off to China again, this time sent by the Court of Directors of the East India Company 'for the purpose of obtaining the finest varieties of the Tea-plant, as well as native manufacturers and implements, for the Government Tea plantations in the Himalayas'. He wrote an account of his travels, *A Journey to the Tea Countries of China*, in 1852.

He was aiming to visit the tea district of Hwuy-chow, but it was 200 miles inland, a sealed country to Europeans, with the exception of a few Jesuit missionaries. He considered sending Chinese agents to collect the plants, but did not trust them: 'No dependence can be placed upon the veracity of the Chinese.' So he decided to go himself, disguised once more in Chinese dress and travelling either by boat or in a sedan-chair.

'Mountain Chair' from Robert Fortune's Three Years' Wanderings in the Northern Provinces of China, *1847.*

103

'The Funereal Cypress' from Robert Fortune's A Journey to the
Tea Countries of China, *1852.*

On his way to the tea districts he came across a funereal cypress
for the first time, covered in ripe fruit. It was growing in the
walled grounds of a country inn and belonged to the innkeeper.
He was about to climb over the wall when he suddenly realised
that he was dressed as a Chinaman and that 'such a proceeding
would have been very indecorous, to say the least of it'. So he
planned a different, more subtle approach:

We now walked into the inn, and, seating ourselves quietly down at one of the tables, ordered some dinner to be brought to us. When we had taken our meal we lighted our Chinese pipes, and sauntered out, accompanied by our polite host, into the garden where the real attraction lay. 'What a fine tree this of yours is! we have never seen it in the countries near the sea where we come from; pray give us some of its seeds.' 'It is a fine tree,' said the man, who was evidently much pleased with our admiration of it, and readily complied with our request. These seeds were carefully treasured; and as they got home safely, and are now growing in England, we may expect in a few years to see a new and striking feature produced upon our land-scape by this lovely tree.

On later occasions he did not hesitate to *steal* seeds and cuttings:

My coolie and myself were busy collecting tea-seeds on a small hill not far from the town. After collecting all the seeds we could find, I happened to get a glimpse of a very fine specimen of the funereal cypress, with which I was so charmed, that I determined to go to the spot where it was growing and enjoy a nearer view. I desired my attendant to accompany me, in case any ripe seeds might be found upon it. As we approached the village we discovered that the tree was inside a garden, which was surrounded by very high walls. Naturally supposing that there must be a gate somewhere, we walked round the walls until we came to a little cottage, which seemed to have served the purpose of a lodge. We passed in here with all the coolness of Chinamen, and soon found ourselves in a dilapidated old garden. A large house, which had formerly been the mansion, was, like the garden, in a ruinous condition. The funereal cypress which I had seen in the distance stood in the midst of the garden, and was covered with ripe seeds, which increased the collec-tion I had formerly obtained.

Having taken a survey of the place, we were making our way out, when an extraordinary plant, growing in a secluded part of the garden, met my eye. When I got near it I found that it was a very fine evergreen Berberis, belonging to the section of Mahonias, and having of course pinnated leaves. Each leaflet was as large as the leaf of an English holly, spiny, and of a fine dark, shining green colour. The shrub was about eight feet high, much branched, and far surpassed in beauty all the other known species of Mahonia. It had but one fault, and that was, that it was too large to move and bring away. I secured a leaf, however, and marked the spot where it grew, in order to secure some cuttings of it on my return from the interior.

In the Bohea mountains he dug up species of hydrangea, spiraea and abelia. He had them carried several hundred miles to

105

Shanghai and then shipped to Europe. It was this love of plants that he thought would cement bonds of friendship between the Chinese and the British: 'Nothing, I believe, can give the Chinese a higher idea of our civilisation and attainments than our love for flowers, or tend more to create a kindly feeling between us and them.'

The twin arms of colonialism – the Bible and the gun – were never far from Fortune's thoughts:

> it may be that another war and all its horrors is inevitable, and whenever that takes place this vast country will be opened up to foreigners of every nation. Then the Christian missionary will be able to extend his labours to those far-distant stations amongst the Bohea hills which I have just been describing.

As a Protestant, he even managed to admire the self-denial and heroism of the Roman Catholic missionaries who had left friends, home and country to 'preach the Gospel to the heathen'. The Protestant missionaries he found a little timid in not pressing further afield than the five ports.

THE TEA TRANSFER

The main reason his sponsors sent Fortune to China, however, was to find out more about the tea industry. A lengthy chapter in his book deals with this in detail: the size of farms and the mode of packing, the route of the tea from the black-tea country to Canton and Shanghai, how long it took and how much it cost. He worked out that the Chinese dealers made considerable profits and so argued that they could be 'amply remunerated by a lower price than any yet quoted': 'if the above calculations are near the truth, we may still hope to drink our favourite beverage, at least the middling and finer qualities of it, at a price much below that which we now pay'.

The ultimate aim was to develop the Indian tea industry and so all the tea plants he had collected were assembled in Shanghai, packed in sealed glass boxes, called Wardian cases, and sent to the Botanic Garden in Calcutta by four different ships, in case of accident. He then had to engage 'some first-rate tea manufacturers' and procure a supply of implements for the manufacture of tea: 'As a result of this mission, nearly twenty thousand plants from the best black and green tea countries of Central China have been introduced to the Himalayas.'

He recommends that the existing manufacturers should be sacked and the new ones used to teach the Indians. When the Indians had learned the Chinese skills, then the new manufacturers should also be dispensed with, because of their high wages.

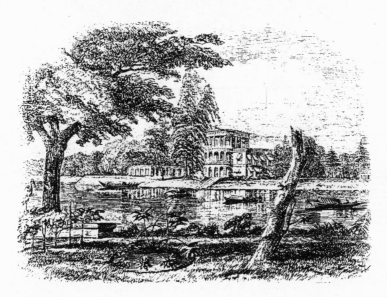

Nineteenth-century view of the Calcutta Botanic Gardens.

A similar chain of events took place in Brazil. Tea was introduced to the country through the botanic garden in Rio de Janeiro, which was set up in 1808, and Chinese workers were brought in to teach the Brazilians how to grow the plant. The garden in Rio was worked by slave labour up until about 1860. The Calcutta Botanic Garden used to be cultivated by 'convicts in chains' but, according to Bishop Heber, their labour was replaced by peasants hired by the day or week: 'the labour of freemen here, as elsewhere, being infinitely cheaper than that of slaves'.

Fortune argues that the results of his tea transfer would be beneficial both to England and to India:

In these days, when tea has become almost a necessary of life in England and her wide-spreading colonies, its production upon a

Rio de Janeiro Botanic Gardens today.

large and cheap scale is an object of no ordinary importance. But to the natives of India themselves the production of this article would be of the greatest value.

The Indians would soon acquire the habit of drinking tea and Fortune would have helped make sure that it was produced at a cheap enough rate. Then 'a boon will have been conferred upon the people of India of no common kind, and one which an enlightened and liberal Government may well be proud of conferring upon its subjects'. A boon would also have been conferred upon the East India Company.

Tea became one of north India's main exports by the end of the nineteenth century and it supplanted Chinese tea in Britain, where the consumption of tea doubled between 1840 and 1860, and doubled again by the end of the century. By 1905 Assam had

206,000 acres under tea cultivation and the all-India total was nearly double that amount.

As Lucile Brockway points out:

> The one sharp difference between the British removal of tea plants from China and the later removal of rubber and cinchona from Latin America is that the tea removal was done in the aftermath of a war, and the Chinese themselves, under this duress, furnished the expert knowledge of tea cultivation and processing. In the later plant removals from Latin America, British botanists neither sought nor received any help from their victims, but Kew Gardens had by then developed the institutional strength to find new cultivation methods.

Tea plants from Loudon's Encyclopaedia of Gardening.

Robert Fortune is celebrated as a great British plant hunter and the plants he brought back soon became popular in English gardens. But, as with Banks and the Tradescants before him, it is impossible to separate his horticultural interests from those of economic botany and politics. His discovery of new plants is inextricably linked to the opening up of China for economic exploitation and to the colonisation of India. The manner in which many of the plants were taken is indicative of the developing power relations between Britain and its empire. It is also symptomatic of imperialism that racism should accompany its march across the world.

6

Joseph Hooker and Kew Gardens

The sluggish inertia of the people often presents a great hindrance to the scientific collector. It is difficult to find any inducement sufficiently tempting to overcome the laziness of the common people in many tropical regions.

P.H. Gosse, *Wanderings through the Conservatories at Kew* (1856)

A romantic story could be written about Kew's share in the encouragement of industries in the British Commonwealth by the distribution of seeds and plants. For instance, cinchona, the quinine tree, was introduced from South America via Kew to India, thus saving millions of lives. Rubber seeds were sent home by collectors, and thousands of plants were raised from them at Kew. These were then despatched to Malaya and Ceylon, and multiplied into great rubber plantations.

Gladys Taylor, *Old London Gardens* (1953)

The heroic days of plant collecting are famous and the name of Kew echoes throughout them. The transfer of the rubber tree from Brazil to Malaya, the discovery and culti-vation of quinine, the collection of rhododendrons from the flanks of the Himalayas and their establishment in gardens from one end of the earth to the other, by such achievements in the last century, Kew and its collectors enhanced the health, the wealth and the beauty of the world.

David Attenborough, in F.Nigel Hepper (ed.), *Plant Hunting for Kew* (1989)

Through its research, its dissemination of scientific infor-mation, and its practical activities, which included plant

110

smuggling, Kew Gardens played a major part in the devel-
opment of several highly profitable and strategically
important plant-based industries in the tropical colonies.
These new plantation crops complemented Britain's home
commodity exchange which for a time, in the nineteenth
and early twentieth centuries, made Britain the world's
superpower.

Lucile Brockway, *Science and Colonial Expansion* (1979)

After Joseph Banks's death in 1820 Kew Gardens declined and fewer collectors were sent out. Then in 1838 the Treasury appointed a committee to 'inquire into the management etc of the Royal Gardens'. This committee, one of whose members was Joseph Paxton, who was gardener to the Duke of Devonshire at Chatsworth and who later designed the Crystal Palace in Hyde Park, stressed the need for a well-equipped botanic garden. The committee's report was presented to parliament in 1840 with the result that Kew was transferred from the Crown to the government. No longer were the gardens to be in the hands of a wealthy amateur like Joseph Banks, but in those of professionals with salaries paid by the state.

WILLIAM HOOKER

In 1841 William Jackson Hooker was appointed Director, coming from Glasgow University where he had been professor of botany, a post he had obtained through the recommendation of Joseph Banks. In 1855 Joseph Hooker joined his father and became Assistant Director. For over 60 years, at the height of its importance, Kew Gardens seemed like a family business. When William Hooker died in 1865 his son took over for 20 years, and on Joseph Hooker's retirement his son-in-law, Thiselton-Dyer, took over as Director, holding the post until 1905.

Dawson Turner
|
WILLIAM J. HOOKER = Maria Turner   John Stevens Henslow
| |
JOSEPH D. HOOKER = Frances H. Henslow
|
Harriet Hooker = W.T. THISELTON-DYER

Kew Directors are indicated by all caps

111

The world-wide system of botanic gardens, which Banks had initiated, was developed in line with the Royal Commission report which called for a National Botanic Garden to be the 'centre around which lesser establishments should be arranged'. These colonial gardens would help the 'mother-country in everything useful in the vegetable kingdom: medicine, commerce, agriculture, horticulture, and many branches of manufacture would derive considerable advantage from the establishment of such a system'. Information would be provided to enable new colonies to be established.

The Palm House at Kew Gardens, designed by Decimus Burton in association with Richard Turner, built 1844–8. Engraving from The Illustrated London News, *August 1859.*

Within five years William Hooker had increased the area for botanical purposes at Kew from 15 to over 250 acres and in 1848 the Palm House was completed, measuring 363 feet long, 100 feet wide and 60 feet high. In the same year the first Museum of Economic Botany at Kew was opened to the public. Plant hunters were once more sent out and the Royal Horticultural Society arranged for seeds and plants from their collectors to be shared with Kew.

JOSEPH HOOKER

Joseph Hooker (1817–1911) was the most celebrated European botanist of the nineteenth century. A medal he received from the Linnean Society describes him as 'the most illustrious living exponent of botanical science' and Mea Allan calls him 'the most honoured British botanist of all time'. The list of his degrees, diplomas and honours, awarded from nearly 30 different countries, takes up over ten pages in Leonard Huxley's *Life and Letters of Sir Joseph Dalton Hooker*. Joseph Hooker was Director of Kew Gardens from 1865 to 1885. From 1873 to 1878 he was President of the Royal Society.

Rhododendron edgeworthii: lithograph by W.H. Fitch (1817–92), from a drawing by Joseph Hooker, from The Rhododendrons of Sikkim Himalaya, *1849.*

Hooker botanised in every continent and introduced into this country 43 new species of rhododendron from the Himalayas. He is credited by Miles Hadfield with being 'one of the principal originators of British rhododendronomania, which has given a distinct quality and feeling quite singular to British gardens on acid soils, and played an important part in the movement for "natural" gardens in later periods'. Mea Allan claims that he 'turned the dull Victorian shrubbery and green woodland into places glorious with colour'. By the end of his life he had named 303 new species of plants.

Rhododendrons became so popular that according to Shirley Hibberd in 1871: 'The money spent on rhododendrons during twenty years in this country would nearly suffice to pay off the National Debt.' So fashionable had they become by this time, often planted in unsuitable alkaline soil, that Hibberd argued for a return to the green shrubbery: 'We therefore protest against the wasteful and ridiculous practice of treating the rhododendron as adapted for any and every position in which a handsome evergreen shrub may be required.'

Sometimes whole hillsides would be planted with rhododendrons. In 1892 the *Gardener's Magazine* notes that at Cragside in Northumberland 'several hundred thousands have been planted, forming impenetrable thickets, and blooming so profusely as to light up the whole hillside with their varied colours'.

EXPEDITION TO THE HIMALAYAS

It was between 1847 and 1851 that Joseph Hooker made his famous expedition to the Himalayas. After an earlier voyage to the Antarctic, the main purpose of which was to discover the south magnetic pole before the French and Americans did, he now wanted to botanise in a temperate zone. His choice lay between India and the Andes. He chose India because of the contacts he had there and the assistance that would be available.

His father contacted both the Chief Commissioner of Woods and Forests, the Earl of Carlisle, and also the First Lord of the Admiralty, the Earl of Auckland, and between them they persuaded the Treasury to grant Hooker £400 per annum for two years so that the 'journey assumed the character of a Government mission'. Lord Auckland also wanted him afterwards to visit Borneo

for the purpose of reporting on the capabilities of Labuan, with reference to the cultivation of cotton, tobacco, sugar, indigo, spices, gutta-percha, etc. To this end a commission in the navy (to which service I was already attached) was given me, such instructions were drawn up as might facilitate my movements in the East, and a suitable sum of money was placed at my disposal.

This trip to Borneo was later cancelled and he was asked to stay in India for an extra year instead.

In India he received 'every assistance' from Dr Falconer, the superintendent of the East India Company's Botanic Garden in Calcutta, which was the garden that had been used to transfer tea from China to the Himalayas and Assam. According to Hooker its name was 'renowned throughout Europe' and during its first 20 years 'it had contributed more useful and ornamental tropical plants to the public and private gardens of the world than any other establishment before or since'.

Before leaving Calcutta for Darjeeling he went with a Geological Survey party to inspect a recently discovered coalfield. On arriving in Darjeeling he received the support of the Governor-General's agent, Dr Campbell, whose 'whole aim was to promote my comfort, and to secure my success, in all possible ways'. In particular Dr Campbell arranged access to Sikkim by negotiating with the Rajah who was 'all but a dependant of the British Government'. Both Hooker and Campbell were later to be captured and held hostage by a faction of the Sikkim court under the Dewan, or Prime Minister.

Most significant of all, perhaps, was the support of Lord Dalhousie, the new Governor-General of India. They had travelled out to India together and Lord Dalhousie had promised Hooker 'every facility he could command'. This was no idle promise, for when Hooker was captured in Sikkim he sent a letter to Lord Dalhousie in Bombay. It had immediate results – 14,000 troops were dispatched to Darjeeling. The troop movements were enough to effect Hooker's release. He was then, with some reluctance on his part, put in charge of 500 men and took possession of the bridge over the Great Rungeet River prior to the advance into Sikkim. Hooker acknowledged the help of all these men by naming rhododendrons after them, or after their wives – *R. aucklandii, R. dalhousiae, R. falconeri, R. campbellae.*

Before his capture Hooker had been asked to make a map of the area and he gave this to General Young to help the troops march into Sikkim. He had surveyed the whole country and provided Campbell with the 'knowledge of its resources which the British government should all along have possessed, as the protector of

115

the Rajah and his territories'. The whole southern part of Sikkim was then annexed. The aim of controlling Sikkim was to keep a buffer between Nepal and Bhutan and, 'but for this policy, the aggressive Nepalese would, long ere this, have possessed themselves of Sikkim, Bhotan, and the whole Himalaya, eastward to the borders of Burmah'.

A few years later Hooker comments that 'the revenues of the tract thus acquired have doubled and will very soon be quadrupled: every expense of our detention and of the moving of troops, etc., has been already repaid by it, and for the future all will be clear profit'.

In a book on Hooker published in 1919, F.O. Bower writes:

His topographical results especially were of the highest importance. They formed the basis of a map published by the Indian Topographical Survey, and by its aid the operations of various campaigns and political missions have since been carried to a successful issue.

For his travels Hooker was provided with a 'completely equipped palkee', a palanquin or sedan chair, by Sir James Colvile, President of the Asiatic Society, which 'for strength and excellence of construction, was everything a traveller could desire. Often en route did I mentally thank him when I saw other palkees breaking down, and travellers bewailing the loss of those forgotten necessaries, with which his kind attention had furnished me.' Twelve bearers were employed to carry him in the palkee while at other times he travelled on a pony. Occasionally he walked and 'picked up a few plants' on the way.

On his three-month expedition in Nepal he had a party of 56 people, including porters, servants, guards, an interpreter, someone to shoot and stuff birds and animals, and 'three Lepcha lads to climb trees and change the plant-papers', between which the plants were pressed for their preservation. His comments on these people as 'savage and half-civilised' are reminiscent of Fortune's on the Chinese and Banks's on the Aborigines.

His views reflected and contributed to the ideology of racism which accompanied British colonialism. He writes that the Bhutan coolies 'complained unreasonably of their loads' which was 'typical of the turbulent, mulish race to which they belong'. The Tibetans are described as a 'wild, black, and uncouth-looking people', 'intolerantly indolent and filthy', 'insolent and bullying':

'A Tibetan household is very slovenly; the family live higgledy-piggledy ...'

When Hooker returned to England with Dr Thomson in 1851, they brought back a herbarium of between 6,000 and 7,000 species of Indian plants. In his *Himalayan Journals* Hooker sums up his feelings:

> Now that all obstacles were surmounted, and I was returning laden wih materials for extending the knowledge of a science which had formed the pursuit of my life, will it be wondered at that I felt proud, not less for my own sake, than for that of the many friends, both in India and at home, who were interested in my success?

Later as President of the Royal Society he made the annual address to his fellows, on 30 November 1875, urging them to 'endeavour never to allow scientific investigation to be subordinated to practical results'. Similarly Banks had earlier claimed that his scientific work should not be interrupted by the wars with France, while at the same time his voyages with Cook, and their navigational discoveries, had paved the way for the defeat of the French and the capture of many of their colonies.

This myth of scientific independence and pure research is still powerful and owes much to an aristocratic conception of knowledge untainted with commerce and politics. That it is a myth in this case is clear from Hooker's close involvement in Indian trade and colonialism. Referring to an area below Darjeeling, he comments: 'The tea-plant succeeds here admirably, and might be cultivated to great profit, and be of advantage in furthering a trade with Tibet.'

THE CINCHONA TRANSFER

One of the most important of Kew Garden's plant transfers which took place at this time was that of the cinchona tree. The bark from this tree is the source of quinine which cures malaria, a disease which has killed more people than any other in human history.

Cinchona trees grow naturally in the northern Andes, in Colombia, Ecuador, Peru and Bolivia, and the Indians had long used the bark to treat fevers, though malaria did not exist on the American continent until brought there by Europeans. Medicinal use of plants by the Incas, as by the Aztecs, was well in advance of Europe at that time. The Peruvian bark, in a powdered form, was eventually brought to Europe around 1640 by Jesuits and at first was known as Jesuit's powder. It was used to cure King Charles II of malaria, but Oliver Cromwell, fatally for him, refused to take it because of its Catholic connections. He called it the 'powder of the devil'. In 1685 John Evelyn recorded seeing the cinchona tree in the Apothecaries' Garden in Chelsea.

The cultivation of cinchona plants, from J.M. Cowan's Cinchona in the Empire, *1929.*

In 1929 J.M. Cowan, the Superintendent of Cinchona Cultivation in Bengal, wrote:

We have, however, within the Empire a large proportion of the malarial tracts of the world, and when it is realised that some 800,000,000 people suffer from malaria (as estimated by Professor Muller of Cologne) and that there are, according to Sir Ronald Ross, 2,000,000 fatal cases every year, it is patent that our responsibilities are very great. Leaving aside the humanitarian aspect and taking only the financial, the direct loss sustained by the British Empire due to sickness and death caused by malaria is said by Dr A. Balfour to amount to between £52,000,000 and £62,000,000 each year.

Today malaria still affects more than 1,500 million people, causing the death of four children every minute in Africa alone. George Bridie, a Surgeon-Major in the British army, wrote in 1879 about cinchona:

> To England, with her numerous and extensive Colonial possessions, it is simply priceless; and it is not too much to say, that if portions of her tropical empire are upheld by the bayonet, the arm that wields the weapon would be nerveless but for Cinchona bark and its active principles.

In 1857 the Sepoy Revolt, or Indian Mutiny, took place. In the following year the British government responded by taking over India from the East India Company and reorganising the army, using more British troops. In the same year they called on Kew to obtain cinchona.

Joseph Banks was the first to propose the transfer of cinchona trees to India, where the production of the bark could be controlled by the British, but it was not realised till 1861 with the help of William Hooker and Kew Gardens. Several collectors were sent out and obtained seeds and plants through a mixture of subterfuge, persuasion, bribery and theft. In doing so, they knew they were breaking the laws of Bolivia, where export of cinchona was a government monopoly, and of Ecuador, where it was illegal to export plants.

In the same year William Hooker writes: 'The means adopted for introducing Cinchonas (trees yielding quinine) into the East Indies and our tropical colonies rank first in point of interest and importance of the works of the past year.' At one time there were as many as 10,000 cinchona seedlings in a heated greenhouse that had been specially built at Kew.

The seedlings were then shipped out to India, the Nilgiri Hills and the part of Sikkim annexed by the British, where plantations were prepared by convict labour. Then quinine was produced to benefit the people of India – or so the story is now told. When Joseph Hooker was asked at the turn of the century what his most important achievement had been in economic botany, he replied: 'Quite certainly the getting of cinchona into India. The result is that anyone can get at any post office a dose of pure quinine for little less than half a penny.'

In fact this was true only in Bengal, and the price was still prohibitive for 90 per cent of the Indians suffering from malaria.

Most of the quinine produced in India went to the British army and civil servants or was sold to private planters for mass treatment of their Indian workers.

The Dutch in Java developed a higher-yielding species which had been smuggled out of Bolivia in 1865 by Charles Ledger. The Indian whom Ledger had persuaded to bring him the cinchona seeds was later executed for the crime. In a similar way a total of 18 Japanese lost their lives helping the smuggling activities of botanist Andreas Cleyer. He was Governor of the artificial trading island off Nagasaki, used by the Dutch East India Company at the end of the nineteenth century.

By 1929 Java was producing over 90 per cent of the world's quinine, compared with about 4 per cent from India, many planters in India having changed over to the more profitable cultivation of tea. Between them, these two European powers undercut and destroyed the South American market. During the two World Wars the whole of the Indian production of quinine was used for the war effort and not available to the Indian public. Quinine enabled Britain to colonise West Africa by reducing the death rate from malaria of its troops from an average of nearly 50 per cent at the beginning of the nineteenth century to 6 per cent or 7 per cent by the end of the century.

THE RUBBER TRANSFER

Another crucial plant transfer organised by Kew took place when Joseph Hooker obtained rubber seeds, *Hevea brasiliensis*, from Brazil in 1876. Columbus saw bouncing rubber balls for the first time in Haiti, and *caoutchouc*, the original word for rubber, comes from the Carib word *cahuchu*. It was first called rubber by Joseph Priestley in 1770. The Indians from the Amazon to Arizona had been the first to learn how to smoke the latex to produce rubber and with it they made torches, jars, syringes, toys, breastplates, quivers, raincoats, shoes and rubber-headed drumsticks. They also used the gum to heal cuts and bruises.

Once again the rubber seeds were smuggled out, this time by Henry Wickham. He had heard of the difficulties of getting cinchona out of Peru and was determined to avoid any delay which would render his 'precious freight quite valueless and useless'. The seeds, estimated at 70,000, arrived at the Liverpool docks where they were put aboard a night goods train which had been sent there specially by Joseph Hooker. Wickham described the scene at Kew:

> Sir Joseph was not a little pleased. The Hevea did not fail to respond to the care I had bestowed on them. A fortnight afterwards the glass-houses at Kew afforded (to me) a pretty sight – tier upon tier – rows of young Hevea plants – seven thousand odd of them.

A total of 1,900 young plants was then sent in the care of a Kew gardener to the Peradeniya Botanic Garden in Ceylon, now Sri Lanka, and 22 of these seedlings were sent on to the Singapore Botanic Garden for distribution to Malaya, now Malaysia. In Malaya indentured Chinese labour was imported to clear and plant the new plantations and Tamils from South India to do the tapping and weeding.

At the turn of the century Brazil produced 98 per cent of the world's rubber; it has now dropped to around 5 per cent. By 1934 1,090,000 tons of crude rubber was coming from South-East Asia, 75 per cent of it originating from those 22 seedlings, compared with 14,000 tons from all other sources.

The development of the rubber industry exemplifies the disastrous results of capitalist and colonial exploitation of raw materials. In Brazil it led to the annihilation of whole groups of Indians and the enslavement of many others. When the industry was destroyed by South-East Asian competition, more Indians died through starvation.

The wholesale introduction of rubber into Malaysia has not been in the interests of the people in that country either, as the President of the Consumers' Association of Penang, Mohamed Idris, points out:

> The best lands in Malaysia are being used to grow export crops such as rubber and palm oil while food crops such as padi, vegetables and fruit are given low priority or even squeezed out by development activities. In 1978 Malaysia had to import 718,000 tons of rice or 44 per cent of the total food requirements in the country.

Kew Gardens and the Empire

The examples of cinchona and rubber show how important Kew and its network of colonial counterparts were in the economic development of the Empire. Kew's role in appropriating new plants for English gardens was matched by its development of economic botany. Joseph Chamberlain as Secretary of State for the Colonies stated in the House of Commons, on 2 August 1898: 'At the present time there are several of our important colonies which owe whatever prosperity they possess to the knowledge and experience of, and the assistance given by, the authorities at Kew Gardens.'

It is also interesting to note the spread of English gardening style through this activity. Kew had originally been designed by William Kent in 1730, and redesigned later in the same century by 'Capability' Brown. This form of garden landscaping introduced at Kew was taken up by those who designed the colonial botanic gardens, such as those in Sri Lanka, Singapore and Melbourne.

Horace Walpole, son of Prime Minister Robert Walpole who was the instigator of the Black Acts, said of Kent: 'He leaped the fence, and saw that all nature was a garden.' Similarly British explorers and naturalists crossed the seas and saw that all the world was ripe for exploitation. Walpole also wrote: 'We have given the true model of gardening to the world ... let it reign here on its verdant throne, original by its elegant simplicity, and proud of no other art than that of softening nature's harshness, and copying her graceful touch.'

Many of the enlarged and rebuilt country houses of the eighteenth century and their new landscaped gardens were built from the profits of overseas trade, including the slave-trade. In 1700 15 per cent of British commerce was with the colonies. In 1775 it was as much as a third.

KEW GARDENS OPEN TO THE PUBLIC

In the eighteenth century there was a right of way through Kew Gardens called Love Lane. In 1765 King George III obtained powers from parliament to close it, though it was not effectively closed until 1802.

In 1773 a young boy from Farnham, aged eleven, heard of Kew Gardens and walked all the way there, 30 miles as the crow flies, to see them. He was given work by the gardener. The boy's name was William Cobbett, the radical campaigner and journalist, famous for his *Political Register*, but perhaps not so well known for his book *The English Gardener*. His passion for gardening had begun when he was six years old.

The gardens were not really open to the public, however, until 1841 when William Hooker opened part of the grounds on weekdays from 1pm to 6pm in the summer and until sunset in the winter. Even then he encountered royal opposition which claimed that the gardens provided the only exercising place for the Queen who by then was established at Kensington. It took 16 more years before people were allowed entry on Sundays, and then only in the afternoons. Over 9,000 visitors came in the first year of opening; in 1845 – 20,139, in 1846 – 46,574, in 1847 – 64,282. By 1865 it had risen to half a million; in 1900 over a million; and by 1907 nearly three million. The largest attendance on one day was 80,000, on a Whit Monday.

Sunday opening at the Royal Botanic Garden in Edinburgh took even longer to achieve. In 1862 a petition signed by over 14,000 working men of Edinburgh called for the garden to be opened on a Sunday after the normal hours of public worship, namely 2pm. They argued that the garden had been established to promote useful knowledge and that it was financed by taxes which they paid. They could not visit it during the week because they were working. The Sabbath Alliance opposed them and in 1863 it was debated in the House of Commons.

In the debate Palmerston, aged 80, while agreeing with Sunday opening, argued to defer to Scottish opinion. The Sabbath Alliance had eventually obtained 48,522 signatures, as against 36,897 for opening. He maintained that Edinburgh provided the working classes with 'the amplest opportunities for air, exercise, and recreation' and implied that they would not be interested in the Botanic Garden because 'the centre is occupied with flower beds and plants intended for scientific instruction'. The motion to open the garden on Sunday was lost by 123 votes to 107.

Not until 1889 was Sunday opening allowed, when the garden was placed under the Public Parks Regulations. *The Scotsman*, 6 April, approved:

> Another benefit, which will become more and more apparent as the summer advances, is that the Garden, like other Public Parks, will be open all week from dawn to dusk, instead of being closed while there is still a great part of the best time of the day to come; the time, too, when working men and their families are best able to take advantage of the humanising, innocent, and elevating pleasure of strolling through a Botanic Garden.

Over 27,000 people visited the garden during the first four Sundays of opening.

Meanwhile at Kew in the 1870s there was growing public agitation for the gardens to be opened at 10am, instead of noon. Joseph Hooker rejected this idea as it would interfere with the work of his gardeners and botanists. In 1877 the Kew Gardens Public Rights Association was formed to campaign for earlier opening. On 15 September 1877 the *Richmond and Twickenham Times* reported:

> A large number of people came down in the morning of the last Bank Holiday expecting admission to the Gardens, but finding the Gates shut, betook themselves, in true British fashion, to drinking and dancing, and then some 2 hours later sought to refresh exhausted nature by falling asleep on the grass.

A local clergyman supported early opening to prevent such drinking. A similar argument had been put earlier in the century by Rev. J.G. Morris, chairman of the Wakefield Horticultural Society. In his opening address, which was reported in the *Gardener's Magazine* of August 1828, he argued that

> by diffusing a love of plants and gardening, you will materially contribute to the comfort and happiness of the laborious classes; for the pleasure taken in such pursuits forms an unexceptionable relaxation from the toils of business, and every hour thus spent is subtracted from the ale-house and other haunts of idleness and dissipation.

In 1879 the issue of earlier opening was raised in the House of Commons and it was decided to open at 10am on Bank Holidays. Not until 1921 did the gardens open at 10am throughout the year. Closing time was strictly enforced. On 21 September 1887 Charles Tryan was fined 36 shillings for remaining in the gardens after they had closed.

The opening time was not the only controversial regulation at Kew. At various times there were rules against smoking in the gardens, walking on the grass verges and taking in parcels over a certain size. Visitors were not allowed to picnic in the gardens and in 1887 this issue was raised in Parliament, as reported in *The Times* on 21 June:

> Dr Tanner asked whether the First Commissioner of Works would consent to relax the regulation with regard to Kew-gardens so that people should be allowed to take their lunch into the gardens with them. Mr Cremer said that the proposal of the hon. member would be regarded as a great boon by the working classes.

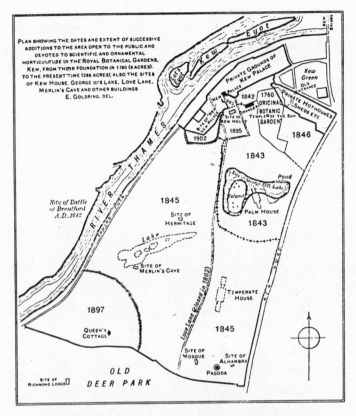

Plan of the development of Kew Gardens, from W.J. Bean's
The Royal Botanic Gardens, Kew, *1908.*

The next year it was decided, instead, to provide a kiosk for refreshments. In 1909 a resolution from Richmond Trades and Labour Council was successful in proposing that a supply of drinking water should be made available.

However, even in a garden where you could not take your picnic and only had water or tea to drink, activities could still take place that were far from innocent. On 18 December 1921 John D. Batten MA, LL.B. wrote a letter to the Director of Kew complaining that 'a visitor may suddenly come upon a man and a girl lying on the ground in a manner as nearly approaching copulation as their garment will permit'. He suggested a new rule that visitors should be forbidden to lie on the grass. This was eventually rejected because it would be impossible to enforce and they were afraid of press criticism. Nevertheless a long debate took place as to which positions on the grass were indecent, and liable to prosecution, and which were just in bad taste.

In the eighteenth century the same problem had worried the authorities of Leyden University Botanic Garden in Holland. Their solution was pre-emptive: 'All days and even on Sundays the garden may be visited, such at the discretion of the Head Gardener. Couples openly in love are on no account to be admitted.'

Photograph of Sir Joseph and Lady Hooker, taken at Kew in the Royal Botanic Gardens on Sir Joseph's 90th birthday, 30 June 1907.

The year 1865, when Joseph Hooker took over from his father as Director of Kew, seems to have inaugurated a stricter regime. A few months before his father died, Hooker in a letter to Darwin dated 7 April wrote: 'We have been robbed much by our own people and I discharged two foremen, dismissed half a dozen gardeners and labourers, and clapped one fellow in jail for six months.'

Theft was a recurring problem. In 1885 the *Richmond and Twickenham Times*, 28 March, reported: 'Frances Pryor aged 10 was charged, on a warrant, with unlawfully plucking flowers in Kew Gardens on the 7th March; and Eliza Pryor, her mother ... was charged with aiding and abetting, contrary to the Parks' Regulation Act.' They failed to appear in court because of ill-health and ended up being locked up for the night. They eventually pleaded guilty and the girl was fined two shillings. The paper reported that Mr J. Smith, the curator at Kew, had said, 'Of late these petty offences had been frequent, and it was necessary that a stop should be put to them.'

It is not a little ironic that a girl aged ten should be locked up and fined for picking flowers from Kew Gardens, considering the world-wide theft of plants associated with Kew and its collectors. One famous plant collector of the early twentieth century, F. Kingdon Ward, even argued for a copyright law to protect his profits: 'it seems only just that there should be a law of copyright to every certified new plant, destined for the market. Only by some such means can the original finder, or owner of a new plant, hope to reap his just reward.'

JOSEPH HOOKER AND CHARLES DARWIN

In the theoretical field Joseph Hooker is most famous for his association with Charles Darwin's theory of evolution. Just before Hooker left on his voyage to the Antarctic he met Darwin by chance in Trafalgar Square and they became life-long friends. They were also connected through the Rev. John Stevens Henslow, the Cambridge professor of botany who had taught Darwin. Hooker married Henslow's daughter. It was partly the connections and influence of this scientific elite which resulted in the theory of evolution being linked to Darwin's name and not that of Alfred Russell Wallace who had developed the theory at the same time. Hooker wrote an essay on the origin of species in 1859, the same year that Darwin's book was published.

Hooker dedicated his *Himalayan Journals* to Darwin and in his turn Darwin acknowledged a debt to Hooker's work on the geographical distribution of plants, as he wrote in a letter to him in 1862: 'For years I have looked to you as the man whose opinion I have valued more on any scientific subject, than anyone else in the world.' As early as January 1844 Darwin had written to Hooker saying that 'species are not (it is like confessing murder) immutable', but despite Hooker's encouragement, Darwin did not publish his theory for another 15 years. In a letter to Harvey around 1860, Hooker wrote: 'I was aware of Darwin's views 14 years before I adopted them and I have done so solely and entirely from an independent study of plants themselves.'

They were not the first to believe that species were mutable. Theophrastus, a pupil of Aristotle, held this view, as did Albertus Magnus, a thirteenth-century German nobleman who studied at Padua and entered the Dominican order. Magnus wrote a treatise *On Vegetables and Plants* about 1260, and he observed that wild plants changed when domesticated, and that cultivated plants could run wild.

At the famous meeting of the British Association of Science in Oxford on 30 June 1860, the Bishop of Oxford asked T.H. Huxley whether it was through his grandfather or grandmother that he was descended from a monkey. Huxley replied that he was not ashamed to have a monkey for an ancestor but that he would be ashamed to be connected with a man who used his great gifts to obscure the truth. Then Hooker seconded the defence of Darwin, who was not present at the meeting. He wrote to Darwin recounting the incident:

> I hit him (Bishop Sam Wilberforce) in the wind at the first shot in ten words taken from his ugly mouth; and then proceeded to demonstrate in as few more (1) that he could never have read your book, and (2) that he was absolutely ignorant of Botanical Science ... Sam was shut up – had not one word to say in reply, and the meeting was dissolved forthwith, leaving you master of the field after 4 hours' battle.

It was a victory against religious obscurantism. The theory of evolution was recognised by Marx as being consistent with his own dialectical theory of history. In a letter to Engels of 18 June 1862, Marx writes: 'It is remarkable how Darwin recognises among beasts and plants his English society with its division of labour, competition, opening up of new markets, "inventions", and the Malthusian "struggle for existence".'

As Marx saw, the theory also had a reactionary side, reflecting its origins in Malthus's theory on population control. Hooker found the arguments of Malthus 'incontrovertible' and saw in the theory of natural selection a justification of aristocratic rule:

> If there is anything at all in force of circumstances and Natural Selection, it must arrive that the best trained, bred and ablest man will be found in the higher walks of life – true he will be rare, but then he will be obvious and easily selected by a discriminating public.

In the same letter to Darwin, on 10 March 1862, he continues: 'Your *Origin* has done more to enhance the value of an aristocracy in my eyes than any social, political or other argument.' It should also be remembered that Darwin's alternative title for his book was *The Preservation of Favoured Races in the Struggle for Life.*

Hooker had similar views about the 'natural' place of women: 'There is no shirking the great fact, that the woman's function is to be wife and mother.' When Francis Galton did his study on heredity, he used Joseph Hooker and his ancestors as one of his examples to prove that intelligence was hereditary. The ensuing theory of IQ has probably been the most influential and damaging educational theory ever put forward. Hooker summed up his views on education: 'I am for compulsory reading, writing, arithmetic and cooking, and for a *limited* extension of higher education.'

The 'romantic story' of Kew Gardens, which Gladys Taylor refers to in her book *Old London Gardens*, needs to be reassessed in the light of all this evidence. Far more persuasive is Lucile Brockway's view that Kew in the nineteenth century helped Britain become the 'world's superpower'.

The landscape garden, like the contemporary landscape painting, was for aristocratic consumption. It hid the reality of labour and exploitation. Likewise Kew Gardens was seen by most people, not as the botanical hub of the Empire, but as a landscaped pleasure garden. As Bower observed in 1919: 'Few of the thousands of visitors on Sundays and Bank Holidays have any idea of the position that Kew holds in the world of science, and in the Empire.'

7

Garden Cemeteries

A garden cemetery and monumental decoration, are not only beneficial to public morals, to the improvement of manners, but are likewise calculated to extend virtuous and generous feelings.

John Strang, *Necropolis Glasguensis* (1831)

The greater number of present cemeteries, the greater the number of future public gardens.

John Claudius Loudon, *Gardener's Magazine* (1843)

The huge cemeteries laid out in the nineteenth century provide badly needed open spaces in populous areas, and they contain fine planting that has now matured, so that their benefits as amenity spaces are incalculable. It is my contention that the cemeteries of the past will become the sanctuaries of sanity and peace for the future within the turmoil of city life ...

James Stevens Curl, *Garden History* (1975)

In opening Kew Gardens to the public in 1841, William Hooker was responding to a movement of the times. There was an urgent need for open spaces and public parks for the rapidly growing urban population. By mid-century, for the first time in the history of the world, the majority of a country's population lived in towns rather than the country. The increase had been phenomenal. Most industrial towns doubled their population in the first three decades of the nineteenth century. Manchester had risen from 17,000 in 1760 to 180,000 in 1830, and from 280,000 in 1841 to 400,000 in 1844. London had three quarters of a million in 1760, two million in 1841 and five million in 1881.

In 1833 a Select Committee on Public Works had reported on what open spaces were available for public use in major towns. It concluded that only in the West End of London was the provision adequate. Manchester became the first major industrial town to acquire a municipal park, although public parks had already been created in Preston in 1833, Gravesend in 1836, Birkenhead in 1843, and Derby and Southampton in 1844. In the same year that the land was bought for the Manchester and Salford parks, 1845, Engels finished his book *The Condition of the Working Class in England*, which is particularly concerned with the Manchester area where Engels lived.

URBAN HOUSING AND DISEASE

Engels describes the appalling housing conditions in the older parts of Manchester, where every spare space was built on: 'If any one wishes to see in how little space a human being can move, how little air – and *such* air! – he can breathe, how little of civilization he may share and yet live, it is only necessary to travel hither.' In the newer working-class areas the same overcrowding occurred, though more formally organised, in the new method of building cottages. One row of houses had back yards, then came a narrow back street and beyond that two rows of back-to-backs.

Engels concludes: 'If the totally planless construction is injurious to the health of the workers by preventing ventilation, this method of shutting them up in courts surrounded on all sides by buildings is far more so.' In a footnote he adds, 'And yet an English Liberal wiseacre asserts, in the Report of the Children's Employment Commission, that these courts are the masterpiece of municipal architecture, because, like a multitude of little parks, they improve ventilation, the circulation of air!' Meanwhile in the suburbs, 'in free, wholesome air', lived the 'upper bourgeoisie in remoter villas with gardens'.

The insanitary conditions of the working-class areas are described in grim detail, nothing having changed since the 1831 cholera epidemic. Yet it was the fear of disease which was to lead to the movement for public parks. The city of Manchester was constructed with a business centre connected to the suburbs by shop-lined thoroughfares which cut through the working-class districts. As Engels points out: 'A person may live in it for years, and go in and out daily without coming into contact with a working-people's quarter or even with workers.' But although the classes were segregated, cholera was no respecter of boundaries:

131

When the epidemic was approaching, a universal terror seized the bourgeoisie of the city. People remembered the unwholesome dwellings of the poor, and trembled before the certainty that each of these slums would become a centre for the plague, whence it would spread desolation in all directions through the houses of the propertied class.

An epidemic of typhus in London in 1837 was attributed directly by the official report to the 'bad state of the dwellings in the matters of ventilation, drainage and cleanliness'. Engels comes to the same conclusion, that the fever 'is to be found in the working-people's quarters of all great towns and cities, and in single ill-built, ill-kept streets of smaller places, though it naturally seeks out single victims in better districts also'.

THE GARDEN CEMETERY MOVEMENT

The fear of pollution and disease led to a movement which developed earlier and more rapidly than that of public parks. More urgent than the problem of providing recreation for the living was that of finding a suitable resting-place for the dead. The graveyards and church crypts were filled to bursting. Many corpses were dug up before they had rotted. Air escaping from the graves was thought to be full of 'miasmas' which spread disease. According to John Loudon, grave-diggers had to be 'plied constantly with rum to induce them to proceed'.

James Curl, in an article entitled 'The Architecture and Planning of the Nineteenth Century Cemetery', describes the situation in London's Enon Chapel where coffins were piled on top of each other and the smell was appalling:

In a space about 60 feet by 29 feet by 6 feet twelve thousand bodies were estimated to have been interred. Quicklime was used to hasten the destruction of the flesh, and the coffins were removed by the chapel staff and burnt. The custodians of many of the graveyards made a substantial profit out of stripping lead, handles, nails, and screws, and even the complete coffins themselves.

The solution was to build cemeteries, and this led to the garden cemetery movement. There had been earlier cemeteries, such as the one at Bunhill Fields in London, created by the Dissenters in the seventeenth century, where Daniel Defoe and William Blake are buried. In the same period, after the plague, John Evelyn had campaigned for cemeteries to be built outside the city. In the eighteenth century cemeteries, such as the one at Calton Hill, had been made in Scotland, and Friar's Bush and Carlisle Circus in Belfast.

St. James's Cemetery, Liverpool, from Loudon's revised edition of his Encyclopaedia of Gardening, *1834: 'It is formed in the bottom and sides of an immense stone quarry, the general form of which is winding and irregular. The sides are planted in some places, and hollowed out into catacombs in others. The bottom is reduced to a level, surrounded and crossed by gravel walks, with groups and clumps of shrubbery on glades of lawn.'*

In England Liverpool began the process by opening St James's Metropolitan Cemetery in 1829, built at a cost of £21,000. By the following year the Joint Stock Company that formed it was paying a dividend of 8 per cent, higher than contemporary speculation in housing or railway stock. As the economic historian Eric Hobsbawm has shown, 'by the 1830s there were vast accumulations of capital burning holes in their owners' pockets, that is seeking any investment likely to yield more than the 3.4 per cent of public stocks'.

In 1830 the General Cemetery Company was established in London and the next year it purchased 54 acres at Kensal Green. The cemetery which was built there shows the influence of the eighteenth-century landscape garden. This style had been exported world-wide and had influenced the famous Père Lachaise Garden Cemetery in Paris, which in turn was copied by some designers of British cemeteries. Later the style was also to be influential in the re-designing of both the Bois de Boulogne, 1853–8, and the Bois de Vincennes, 1857–64, in Paris.

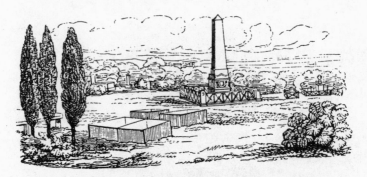

The Cemetery of Père Lachaise in Paris, from Loudon's
Encyclopaedia of Gardening: *'Some of the graves are enclosed
with iron palisades, within which grow roses, weeping willows,
lilacs, honeysuckles, etc., with a variety of
different kinds of flowers.'*

JOHN CLAUDIUS LOUDON

John Loudon (1783–1843) was 'the greatest gardener in the nine-teenth century's first 50 years' according to Geoffrey Taylor. He was the author of several gardening books and editor of various gardening magazines, and was closely involved in the design of both cemeteries and public parks. He thought that the cemetery could serve also as a botanical garden and saw Kensal Green Cemetery as 'rapidly becoming a school of improvement in archi-tectural taste, and of instruction in trees and shrubs'. Cemeteries were necessary for public health, but also for education and morality, for 'the improvement of the moral sentiments and general taste of all classes, and more especially of the great masses of society'. In 1840 Abney Park Cemetery in Stoke Newington, East London, was opened. It was laid out like an arboretum, with each tree labelled for the 'edification of the working classes'.

Loudon did not recommend flowers for a cemetery, though it was common at the time to have flowers growing in graveyards and on the graves themselves. He preferred trees and shrubs, but not the clumps and belts of trees found in 'Capability' Brown's landscape gardens. He wanted them planted singly and alongside roads and walks, favouring evergreens such as pine, cypress, juniper and cedar, because they produced less litter. However, in

John Claudius Loudon (1783–1843) by an unknown artist c.1812.

his series of articles on cemeteries, published in *The Gardener's Magazine* in 1843, the year that he died, Loudon listed literally hundreds of trees and shrubs, climbers, bulbs, herbaceous plants and ferns which he considered suitable for a cemetery.

The move away from serpentine design, which was so influential in the eighteenth century when straight lines were avoided, can be seen in Loudon's recommendation that cemetery walks 'ought to be straight, or, if curvilinear, the curves ought to be few'.

He thought straight lines were more solemn, a winding road being too much like that in a landscape park leading to a country residence. The designs which he himself made, for a private cemetery in Cambridge and a municipal one in Southampton, each had a formal, geometric pattern. This was different from the Highgate Cemetery in London, for example, which was opened in 1838, or the Glasgow Necropolis of 1833, both built on hills in a more romantic style.

Melanie Simo describes Loudon's plan for Southampton Cemetery:

> The ground was to be sown with rye grass and white clover. The trees – hollies and thorns already existing in the cemetery grounds – would remain largely intact. The central road and main walks were to be lined with cypresses or Irish yews planted at regular intervals, thirteen or fourteen feet apart. This regularity was not sacred, however. As graves, gravestones, and tombs were needed, trees might be transplanted to accommodate them. Irish yews were preferable to cypresses for this purpose, since they could withstand transplantation at any size.

The style of the garden cemeteries was also influenced by Turkish cemeteries, such as the one at Eyub, near Constantinople. Coleridge compared the 'unsightly manner in which our monuments are crowded together in the busy, noisy, unclean, and almost grassless churchyard of a large town' with the 'still seclusion of a Turkish cemetery'. Turkish cemeteries were used by the

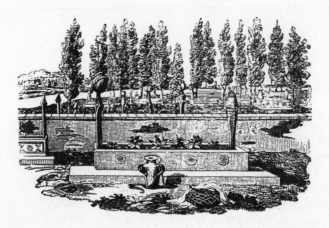

The Cemetery of Pera, Turkey, from the Gardener's Magazine.

public as places to walk. They were usually on the outskirts of towns, on rising ground, planted with cedars, cypresses and scented shrubs. Most of the tombstones had plants growing on them. Loudon refers in particular to the cemetery of Pera in Turkey, 'planted with noble cypresses', which was the main promenade in the evenings for the inhabitants of the town.

COMMERCIAL CEMETERY COMPANIES

In 1832 the bill for establishing General Cemeteries received the Royal Assent and between 1832 and 1847 parliament authorised eight commercial cemetery companies in London alone. There was no shortage of people buying shares and by 1839 the original shares in the General Cemetery Company had doubled in value. The only people to suffer were the clergy, who objected to losing their money for burials. At Kensal Green they were compensated by a fee being given to the rector of the parish from which each burial originated.

Also in 1832 the Anatomy Act was passed, to provide corpses for the medical schools and to stop body-snatching. The act had failed to be passed in 1829 as the government feared an insurrection, but in 1832 it was hidden by the Reform Bill. It decreed that people who died in the work house could be dissected if they were not claimed by relatives. The act was supported by Whigs and free trade Tories, and opposed by traditional Tories and radicals.

The 10 per cent of the population who were paupers, of course, rarely came near these new cemeteries in death. In 1845 Engels graphically described the pauper burials:

The poor are dumped into the earth like infected cattle. The pauper burial-ground of St. Brides, London, is a bare morass, in use as a cemetery since the time of Charles II, and filled with heaps of bones; every Wednesday the paupers are thrown into a ditch fourteen feet deep; a curate rattles through the Litany at the top of his speed; the ditch is loosely covered in, to be re-opened the next Wednesday, and filled with corpses as long as one more can be forced in. The putrefaction thus engendered contaminates the whole neighbourhood. In Manchester, the pauper burial-ground lies opposite to the Old Town, along the Irk: this, too, is a rough, desolate place. About two years ago a railroad was carried through it. If it had been a respectable cemetery, how the bourgeoisie and the clergy would have shrieked over the desecration! But it was a pauper burial-ground, the resting-place of the outcast and superfluous, so no one concerned himself about the matter. It was not even thought worth while to convey the partially decayed bodies to the other side of the cemetery; they were heaped up just as it happened, and the piles were driven into newly-made graves, so that the water oozed out of the swampy ground, pregnant with putrefying matter, and filled the neighbourhood with the most revolting and injurious gases. The disgusting brutality which accompanied this work I cannot describe in further detail.

In 1842 the directors of Kensal Green Cemetery offered seven acres of their grounds for the interment of paupers. They calculated that seven acres could contain 133,500 graves and each grave could hold ten coffins, so they could cope with 1,335,000 deceased paupers. At an annual intake of 1,000, the seven acres would take 1,335 years to fill. Loudon ridiculed the offer and with typically meticulous calculation showed it to be exaggerated at least sevenfold.

Kensal Green Cemetery today.

In 1843 John Loudon died and was himself buried in Kensal Green Cemetery. Jane Loudon was buried beside him in 1858. Many famous graves are there, including those of Leigh Hunt, Cruikshank, Brunel, Thackeray and Browning. In 1855 the last Chartist demonstration ever held was the great funeral procession that followed the body of the Chartist leader Feargus O'Connor to the same cemetery.

Loudon criticised the big cemetery companies for their inadequate drainage and their overcrowding. Some admitted sheep into the cemeteries at night to avoid the cost and the difficulty of mowing the grass, but this had the effect of destroying the shrubs and flowers placed on the graves, which was the only way the poor had of showing respect for the dead. He advocated municipal ownership of cemeteries, but public cemeteries were not created till the 1850s. Cremation was not made legal in England till 1885, though it had existed amongst the Aborigines for at least 26,000 years.

In the last quarter of the nineteenth century Octavia Hill, the capitalist philanthropist who founded the Charity Organisation Society in 1869, campaigned to prevent disused burial grounds from being built on by developers. She saw these graveyards as 'open air sitting rooms for the poor', and in 1884 the Burial Ground Act was finally passed prohibiting building on any such ground unless it was for extending a place of worship. Octavia Hill failed in her attempt to preserve Swiss Cottage fields in 1875, and in her plan to plant an avenue the length of the Mile End Road in East London. But, working with the Commons Preservation Society, which had been founded in 1865, she was instrumental in the late 1880s in saving Parliament Hill Fields as part of Hampstead Heath, as well as preserving Wandsworth Common and Tooting Common. Many small London gardens, which once were churchyards, owe their continuing existence to her campaigns. In 1894 she was one of the co-founders of the National Trust.

Today many cemeteries are still in private hands, others are owned by local authorities. In March 1988 it came to light that

The Guardian, *3 March, 1988.*

Conservative-controlled Westminster city council had sold off three cemeteries for 15p, to avoid the maintenance costs of £350,000 a year. They were re-sold by property speculators for £1.2 million, and later valued at £10 million.

FERTILISERS

Another connection between bones and gardening also developed in the nineteenth century. Bones, which are rich in phosphates, had been used as a fertiliser at the end of the eighteenth century and in 1829 Mr Anderson of Dundee invented a machine to break them up. In a book called *The Kitchen Garden*, published in 1855, E.S. Delamer writes:

> Bones, for instance, are mostly sold by the cook or kitchen-maid; but wherever there is a garden, not a bone ought to be allowed to leave the premises. Bone dust, pounded bones, bones in almost any shape, are essential manures for turnips, asparagus and most other culinary plants.

British supplies of bone manure were limited, so it soon became necessary to import it on a massive scale. In 1842, 1,200,000 oxen were slaughtered in South America to provide fertiliser for British farms and gardens. Earlier in 1826 Loudon wrote about the immense loads of bones being brought to Hull by the Dutch: 'It is more than probable that they are carefully collected from the fields of warfare.' Some 30,000 tons of bones were imported from Europe every year.

This led Baron Liebig of Munich to a remarkable conclusion – a variation on a familiar theme, that of English exploitation of foreign resources:

> England is robbing all other countries of the condition of their fertility. Already, in her eagerness for bones, she has turned up the battlefields of Leipzig, of Waterloo, and of the Crimea; already from the catacombs of Sicily she has carried away the skeletons of many successive generations. Annually she removes from the shores of other countries to her own the manurial equivalent of three millions and a half of men, whom she takes from us the means of supporting, and squanders down her sewers to the sea. Like a vampire, she hangs upon the neck of Europe – nay, of the entire world! – and sucks the heart-blood from nations without a thought of justice towards them, without a shadow of lasting advantage to herself.

In 1840 Liebig discovered that adding sulphuric acid to bones made the phosphate in them water-soluble, doubling the efficiency of bones as manure. This discovery was applied commercially by John Bennet Lawes in 1842 when he opened his Deptford factory to make 'Super Phosphate of Lime'. According to H.G. Wells, in his *Short History of the World*, the use of fertilisers in the nineteenth century led to the soil producing 'quadruple and quintuple the crops got from the same area in the seventeenth century'.

A similar case of expropriation in the twentieth century is illustrated by Edward Hyams in his book *Soil and Civilisation*. Between 1920 and 1950 Britain imported 11,683,000 tons of beef from Argentina, the equivalent of 50 million head of cattle, each with an average age of three years. In that time each would have consumed about ten tons of grass, taking plant nutrients from the soil, changing its texture and removing vast quantities of organic material:

> What then, has happened as a result of this export of meat? A quantity of top-soil equal to about a million fertile acres has been sent away from the soil community to which it belonged, eaten by the English, assimilated into their flesh, or, by way of their sewers, thrown into the sea.

Guano, which was to be found in deposits sometimes 100 feet thick on the coastline of Peru and Chile, was also imported on a large scale in the nineteenth century. Guano means dung and comes from the Quecha word *huano*. It had been used as a fertiliser for centuries by the Incas, who had imposed the death-penalty on anyone disturbing the birds which created it. Guano is rich in nitrogen and phosphates, one ton being equal to 33 tons of farmyard manure, or as Jane Loudon puts it: 'It is so strong that a table-spoonful of it dissolved in water will go as far as three trowels-full of horse dung.' It was first imported to England in 1840. The dusty, back-breaking work of excavating it was carried out largely by Chinese labourers. Some 283,300 tons were imported in 1845 and in 1853 it was calculated that at that rate the deposits would be worked out in the next eight or nine years. By the end of the century five million tons had been imported from Peru alone.

An alternative to Peruvian guano.

PUBLIC PARKS

The fact that life springs from death is not news to gardeners, who are used to making compost heaps to fertilise their gardens. But it is not so well known that the movement for garden cemeteries spear-headed the campaign for public parks. Loudon had long criticised the lack of public gardens in England, putting it down to the 'comparatively anti-social character of the British people':

It has justly been observed by foreigners, that the parks of London are calculated exclusively for those who possess horses and carriages; and that no provision is made for the enjoyment of the open air by pedestrians, invalids, or children. In the Regent's Park there is not a single gravel walk for persons on foot; not one place of shelter; and

142

only a few rough benches, as seats, by the side of the carriage road; liable, when the weather is such as to admit of their use, to the inconvenience of being covered with the dust raised by the passing carriages and horses. From the whole of the interior, from the verdure and softness of turf, from the shade of trees, and the beauty of shrubs, the public are completely excluded by a close fence, with locked gates.

Loudon hoped that our increasing 'intercourse with the Continent' would change 'this peculiarity in our manners'. By the second half of the nineteenth century Loudon's wishes had come true. It eventually became accepted that parks should be open to the public and maintained by local authorities, but not without a struggle.

8

Public Parks

Who, that has reason, and his smell,
Would not 'mong roses and jasmin dwell,
Rather than all his spirits choke,
With exhalations of dirt and smoke,
And all th' uncleanness which does drown
In pestilential clouds a pop'lous town?

Abraham Cowley (1618–67) 'The Garden'

To one who has been long in city pent,
'Tis very sweet to look into the fair
And open face of heaven.

John Keats (1816)

To sit in the shade on a fine day and look upon verdure is
the most perfect refreshment.

Jane Austen, *Mansfield Park* (1814)

The increasing population of the cities in the nineteenth century led to more enclosure of land to build houses. The danger of losing touch with the country was clearly seen by Engels: 'A town, such as London, where a man may wander for hours together without reaching the beginning of the end, without meeting the slightest hint which could lead to the inference that there is open country within reach, is a strange thing.'

William Robinson also criticised the 'flat monotony' of expanding suburbia:

To-day the ever-growing city, pushing its hard face over our once beautiful land, should make us wish more and more to keep such beauty of the earth as may still be possible to us, and the horrible railway embankments, where once were the beautiful suburbs of London, cry to us to save all we can save of the natural beauty of the earth.

144

Eighteenth-century Pleasure Gardens

In the eighteenth century, as well as being much smaller and closer to the countryside than it is today, London had dozens of pleasure gardens. Many of these were built around wells, for instance Islington Spa, where there were mineral springs, and people went to them to drink the water or meet in the tea gardens. There were often places to play games like bowls, skittles, archery or cricket, and also various performances such as fire-eating, juggling, tight-rope walking or acrobatics. Concerts and firework displays took place, while people could also eat, drink and dance.

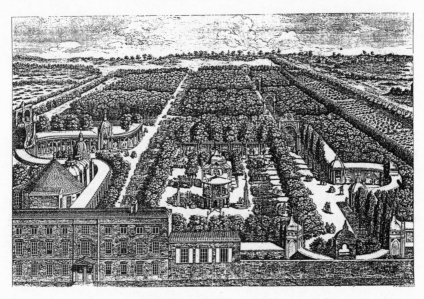

Vauxhall Gardens, 1751.

The gardens consisted of shaded walks and arbours, shrubs and fruit trees. At Sadler's Wells there were poplars and willows and sloping banks of flowers. Bagnigge Wells had formal walks with hedges of box and holly, a flower garden, elder bushes and other shrubs, and also gooseberry and currant bushes. Ranelagh Gardens in Chelsea, one of the most fashionable resorts, had gravel walks shaded by elms and yews, and a flower garden. It was here, on 29 June 1764, that the eight-year-old Mozart played several of his own compositions on the harpsichord and organ. The most famous gardens were probably at Vauxhall, consisting of twelve acres, where the main avenue of elms extended for 900 feet.

Most of these pleasure gardens had ceased to exist by the end of the eighteenth century as the industrial revolution began to get underway, though Ranelagh survived until 1803 and Vauxhall till 1859. Land was needed to house the increasing population, to build roads and railways, and also to bury the dead. The Spa Fields Pantheon, for example, was turned into a Church of England chapel in 1777 and the gardens converted into a burial ground. Later, in 1843, it became notorious, as Warwick Wroth recounts, for 'its over-crowded and pestilential condition, and for some repulsive disclosures as to the systematic exhumation of bodies in order to make room for fresh interments'. Cuper's Gardens were destroyed in order to build Waterloo Road, the southern approach to Waterloo Bridge, and Pancras Wells were taken over by the Midland Railway to build St Pancras station.

The pleasure gardens were privately owned and usually charged for admission. Ranelagh Gardens, for example, charged one shilling for most of the eighteenth century, rising to two shillings in 1792. A protest against charges took place at the opening of the 1764 season at Vauxhall Gardens when a group of 50 young men 'tore up the railings in order to lay the walks open'. They took their protest further. Chancellor, in *The Pleasure Haunts of London*, indignantly describes how 'they played havoc in the wildernesses; even irrupting into the private boxes where parties were seated peacefully eating their suppers surrounded by the pictorial representations of plays and sylvan amusements'.

JOHN LOUDON AND THE DERBY ARBORETUM

As early as 1803, the year when the Ranelagh Gardens were closed, Loudon, then aged 20, wrote an article in the *Literary Journal* on London's public squares: 'It will be allowed by everyone that the Squares of London are of the greatest consequence to the health of its inhabitants, and to the beauty of that city.' He advocated planting them with hardy trees and flowering shrubs, particularly scented evergreens. He also wanted botanical labels placed next to certain specimens for the instruction of the public.

In 1811 he presented a scheme to the Linnean Society for a 'living museum', a garden of about 100 acres, containing every known species and variety of plant. It would include a research library, and the collection of plants would be arranged so as to appeal to the general public as well as the scientist. This national garden never materialised, but a similar spiral design was used in the arboretum of the Loddiges' Botanical Nursery Garden in Hackney, East London, which Loudon visited in 1833.

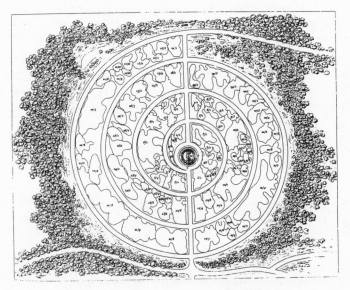

Loudon's design for a botanic garden, 1811.

In his *Encyclopaedia of Gardening* of 1822 Loudon again argued the case for creating new public open spaces and gardens. Many of London's squares at this time were only open to the surrounding houseowners, as was Regent's Park. Loudon observed that

> our continental neighbours have hitherto excelled us in this depart-
> ment of gardening; almost every town of consequence having its
> promenades for the citizens *en cheval* and also *au pied*. Till lately,
> Hyde Park, at London, and a spot called The Meadows, near
> Edinburgh, were the only equestrian gardens in Britain; and neither
> were well arranged.

In 1829 the Lord of the Manor of Hampstead, Sir Spencer Maryon Wilson, tried to enclose Hampstead Heath, claiming his right under the thirteenth-century Statute of Merton. He wanted to excavate sand and gravel and then develop housing on the heath. It provoked a public protest. Loudon joined the protest and in December of that year wrote an article in his *Gardener's Magazine* entitled 'Hints for Breathing Places for the Metropolis'. His main plan was to create concentric bands of parks and open spaces in London, similar to the idea of the green belt, which was eventually established in 1938.

The struggle over Hampstead Heath continued throughout the century, though it eased after Wilson's death when his successors agreed to transfer the manorial rights to the Metropolitan Board of Works. Octavia Hill, who was involved in the later campaign to preserve the heath, wrote: 'It is especially important to keep the hill tops free from buildings so that the purity of the air blowing in from the country may be thus preserved.'

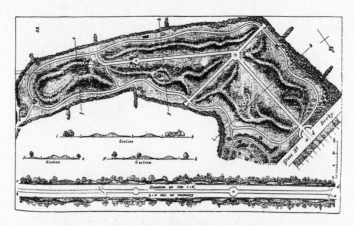

Loudon's plan of the Derby Arboretum, from the
Gardener's Magazine, *1840.*

Loudon also argued continually for the creation of public parks to improve people's health, both mental and physical, so that 'the pale mechanic and the exhausted factory operative might inhale the freshening breeze and some portion of recovered health'. In 1839 he had the opportunity to design a smaller version of his 'living museum', in the Derby Arboretum, laid out in 1840. The eleven-acre site was provided by Joseph Strutt, son of a wealthy industrialist, who donated the park to the Corporation of Derby, but gave no endowment for its upkeep. In the early 1840s municipal corporations were not yet able to use rates to maintain public parks, so on five days a week people had to pay an entrance charge. Only on Sunday afternoons and on Wednesdays, from sunrise to sunset, was the park open free of charge. By 1850 it was freely open to the public five days a week.

The Derby Arboretum today.

Toilet facilities were available and visitors were allowed to bring their own refreshments. For a small charge they were provided with knives, forks, crockery and hot water for tea. Several open spaces were reserved for bands and dancing. Strutt wanted to wean people from 'brutalising pleasures' by offering them new forms of 'rational enjoyment'. Fears that the park would be vandalised, however, proved unfounded. The private inauguration was on 16 September 1840, and the next day the working classes celebrated the opening, marching with banners to the park. Although an estimated 9,000 people filled the arboretum, not a single tree or shrub was destroyed. The third day was the Children's Celebration, attended by a further 6,000 people.

Loudon's catalogue for the Derby Arboretum included a complete account of the three-day celebrations and also gave botanical and historical information about the plants. The park was seen to encourage social well-being as well as providing scientific education, and it served a wide region. On Sundays people would arrive in Derby, having travelled 60 miles or more in third-class railway carriages, from Nottingham, Sheffield, Birmingham or Leeds, to enjoy the arboretum. Four years after it opened, a parliamentary commissioner, J.R. Martin, concluded: 'The Arboretum, as these gardens are designated, is much frequented, and has already produced a perceptible effect in improving the appearance and demeanour of the working classes, and it has, doubtless, conferred an equal benefit upon their health.'

MORAL AND ECONOMIC RATIONALE

In the previous century a similar aim was put forward by Whately in his *Observations on Modern Gardening* (1770), that people should be able to recuperate and enjoy nature. The first people's park, built in Munich in 1789, was called the 'Englischer Garten', indicating its stylistic origin. Ludwig von Skell, its landscape architect, saw it as a place for exercise and also where the different classes could meet each other.

The class aspect of parks is a recurring theme. They were thought to have a civilising influence and symbolised peace and tranquillity in a violent and revolutionary period. Even a radical like Francis Place believed they could 'instil a hallowed calm, and a spirit of reverence into the mind and heart of Man'.

Agitation over the Reform Bill eventually led to the Municipal Reform Act of 1835 which created locally elected town councils, though with a very limited franchise. The government, however, was slow to get involved in creating public parks, as was pointed out by the *Botanical Magazine* of the same year:

> Public gardens are just beginning to be thought of in England; and, like most other great domestic improvements in our country, they have originated in the spirit of the people, rather than in that of the government. On the Continent, the contrary has generally been the case.

The 1848 Public Health Act eventually empowered councils to establish public walks and open spaces as a 'means of exercise for the middle and humbler classes', though it was not until 1860 that local authorities were allowed to levy rates to maintain such spaces.

In Edinburgh recreation in a park was thought to cure drunkenness; in Macclesfield they considered that it led to a decrease in crime and a fall in the death rate; and after the Leeds Botanical Gardens had been opened to the public on Sundays, drunkenness was said to have decreased and 'manners improved'. The object of the Derby Arboretum was 'to give the people of Derby an opportunity to learn botany, to enjoy the pure air of the park as an alternative to the debasing pursuits and brutalising pleasure of drinking and cockfighting'.

It was even suggested by one writer in 1854 that public parks and gardens had the power to stop a revolution:

> The more people have of new plants, and the more they delight in them, the happier and the better they will be; we let them in to Kew Gardens unwatched, and yet not a leaf is rifled; we build, or they build for themselves, Crystal Palaces, and we make for them parks and gardens, where they may walk unrestrained and roll upon the grass even, and bask in the sunshine, and revel in pure air. And what is the consequence of this? We must condense the reply into one sentence – We have had no Revolution.

There was also, of course, a shrewd economic motive for building parks, connected with land speculation and development. Nash's improvement scheme for the West End of London, which included Regent's Park and St James's Park, had three aims, in this order: 'to assure the greatest possible revenue to the crown and secondly to add to the beauty of the metropolis and thirdly to study the health and convenience of the public'. The villas built next to Regent's Park gave the inhabitants the illusion of living in country houses and their values, in property terms, were correspondingly enhanced.

Birkenhead Park, designed by Joseph Paxton and Edward Kemp in 1843, was built primarily to raise land values in the area, though the aim, spelt out in a contemporary guide to the park, was to make people 'virtuous and happy' through 'innocent amusement and healthy recreation'. Be that as it may, the value of leasehold land round the park rose in two years from one shilling to eleven shillings a square yard.

The American Frederick Law Olmsted was impressed by the park and wrote in his *Walks and Talks of an American Farmer in England*: 'All of this magnificent pleasure ground is entirely, unreservedly and for ever, the people's own. The poorest British peasant is as free to enjoy it as the British Queen.'

151

The Princes Street Gardens in Edinburgh were built for the same commercial reason. Loudon acknowledges the economic argument: 'The ground-rents of the houses contiguous to the park would be higher and the sites would be more readily occupied by the wealthy citizens.'

The different origins, organisation and purposes of the new parks can best be seen by looking at three examples: the Manchester and Salford public parks, Birmingham Botanical Gardens and Victoria Park in the East End of London. They also illustrate the class conflicts involved in the movement for public parks.

MANCHESTER AND SALFORD PUBLIC PARKS

On 8 August 1844, a public meeting was held in Manchester Town Hall, chaired by the Mayor, to raise subscriptions for public parks. The meeting agreed a resolution that the formation of parks 'would contribute greatly to the health, rational enjoyment, kindly intercourse, and good morals of all classes of our industrious population'. The MP for Manchester, Mark Philips, spoke on a similar theme: 'The mutual improvement of all classes must be the result ... the more they mix with one another ... the more they will understand one another.' Philips was later to be instrumental in securing the passing of the act empowering local authorities to provide public parks and open spaces out of local rates.

One speaker at the meeting stressed the calming influence of parks, 'the more amusements were given to the people, the more contented they were'. Another said that playing cricket, bowls and quoits were good alternatives to 'the temptations of the tavern and the beerhouse, and their frequent accompaniments of immorality and vice'. A total of £7,000 was raised at the meeting and a month later the Prime Minister, Robert Peel, added £1,000 to the fund.

On 10 September 1844, 5,000 working people met in the Free Trade Hall to discuss the same matter. They concluded: 'Parks must be established, life preserved, health confirmed or restored, intellect cultivated and morals improved, and working men and women must each cast in their mites and work heartily in the cause.'

The following year enough money had been collected to buy

152

land to make three parks, Queen's Park and Philips Park in Manchester and Peel Park by the river Irwell in Salford. On 22 August 1846, the parks were opened. They were free of charge and open every day of the week. Closing time was an hour after sunset each evening.

The style of the parks showed traces of the eighteenth-century landscape gardens: informal lawns and lakes, shrubs and trees, though bedding plants began to be introduced into the flower-beds in the 1850s. Nevertheless the parks were criticised for their incongruity and lack of consistent style. In 1847 a correspondent in the *Gardeners' Chronicle* attacked Queen's Park for having straight paths, uniform grass borders, tiny lakes and small streams crossed by large bridges. The editor of the magazine, John Lindley, also criticised the park for its discrepancies of scale, contrasting the lakes in it, rather unfairly, with those in the Lake District and concluding ironically: 'And this is *landscape gardening* in the nineteenth century.'

Commemoration sign in Queen's Park,
Manchester, 1989.

Joshua Major, who designed all three parks, not surprisingly defended himself by arguing that he had only a limited space. The inclusion of sports facilities also meant that straight walks were more appropriate.

These sports facilities were the main new development in the parks. Special areas were set aside for sports, or what Major called 'innocent athletic games'. They tended to be of the more sedate kind such as archery, quoits, skittles, bowls, badminton and cricket. Football was not allowed. Gymnasia were built and swings were provided for children, but as usual these were monopolised by boys. A month after the parks were opened, the Manchester borough council proceedings record that it was recommended to build two additional sets of swings in Queen's Park and Philips Park, 'one for girls only, in a situation remote from the one used by the boys, and the other for boys; it having been already found where boys and girls are mixed together, the former exclude the latter from the use of the swings'.

As well as gender conflict in the use of the parks, there was class conflict too. The pious hopes of 'kindly intercourse' between the classes were not always fulfilled. In 1865 the park keeper, Mr Harrison, complained that in fine weather the park was visited by

The summer bedding in Philips Park, Manchester, 1913, during a visit by the Parks Committee.

a 'number of exceedingly ill behaved young men and women whose dress, language and conduct were both disgusting and filthy'. It was argued that they may have behaved as they did because they thought the park belonged to them. When the parks had opened, a notice had been posted saying: 'This park was Purchased by the People, was made for the People and is given to the People for their protection.'

In 1868 by-laws were passed so that people not dressed in clean and decent clothes could be excluded. No alcohol was to be permitted in the parks, no gambling and no indecent language. A rich Manchester businessman claimed to Hippolyte Taine that Peel Park 'keeps our working men occupied and gives them something to think about. They must have something to amuse them; and besides, every hour spent here is one hour less in the public houses.'

By 1880 a speakers' corner had been established, like the one in Hyde Park. Around 1900 the proceedings were put on a regular footing and the forum became known as Queen's Park Parliament. The programme for 1910 included debates on the British Empire, unemployment, tariffs and the cotton trade, the state and the child.

Philips Park today.

BIRMINGHAM BOTANICAL GARDENS

Unlike the Manchester and Salford parks, the Birmingham Botanical Gardens were largely a middle-class preserve. Consisting of 15 acres and situated in Edgbaston, a wealthy suburb of Birmingham, they opened in 1832. In 1839 Loudon noticed their impact on the surrounding area, where people's gardens contained 'more choice plants' than when he was there in 1831: 'The botanic garden has already had a considerable effect in improving the general taste of the Birmingham people for plants.'

The Edgbaston estate was owned by Lord Calthorpe and he was persuaded to charge a low rent for the gardens, knowing that they would encourage applicants for leases to build villas on his land. Middle-class shareholders subscribed the capital. Similar gardens were set up in the first half of the nineteenth century in a number of major cities: Liverpool 1802, Hull 1812, Glasgow 1817, Kensington 1818, Manchester 1829, Bath 1834, Sheffield 1836, Leeds 1840, London's Regent's Park 1841. The shareholders in Birmingham wanted a botanic garden both for scientific study and as a semi-private garden for recreation. As the *Gardeners' Chronicle* of 28 September 1877, reported: 'In the Birmingham Botanic Gardens one feels in the country, far away from the din of commerce, the roar of trade, and the contentions of politics.'

Birmingham Botanical Gardens being used for a
wedding reception, 1989.

The committee of management of the gardens consisted of land-owners, who were either earls or lords, and also included manufacturers, Anglican clergymen, bankers and physicians. Shareholders and their families were admitted free and they could each bring in four other people without charge. From 1833 there were also free open-air concerts.

In 1844, when there were still no public gardens in Birmingham, it was decided to open the gardens to the working classes on Mondays and Tuesdays at a charge of one penny per person. This was done for both philanthropic and economic reasons. In 1847 working-class entry was restricted to Mondays only. They were excluded from the hot-houses, however, and no picnics or games were allowed, and no smoking. Two policemen were placed on duty.

Middle-class people also took advantage of the one penny entry charge. A certain Mr Cadbury had seen parties getting out of carriages and entering the gardens on a Monday. Apparently nothing could be done about it. In 1851 the Annual Report of the Birmingham Botanical and Horticultural Society recorded 35,708 Monday visitors, but complained: 'At the same time it is to be regretted that persons moving in the higher ranks of life should still continue to make use of a privilege which is intended solely and exclusively for the working classes.'

Public games were eventually permitted and in 1853 it was noted that playing games had caused damage to the main lawns and borders. This was in the peak year of attendance when between June 1853 and May 1854 over 45,000 people visited the gardens. The annual average was 25,000. In 1865 it was decided to raise the entrance fee to two pence in order to limit attendances and in the following year the number of visitors immediately dropped to 9,789. Between 1868 and 1874 the average had risen again, however, to around 20,000. In 1874 the Monday visitors were finally allowed access to the conservatory and hot-houses. The worst fears of the committee were not realised, as the Annual Report recorded: 'No damage to the property of the Society has resulted.'

VICTORIA PARK

Victoria Park, in the East End of London, originated from working-class pressure. In 1838 an organisation called the London Democratic Association was formed with a radical programme of reform. It found support amongst some of the poorest-paid workers in the East End, weavers, dockers and labourers. The society campaigned for a public park and recreation area. Land was eventually acquired in Hackney, called at first Tower Hamlets Park, later to become Victoria Park.

The East End of London at this time had the same population as the whole of Manchester, about 400,000. Industry and the new railways had brought smoke and pollution. Overcrowding, unemployment and poverty led to insanitary conditions, death and disease. In 1848 a doctor, named Hector Gavin, describes the lack of drainage and fresh water, the filth and unendurable stench of the cess pools, the pestilence and fever. At the same time, in *Sanitary Ramblings: Sketches and Illustrations of Bethnal Green*, he comments on

> the love of the beautiful, and the sense of order which are readily accorded to the artisan in his neat garden. When seen in his damp and dirty home, he is generally accused of personal uncleanliness ... yet in his garden he displays evidence of a refined taste and a natural love of beauty ... we are irresistably led to regard the personal uncleanliness of the poor, and the impurities which surround their houses, as the results of agencies foreign to the individuals.

In 1839 the newly appointed Registrar-General of Births, Deaths and Marriages made his first report. It shows that the mortality rate in East London far exceeded that of the rest of the city. The appendix of the report contains recommendations from William Farr, a well-know reformer and authority on public health:

> A park in the East End of London would probably diminish the annual deaths by several thousands ... and add several years to the lives of the entire population. The poorer classes would be benefitted by these measures, and the poor taxes reduced. But all classes of the community are directly interested ... for the epidemics ... which arise in the east end of the town do not stay there, they travel to the west end and prove fatal in wide streets and squares: the registers show this.

Although the Municipal Reform Act was passed in 1835, it did not apply to London. There was no overall London local authority. The only authority to appeal to was parliament or the queen. In 1840 a local MP, George Frederick Young, got involved in the campaign. After a public meeting 'to advocate the formation of an East London Park', he was given the task of drawing up a petition to Queen Victoria, who was then 21 years old and in the third year of her reign.

The petition refers to the 'Poor People, closely crowded in confined districts' who 'have no open spaces in the vicinity of their humble dwellings for air, exercise or healthful recreation;

circumstances which produce the most painful effects on their physical and moral condition.' It continues:

> From official documents it appears that the mortality in towns, in general, from epidemic diseases, is double that of agricultural districts. But, in the neighbourhood for which we implore your Majesty's gracious interposition, the mortality is more than double that of those parts of the Metropolis which are more effectually ventilated. Fever is constantly prevailing in these places, which are indeed declared on competent authority to be 'the main sources and seats of the Fevers of the Metropolis'.

After the petition was circulated throughout Tower Hamlets for a few weeks it collected more than 30,000 signatures.

Other reasons for creating a park were put forward. It would reduce drinking and gambling and it would raise land values and rents. The tone of the East End would be raised by attracting middle-class people to live in the area, as a local magistrate, George Offer, explained:

> To land and house owners in this Eastern district it is of the greatest importance that emigration to the west should be checked by providing a rational and wholesome place of recreation similar to those enjoyed by the Northern and Western districts. A Public Park, surrounded by good houses, would attract wealthier residents, improving the tone and behaviour of the area.

Construction of the Park

By 1841 the decision to build the park had been taken by the government and it was decided to sell some Crown property to raise the money to finance it. It was initially a royal park, though in 1887 it lost its royal title and was financed from the rates. The workers who built it were paid 3s 3d a day if they were unskilled labourers and 5s 5d if skilled workers, such as bricklayers, carpenters, and painters.

In 1868 the Board of Works decided to extend the bathing lake and a debate took place in the press about the use of public works to provide temporary work for the unemployed. A distinction was made between the 'deserving' and the 'undeserving' poor, between the unemployed who were 'willing' and those who were 'idle'. The Rev. Brook Lambert of St Mark's, Whitechapel, wrote to the board warning them not to encourage 'idlers' to seek work at Victoria Park:

> May I suggest that if the plan is really to be worked as a help to distress, the wage given should be below the ordinary rate, so that there should be no interference with the labour market, and that there may be a certainty that work is given only to those who really want it to keep themselves from starving.

Eventually 100 men, many of them skilled workers, were employed at the unskilled rate. The board complained that progress was too slow, to which the park superintendent, Mr Merrett, who was in charge of the work, replied that the main reason for the delay was the physical weakness of the labourers, many of whom had been close to starvation.

Victoria Park, from Nathan Cole's The Royal Parks and Gardens of London, *1877.*

The park was designed by James Pennethorne, who had worked with Nash on Regent's Park, and the post of chief horticulturist was given to Samuel Curtiss, on the recommendation of William Hooker. Pennethorne envisaged the park in two distinct halves, divided by class. One half would contain lawns and flower-beds, winding paths and clumps of trees, with its western side surrounded by large middle-class houses whose ground rents would help finance the park. The sites for these villas were advertised for sale, but not one was actually sold. The wealthy were not convinced of the desirability of living in the East End, even with a park next door. The other half of the park, to the east, would be mostly open grass for working-class games and recreation.

Nothing much was done till 1845 when the park fences were erected and Curtiss started his planting. He had to cover 16 acres with tree-clumps, at about 2,000 trees to the acre. The 32,000 trees cost £640 and he also bought 400 larger trees, 'for dotting about the park', at a cost of one shilling each. He needed 240 elms and 120 limes for the drives, and 550 hornbeams to screen the canal. As the *Illustrated London News* of 3 January 1846 records: '70–80 men are employed daily, over 10,000 trees and shrubs are planted, the avenues lined with elms and hornbeams, intermixed with laurels, chestnuts, and the true cockspur thorn'.

The park never had an official opening. Local people just took it over in 1845 while it was being built. As Nathan Cole later wrote: 'They look on the park as their own property.'

Sport and Horticulture

The park was certainly popular and surprise is expressed in the *Illustrated London News* of 2 May 1846, at the little damage done by its working-class visitors:

> We are happy to find that this newly-formed 'Public Walk' is progressing well, so as already to afford the Eastern inhabitants of the Metropolis an amusement to which they have, till lately, been strangers ... We may state that on Good Friday, the new park was visited by 25,000 persons, and by a considerably greater number on Easter Monday ... Excellent order was kept, and very trifling injury or damage was done.

The Rev. Suter of All Saints, Bethnal Green, thought that use of the park prevented suicide and praised it in glowing terms:

> It is our sanatorium for invalids, the gymnasium for our young men, the playground for our children, and the only place where our unemployed can go, walk and sit and enjoy God's fresh air without paying for it, and thus be saved in many cases from the despair that leads to suicide.

People also came in their carriages from the West End to visit the park. In 1851 music was allowed in the park as a result of a petition drawn up by 'the inhabitants of Hackney, Old Ford and Bethnal Green', and in 1865 a permanent bandstand was erected. When the band played, crowds of 100,000 might be present in the park. On Whit Monday 1892 the number of recorded visitors reached a total of 303,516.

The park was used for sports and recreation, such as cricket, rounders, archery and boating. Football was not allowed until 1888. A gymnasium was built and, when the lake was constructed, swimming became very popular. It was allowed between 4am and 8am in the summer, though only for men and boys. As many as 25,000 went swimming on a single day. The swimming was in the nude, swimming costumes not yet having been invented. A request by a group of women for a tennis court was turned down.

Victoria Park today.

The flower-beds were also very popular and Victoria Park became famous for its bedding-out schemes, which were displayed without railings, unlike in Hyde Park where they were kept behind bars. Carpet-gardening became fashionable, using plants such as coleus and various cacti to form a continuous pattern like a carpet. By the end of the century 200,000 plants were being bedded out annually.

There was a friendly rivalry between the professional gardeners of the park and the local amateurs, as J.J. Sexby records:

> At Victoria Park the hard-working artisan is a bit of a horticultural critic in his way. Somehow in the small back gardens and crowded yards he manages to rear many a choice specimen, so that the flowers in the adjoining park have to be kept up to the mark.

Every spring, after the young plants had been bedded out, the remainder were given away free to anyone who asked for them.

Political Demonstrations

The other main use of the park, besides sport and horticulture, was politics. In 1848 Victoria Park witnessed the final great Chartist demonstration in support of the third presentation of the Charter which contained two million signatures. On Whit Monday a demonstration was called to take place in the park, to be followed by a march through London linking up with other contingents of Chartists. The government took it very seriously, reacting with organised force and turning Victoria Park into an armed camp. Some 1,600 foot police were stationed in the park, 500 of them armed with cutlasses, 100 mounted police, and 500 recalled police pensioners. A large detachment of cavalry also stood by. Even the park-keepers were sworn in as special police and issued with cutlasses.

Facing this threat of violence, the organisers tried to cancel the demonstration, but people had already begun to assemble and speeches had started. The demonstrators were charged by the mounted police and this, along with torrential rain, eventually dispersed the crowd.

A part of the park, called the Forum, was traditionally used for open-air public meetings, whether religious or political. Famous socialists, such as Henry Hyndman, Bernard Shaw, William Morris, John Burns, Tom Mann and Ben Tillett, were frequent speakers. William Morris wrote to his daughter Jenny in 1886: 'Eastward Ho to Victoria Park ... It is rather a pretty place with water (though dirty) and lots of trees. Had a good meeting, spoke for an hour in a place made noisy by other meetings near, also a brass band not far off.'

South of the Forum was a large assembly place used for mass meetings of dockers and other industrial workers. Suffragettes also

163

demonstrated here. It was to this spot too that Oswald Mosley was leading his fascists in 1936 when they were stopped in Whitechapel by a counter-demonstration.

Most public parks were used for political meetings and demonstrations, though in a few there were by-laws forbidding them. The park superintendent's perspective on this activity is provided by W.W. Pettigrew, in charge of Manchester parks at the beginning of this century. He saw it as a safety valve 'wherein disgruntled folk are enabled to air their grievances'.

HYDE PARK

The most famous park for political demonstrations is Hyde Park and its history marks many of the key moments in English history. It originally belonged to the church, but became a royal park when Henry VIII confiscated it in 1536. He used it for hunting hares, herons, pheasants and partridges, as well as deer. James I opened it to the public in 1603.

During the Civil War fortifications were erected in the east part of the park to defend London from the Cavaliers. The forts and trenches were constructed by women as well as men, as Samuel Butler recounts in 'Hudibras':

> *From ladies down to oyster-wenches*
> *Labour'd like pioneers in trenches,*
> *Fell to their pick axes and tools,*
> *And helped the men to dig like moles.*

In 1649 all the royal parks were declared to be the property of the Commonwealth and thrown open to the public, but three years later this was revoked and the House of Commons 'resolved that Hyde Park be sold for ready money'. The parks were auctioned in lots and sold off to speculators. Anthony Deane bought most of Hyde Park and John Evelyn complains in 1653: 'I went to take the aire in Hide Park, when every coach was made to pay a shilling and every horse sixpence by the sordid fellow who has purchas'd it of the State.' The parks later reverted to the crown, but with public access.

Troops were quartered in the park in 1715 and 1722 when there were fears of Jacobite risings, and again at the time of the Gordon Riots in 1780. In the north-east corner of the park stood Tyburn

Tree where so many public hangings took place in the eighteenth century. According to Horace Walpole, 'no less than 500,000 people were assembled' for the hanging of Dr Dodd for forgery in 1777.

Queen Caroline, wife of George II, was very fond of parks and had the lake, called the Serpentine, built. She also wanted to restrict the use of St James's Park to the royal family, resulting in her reputed conversation with the Prime Minister. She asked Walpole what it would cost and he replied, 'Only a Crown, Madam.' This apparently deterred her.

Loudon had plans for Hyde Park which he spelt out in 1826. He wanted music in the park, in the form of a perambulating band; reading, to be supplied by magazine and newspaper stands; and refreshments such as tea, coffee, milk and fruit. His aim was to soften and refine the manners of the rude working class.

The class conflict in the park was vividly described by Marx in 1855. The Sunday Trading Bill had just been passed, calling for closure of all shops on Sunday. As Marx pointed out, the working class received its wages late on Saturday, so Sunday trading existed solely for them. A demonstration was called to protest and to show up the hypocrisy of the aristocracy who used the road by the Serpentine, particularly on Sundays, to 'parade their magnificent carriages with all their trappings and exercise their horses followed by swarms of lackeys'. As the Chartist poster announced:

An open-air meeting of artisans, workers and 'the lower orders' generally of the capital will take place in Hyde Park on Sunday afternoon to see how religiously the aristocracy is observing the Sabbath and how anxious it is not to employ its servants and horses on that day.

Marx reported the event:

At 3 o'clock about 50,000 people had gathered at the appointed spot on the right bank of the Serpentine in the huge meadows of Hyde Park. Gradually the numbers swelled to at least 200,000 as people came from the left bank too. Small knots of people could be seen being jostled from one spot to another. A large contingent was evidently attempting to deprive the organizers of the meeting of what Archimedes had demanded in order to move the earth: a fixed place to stand on. Finally, a large crowd made a firm stand and the Chartist James Bligh constituted himself chairman on a small rise in the middle of the crowd. No sooner had he begun his harangue than Police Inspector Banks at the head of forty truncheon-swinging

165

constables explained to him that the Park was the private property
of the Crown and that they were not allowed to hold a meeting in it
... After some preliminary exchanges, in the course of which Bligh
tried to demonstrate that the Park was public property and Banks
replied that he had strict orders to arrest him if he persisted in his
intention, Bligh shouted amidst the tremendous roar of the masses
around him: 'Her Majesty's police declare that Hyde Park is the
private propery of the Crown and that Her Majesty is not inclined to
lend her land to the people for their meetings. So let us adjourn to
Oxford Market.'

With the ironic cry of 'God save the Queen!' the throng dispersed
in the direction of Oxford Market. But meanwhile, James Finlen, a
member of the Chartist leadership, had rushed to a tree some
distance away. A crowd followed him and surrounded him instantly
in such a tight and compact circle that the police abandoned their
attempts to force their way through to him... The spectacle lasted
for three hours ... Zealous Chartist men and women battled their
way through the crowds throughout these three hours, distributing
leaflets ...

In 1866 another massive demonstration took place in Hyde
Park. This was part of the Reform agitation demanding the vote
for working-class men. The Tories, according to A.L. Morton, were
convinced that they were 'on the verge of a revolutionary
outbreak' and they passed the Reform Act of 1867 'as a concession
to avert revolution'. In trying to prevent this demonstration, the
government illegally closed the gates of the park, and so,
according to Raymond Williams, 'a number of people very
properly proceeded to take down the railings'. Half a mile of
railings were pulled down and the flower-beds ruined.

The first political May Day celebrations in this country took
place in Hyde Park in 1890. They were part of the campaign for
the eight-hour working day and up to half a million people
marched to the park. The *Star* reported: 'It seemed as though the
whole population of London poured parkwards.'

In 1908 seven marches from different parts of London
converged on Hyde Park calling for Votes for Women. It was
probably the largest ever demonstration in the park. Thirty special
trains were run from 70 towns to bring the demonstrators to
London. This time the authorities themselves agreed to take up a
quarter of a mile of park railings in order to provide more space.
Twenty platforms were set up for the meetings with a woman
presiding on each one. *The Times* said that the organisers had
counted on an audience of 250,000: 'That expectation was

certainly fulfilled; probably it was doubled; it would be difficult to contradict anyone who asserted that it was trebled. Like the distance and numbers of the stars, the facts were beyond the threshold of perception.'

The *Daily Express* reported:

The Women Suffragists provided London yesterday with one of the most wonderful and astonishing sights that has ever been seen since the days of Boadicea ... It is probable that so many people never before stood in one square mass anywhere in England. Men who saw the great Gladstone meeting years ago said that, compared with yesterday's multitude, it was as nothing.

William Morris speaking at a May Day Rally in Hyde Park,
1894, sketched by Walter Crane.

During the General Strike of 1926 food dumps were set up in the park and troops drilled there. In the 1930s, the Hunger Marches, protesting against unemployment, ended in the park. In 1932 mounted police cleared the park, but in 1936 the crowd of 250,000 was too large to disperse. In recent years Hyde Park has seen demonstrations on the scale of the earlier ones, protesting now against nuclear weapons and against apartheid in South Africa.

In 1930 George Lansbury, as First Commissioner of Works, set up the lido in the park, with swimming allowed for men, women and children from 6am till dusk in the summer. Previously swimming was allowed in the Serpentine only for males and only early in the morning, as in the lake in Victoria Park.

In 1958, making Park Lane a dual carriageway swallowed up 23 acres of Hyde Park at one fell swoop, and prior to that a further 27 acres of the royal parks of London had been destroyed to make way for road-widening schemes. To prevent such vandalism, Whitaker and Browne recommend 'the formation of a vigilant local committee for each open space' which 'should be elected by the surrounding neighbourhood'. The history of public parks and commons illustrates the necessity of such vigilance. It has been a history of struggle, both to create and preserve the parks, and also to determine how they should be used.

9

Pollution, Glass and Bedding-out

1845
Tax on glass removed

1845
United Flint Glass Makers' Society founded

1847
James Hartley's sheet glass process

1851
Window tax repealed

1853
Smoke Nuisance Act

1859
30,000–40,000 bedding plants in Hyde Park

The chimney must be cured of smoking.
Ladies' Sanitary Association Annual Report (1859)

Shall I tell you what luxury has done for you in modern Europe? It has covered the merry green fields with the hovels of slaves, and blighted the flowers and trees with poisonous gases, and turned the rivers into sewers; till over many parts of Britain the common people have forgotten what a field or a flower is like.
William Morris, 'The Society of the Future' (Lecture delivered to the Hammersmith Branch of the Socialist League on 13 November 1887 – the evening of Bloody Sunday)

No thing on this earth can be good under adverse condi-
tions – not the river, not the green grass, not the skylark,
nor the rose.   Robert Blatchford, *Merrie England* (1893)

> *A blazing arch of lucid glass*
> *Leaps like a fountain from the grass*
> *To meet the sun!*
>   Alfred Tennyson, 'May-Day Ode' (1851)

The immense number of half-hardy plants which had been
introduced may have accounted for the 'bedding-out'
system which was such a marked feature of the majority of
gardens throughout the nineteenth century. People soon
tired of the flowerless landscape style and the great lawns
were cut up into beds, round, square, diamond and so
forth, and planted to make a display during the summer
months with flowers such as lobelias, calceolarias, gera-
niums, antirrhinums and ageratum. The flat, closely
bunched Victorian bouquet reflected the fashionable beds
of the period. In 1863 a book was published containing no
letterpress, except a brief preface, and consisting wholly of
plans for these ugly beds – Geometrical Flower Beds, *by*
Charles Francis Hayward.
        Eleanour Sinclair Rohde, *The Story of the Garden* (1932)

In the middle of Queen Victoria's reign bedding-out was at the
height of its fashion. Alicia Amherst, writing at the beginning
of this century, describes what it was like in the 1860s. It
consisted of 'large, glaring patches of bright flowers as dazzling as
possible, or minute and intricate patterns carried out in carpet
bedding'.

The bedding system began in the 1830s with the increasing
number of plants arriving from Mexico, South Africa and South
America, and by mid-century it had become firmly established.
Ribbon borders took the place of herbaceous borders, though the
latter never disappeared completely and herbaceous perennials
were still stocked by nurseries. In the 1870s and 1880s carpet
bedding became popular. Using low ground-cover plants such as
arabis, sempervivum and sedum, embroidered beds were made.
William Robinson called them 'mosaic beds' and the style was also
referred to as tapestry bedding. William Morris thought it was 'an
aberration of the human mind'. Emblems, monograms, names
and coats of arms were similarly devised. This emblematic carpet

170

bedding was thought to be based on a French custom of the sixteenth century.

Nearly half of Nathan Cole's book *The Royal Parks and Gardens of London*, published in 1877, consists of designs for flower and carpet bedding on grass. At that time two million plants were bedded out annually in London parks. He points to one of the major influences:

> Our public Parks and Gardens have been adorned with the vegetation of the tropics, and from all parts of the globe these floral treasures have come. Those rich gifts from other countries, gathered together in our own gardens in summer, have fostered a wholesome love of flowers, and stimulated their culture in private gardens.

Carpet bedding at Kew Gardens, 1870.

The new urban formality of ornate and highly structured flower-beds was even applied to the country gardens where it had been fashionable in the seventeenth century. The garden designer William Andrews Nesfield (1793–1881) began in the middle of the century to plan elaborate parterres, which included scroll patterned flower-beds, for both new and well established country houses. Sometimes the patterns would be made up of coloured sand or gravel, edged with box. The designs were often similar to those of the knot gardens of the sixteenth and seventeenth centuries, which in turn probably derived from Arab patterns and from women's embroidery.

Designs for knot gardens from William Lawson's The Countrie House-wife's Garden *first published in 1617.*

FROM LANDSCAPE GARDENS TO BEDDING-OUT

The change from eighteenth-century landscape gardens to mid-nineteenth century bedding-out schemes is related to the change from a rural to an urban way of life, and also to the change in the dominant class, from land-owners to industrial capitalists. As Hobsbawm has pointed out in *Industry and Empire*:

> By the 1840s farming was distinctly a minority interest. It occupied no more than a quarter of the population and less than this share of the national income. When the nobility abandoned agriculture – as happened in 1846, and even more obviously in 1879 – all that was left was a minority pressure group stiffened by a bloc of fox-hunting back-bench MPs.

By mid-century, with the waning of Chartism, British industrialists felt politically more confident and economically no longer so threatened with bankruptcies by fluctuations of trade. This era of confidence was reflected in municipal spending, not only on public parks, but also on monuments and halls. Leeds, in competition with Bradford, spent a 'titanic' £122,000 on its town hall.

Town gardening was partly influenced by the landscape garden, as is clear from the development of some of the garden cemeteries and public parks, but it could not compete with the rolling acres of the countryside. A number of other factors, connected with the rise of industrial capitalism influenced the change in style to the more formal system of bedding-out. One was pollution and its devastating affect on plants, another was the development of glass, both for the Wardian case and for glasshouses, and a third was the exploitation, by the expanding firms of seed merchants and their nurseries, of the plants brought back by the plant hunters.

A list of flower seeds, advertised in 1836 in *The Floricultural Cabinet*, shows that half of them, 74 out of 150, were recent introductions from the Americas, mainly from Chile, Mexico and California. A total of 42 had been introduced between 1820 and 1829, and 22 between 1830 and 1834. They included alstroemeria, clarkia, eschscholtzia, oenothera, petunia, and schizanthus.

The family firm of Veitch sent more than 20 plant hunters around the world, including E.H. Wilson who had earlier worked at Birmingham Botanic Gardens and at Kew. In 1853 Robert Veitch bought his Chelsea nursery in the King's Road to add to the one he owned in Exeter. In a few years, under the direction of his son James, it became the most important nursery in Great Britain, employing many skilled plant hybridisers. Sutton and Sons of Reading also became prominent in the 1850s, and in 1855 William Thompson of Ipswich, now Thompson and Morgan, issued his first seed catalogue.

POLLUTION

Pollution was caused not only by insanitary housing conditions and bad drainage, but also by smoke. As early as 1629 John Parkinson in his *Paradisus* was writing of the 'unwholesome ayres where there is much smoke'. He particularly attacked coal 'which of all other is the worst, as our Citie of London can give proofe sufficient, wherein neither herbe nor tree will long prosper, nor hath done ever since the use of sea-coles beganne to be frequent therein'. John Evelyn, in his *Fumifugium: or the Inconveniencie of the aer and smoak of London dissipated* of 1661, suggests planting fragrant flowers and shrubs to counter the smell of smoke in the city. When William and Mary came to the throne in 1688 they

173

often used to stay at Hampton Court, for William suffered from asthma and could not endure the smoky air of London.

In the nineteenth century the situation became far worse. Between 1830 and 1850 6,000 miles of railways had been built. Between 1850 and 1880 coal production rose from 49 million tons to 147 million. In 1750 there were only two cities in Britain with more than 50,000 inhabitants: Edinburgh and London; in 1851 there were 29, including nine with over 100,000. As Hobsbawm explains:

> Railways, sidings and stations tore wide strips into the centres of cities, pushing the population which had previously lived there into other slums, and covering those that remained with that dense layer of soot and grime which may still be seen in some corners of northern towns to this day. The acrid fog which foreigners found so characteristic wrapped itself ever more firmly round Victorian Britain.

Ironically the railways were essential for the nursery gardens, which depended on this form of transport to deliver their plants. The railways also helped establish the popularity of alpine plants in the second half of the century, as they could now be transported from Switzerland in two days instead of a whole week.

Engels depicts the Manchester conurbation, from Bolton to Stockport, as 'reeking of coal smoke', with Stockport 'renowned throughout the entire district as one of the duskiest, smokiest holes'. The previous year John Loudon wrote of the damage that smoke was doing to market gardeners and how they had presented a petition to parliament. The decline of the florists' societies during this period is attributed by Tom Carter to the effects of pollution: 'The fog and smoke of the manufacturing towns was yet another factor which brought about the decline of floristry in the 1840s and 1850s.' By the mid-nineteenth century pinks had disappeared from Paisley because of factory smoke.

Despite Palmerston's Smoke Nuisance Act in 1853, which tried to impose controls on factory smoke, the pollution worsened. In a lecture entitled 'The Society of the Future', delivered in 1887, William Morris calls London a 'horrible muck-heap', and in 'A Factory As It Might Be' he describes the factory of the future: 'Well, it follows in this garden business that our factory must make no sordid litter, befoul no water, nor poison the air with smoke.'

It was not only the East End that was polluted. In 1853 the

Gardeners' Chronicle writes about 'the smoke-begrimed plains of the west of London', and in 1866 south London is included: 'Even Kennington Common, which now aspires to the name of Park, has its bordering of flowers, as bright as the smoke and vapour from an adjoining factory will let them be.' There was also at this time a plan, which never materialised, to pump fresh air in pipes from Hampstead Heath to the City of London.

In 1851 when the Crystal Palace was erected in Hyde Park, it was discovered how much better trees fared under glass than in the polluted atmosphere of London: 'While the dirty, half-starved Elms, growing as if wild in the open park, made shoots at the most a foot long on the average, the well-fed, well-cleaned, well-lodged trees under the transept, made shoots from 6 to 7 feet long.'

Alicia Amherst in 1907 describes the smoke and hurtful fogs, 'the evil has, of course, become greatly intensified during the last fifty years', particularly because of the 'prodigious quantity of coal consumed'. By this time the number of miners had grown from 200,000 in 1851 to well over a million. The electric power stations proved 'very deleterious to vegetation' because of their suffocating smoke, 'even healthy young shrubs and bushes, such as laurels, are destroyed by it'. Similar devastation by British power stations is experienced today in Scandinavia where whole forests are destroyed by acid rain.

In the second half of the nineteenth century many of the original shrubs and trees in the Derby Arboretum succumbed to the smoke from the town, caused by domestic and industrial coal-burning. They were replaced largely by the hardy common sycamore. As early as 1802 Loudon was criticising the planting of yew and fir in London squares because the smoke made their foliage drab and they grew so poorly. He suggested using deciduous trees instead, such as plane, sycamore and almond. Plane trees in particular managed to survive the polluted atmosphere because of their ability to shed their bark. The London plane is a hybrid between the oriental plane and the American plane and was first introduced in the seventeenth century. It now comprises over half the planted trees of central London.

Another of the plants that seemed to cope with the pollution was the *Rhododendron ponticum*. P.H. Gosse writes in 1856 that it was 'cultivated even in the smoky gardens of London in great abundance'. Similarly the privet proved very resistant, which is why it was so commonly used for hedges. Very few roses, however, could survive the smoke in the centre of London. In some districts they had to be grown under bell jars which could only be removed at the weekend when the air was less polluted by factory smoke.

In 1928 W.W. Pettigrew, superintendent of Manchester parks, gave a lecture to the Smoke Abatement League on 'the influence of air pollution on vegetation'. He provides revealing statistics for Philips Park, which was situated in the worst polluted area of the city:

> Generally speaking, Rhododendrons live only for three years in this park. The first summer after they are planted, a fairly large percentage of them bloom, for the flower buds are already formed on them when they are brought from the nursery in the country. Afterwards, hardly one per cent of them bear blooms ... Philips Park is about 30 acres in extent, and in order to maintain it in present-able condition, so far as furnishing the borders with trees and shrubs is concerned, it has to be planted up each year with 2,500 Rhododendron bushes, 2,500 Poplar trees, 1,000 Willows, 750 Elders and about 300 different kinds of flowering shrub.

The bedding-out system, in which whole flower-beds might be changed two or three times during a season, seems expensive, but not when compared to Pettigrew's catalogue of expenditure for the year.

THE WARDIAN CASE

Changing plants several times a year was a way of avoiding the effects of pollution, but in order to raise these tender bedding plants, such as begonias, salvias and geraniums, glass was needed. Glass was also required in the form of the Wardian case to transport these 'rich gifts from other countries' across the world's oceans.

Nathaniel Bagshaw Ward (1791–1868) was a doctor in the East End of London, a keen grower of ferns, and also interested in moths and butterflies. He tried cultivating ferns in his rockery, but the polluted London air prevented them from growing. In the summer of 1829 he buried the chrysalis of a Hawk Moth in some moist mould in a closed bottle to observe its development:

I observed that the moisture which during the heat of the day arose from the mould, became condensed on the surface of the glass, and returned whence it came; thus keeping the mould always in the same degree of humidity. About a week prior to the final change of the insect, a seedling fern and a grass made their appearance on the surface of the mould.

He realised that the fern could grow because the atmosphere was free from soot, because light came through the glass and because the moisture remained in the bottle. It remained growing in the bottle for nearly four years. The Wardian case, now called a terrarium, had been discovered.

A Wardian case.

According to Ward, it would help in 'improving the condition of the poor' who could grow flowers, ferns and ivies for pleasure, and 'all the vacant spaces may be employed in raising small salads, radishes, etc.', which would 'in the course of a twelve-month pay for the case out of its proceeds'. The *Illustrated London News* records its use, after complaining that it was practically impossible to grow any flowers or vegetables in London:

By simply preventing the access of the London smoke to injure the leaves we have this year succeeded in growing cucumbers in the very centre of the metropolis, showing what may be effected when the deleterious gases which emanate from the combustion of coal are prevented from exercising their baneful influence.

The main use for the Wardian case was in the transportation of plants across the world. Ward constructed two rectangular wooden boxes with sloping glass tops, sealed with putty to make them airtight: 'In the beginning of June 1833, I filled two cases with ferns, grass etc., and sent them to Sydney.' The contents arrived safely six months later. The cases were refilled and sent back, surviving temperatures of between 20 and 120 degrees Fahrenheit. Sometimes 'the decks were covered a foot deep with snow'. The plants had not been watered once and when they arrived, Ward examined them along with the nurseryman George Loddiges of Hackney. Loddiges later told William Hooker: 'Whereas I used, formerly, to lose nineteen out of twenty of the plants I imported, during the voyage, nineteen out of twenty is now the average of those that survive.' Hooker himself imported six times as many plants for Kew Gardens in 15 years as had been imported in the previous century.

The cases would be lashed to the deck and the glass was often protected by a netting of strong wire. They proved indispensable for introducing the Chinese banana to Samoa, Fiji and Tonga, and for the tea, cinchona and rubber transfers.

In 1833, soon after the discovery of the Wardian case, new methods of glass manufacture were invented which enabled a far more transparent glass to be made. Previously the small glass sheets were never perfectly flat, varied in shade and contained air bubbles and streaks. Larger sheets of glass could now also be made and greenhouse building developed fast. Advertisements for sheet glass appeared regularly, as for instance in George Glenny's Garden Almanacs of 1848 and 1849. The removal of the tax on glass in 1845 reduced the price of sheet glass to two pence a foot, one seventh of its previous price.

In 1860 Samuel Hereman advertised 'Hothouses for the Million', invented and patented by Joseph Paxton:

These Buildings are of unparalleled cheapness, and being composed of simple parts can be enlarged, removed, or adapted to any Horticultural purpose by ordinary labourers. They are calculated for gardens of the highest order, or gentlemen's gardens generally, for market gardens where they may be made to cover any extent of surface, and also for suburban, villa, and cottage gardens.

JOSEPH PAXTON

Joseph Paxton was at this time the most celebrated person for his use of glass in design. Not only did he design the Great Conservatory at Chatsworth, but also the Crystal Palace in Hyde Park. *The Times* obituary described him also as the 'greatest gardener of his time'.

Paxton edited the monthly *Horticultural Register* between 1831 and 1835, and in 1834 produced *Paxton's Magazine of Botany.* In 1841 he was a leading light behind the first weekly gardening newspaper the *Gardeners' Chronicle* and he designed a number of public gardens, particularly in Scotland. He took an active part in the development of the railways and organised the building of trenches, roads and railways in the Crimea. He was also Chairman of the Midland Railway: when the Crystal Palace was moved to Sydenham, the original prospectus mentioned a railway station on the site, though this never materialised.

Joseph Paxton was the epitome of the Victorian self-made man. Samuel Smiles, famous for his book *Self Help*, which came out in 1859 and within four years had sold 55,000 copies, describes Paxton's life as one 'of labour, of diligent self-improvement, of assiduous cultivation of knowledge'. Paxton was the son of a poor tenant farmer in Bedfordshire and rose from being a gardener's assistant with very little formal education, to be head gardener to the Duke of Devonshire at Chatsworth, one of the richest men in the land. In the second half of the century the Duke's estate brought in £181,000 a year, equivalent to more then £12 million today. Paxton was knighted for his design of Crystal Palace and was MP for Coventry from 1854 till his death in 1865.

Paxton became head gardener at Chatsworth in 1826 and the patronage and wealth of the sixth Duke of Devonshire enabled him, along with Decimus Burton, to design the famous conservatory. It was 277 feet long, 123 feet wide and 67 feet high, and it covered just over three-quarters of an acre. Eight boilers, heating seven miles of pipes and consuming 350 tons of coal, were needed to heat the building. Coal was brought to the boilers by an underground tramway. As at Kew, the chimneys were placed some

HOTHOUSES FOR THE MILLION.

SAMUEL HEREMAN

BEGS TO INFORM THE PUBLIC THAT HE HAS BEEN APPOINTED SOLE AGENT FOR THE MANUFACTURE AND SALE OF

THE NEW PORTABLE AND ECONOMICAL HOTHOUSES,

INVENTED AND PATENTED BY

SIR JOSEPH PAXTON, M.P.

Paxton's design advertised in the Gardeners' Chronicle and Agricultural Gazette, *January 1860.*

distance from the conservatory, linked to the boilers by a tunnel, in order to prevent the smoke from blocking out the sunlight.

The design was based on the structure of the leaf ribs of the giant water-lily, *Victoria regia* or *amazonica*, the leaves of which are six or seven feet in diameter. Begun in 1836, the conservatory took 500 people four years to build and in 1843 it was visited by Queen Victoria, who drove through it in an open carriage. It became a centre, like Kew, for the exotic plants flooding in from the empire, and in it, according to John Loudon, 'a tropical garden could be enjoyed in the depth of winter'.

Loudon visited Chatsworth in 1839 when the conservatory was nearing completion and he describes it in glowing terms:

In general design it may be compared to a cathedral with a central aile and side ailes. The entrances will be at the ends, through porches, which will be treated as green-houses; and, when the whole is completed, it will cover above an acre and a quarter of ground. There will be a carriage drive through it; which will form part of a general drive through the pleasure-grounds. The conservatory is situated in an open part of a lofty wood, in nearly the centre of the pleasure-grounds, and it is unquestionably the largest structure of the kind in existence or on record.

In 1851 Mrs S.C. Hall saw the Chatsworth conservatory

filled with the rarest Exotics from all parts of the globe – from 'farthest Ind', from China, from the Himalayas, from Mexico; here you see the rich banana, Eschol's grape, hanging in ripe profusion beneath the shadow of immense paper-like leaves; the feathery cocoa-palm, with its head peering almost to the lofty arched roof; the far-famed silk cotton-tree, supplying a sheet of cream-coloured blossoms, at a season when all outward vegetable gaiety is on the wane, the singular milk-tree of the Caraccas; the fragrant cinnamon and cassia – with thousands of other rare and little known species of both flower and fruits.

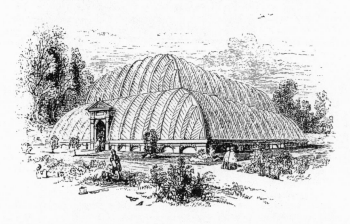

The Great Conservatory at Chatsworth House.

William Hooker followed the lead of Chatsworth and between 1844 and 1848 the great Palm House at Kew, designed by Richard Turner and Decimus Burton, was built, 362 feet long, 100 feet wide and 63 feet high. Competition to produce exotic plants was intense among rich landowners. Vast amounts of money and labour were spent to satisfy their whims. Lord Egremont describes how his grandfather had a greenhouse built to grow bananas, because he was told that they tasted better straight from the tree. The first home-grown banana was presented to him at Petworth House amid a deathly hush:

My grandfather peeled it with a golden knife. He then cut a sliver off and, with a golden fork, put it in his mouth and carefully tasted it. Whereupon he flung dish, plate, knife, fork and banana on to the

'The gigantic water-lily (Victoria regia), in flower at Chatsworth.' From the Illustrated London News, *17 November, 1849.*

floor and shouted, 'Oh God, it tastes just like any other damn banana!' Banana tree and all were ordered to be destroyed. My famous old gardener, Mr Fred Streeter, told me that the banana cost my grandfather some £3,000.

THE CRYSTAL PALACE

Iron and glass came together most spectacularly in the design of the Crystal Palace. Presiding over a Midland Railway committee meeting in Derby, Paxton again used the pattern of the ribbed leaf of the giant water-lily and drew his plan for the Great Exhibition centre on a piece of blotting paper. As he later said: 'It is to this plant that the Crystal Palace owes its direct origin.' The building also owed much to Loudon's invention in 1818 of a curvilinear wrought-iron sash bar.

The Crystal Palace was to cover almost 20 times the area of the Chatsworth Palm House, three times the size of St Paul's cathedral. It was erected by 2,260 men in seven months. Within the first few months there was a strike by the glaziers, but they were dismissed and new workers taken on in their place. Some 500 painters were employed to decorate the interior and 900,000 square feet of glass were used, equivalent to about a third of the country's annual glass output. It needed 3,800 tons of cast iron, 700 tons of wrought iron and 600,000 cubic feet of timber. The building was 1,848 feet long and 408 feet wide.

The exhibition of industrial goods and plants, which took place in the Crystal Palace in 1851, celebrated the spirit of free trade, private enterprise and the superiority of the British Empire. No public money was spent, but a profit was made of £186,437, of which Paxton received £5,000. In less than six months, between 1 May and 11 October, over six million people had visited the exhibition, an average of 43,000 daily. The original admission price of £1 was gradually reduced to a shilling.

The new Palm House in the Edinburgh Botanic Garden, which opened in 1858, also had a very direct connection with the empire, as the *Falkirk Herald* records:

> The tropical aspect of this house is heightened by the fact that the man in attendance upon the visitors is a bona fide African. The presence of such a man gives a consistency to the scene; and, besides, it is found that a native of the sunny climes, where the palm trees grow, is better able to stand the high temperature of such a house than one of our pale-faced race.

The Crystal Palace was likened at the time to a church, with its nave and transepts, though Ruskin called it a 'cucumber frame'. One of the organisers of the exhibition, Henry Cole, describes its purpose:

> A great people invited all civilised nations to a festival, to bring into comparison the works of human skill. It was carried out by private means; was self-supporting and independent of taxes and employment of slaves, which great works had exacted in ancient days.

Strictly speaking he was right about slavery, which had officially been abolished earlier in the century, but during the struggle for emancipation it had often been pointed out that the condition of industrial workers was often no better than that of slaves. Engels bears this out in his description of the manufacture of glass, particularly by children:

> The hard labour, the irregularity of the hours, the frequent night-work, and especially the great heat of the working place (100 to 130 Fahrenheit), engender in children general debility and disease, stunted growth, and especially affections of the eye, bowel

complaint, and rheumatic and bronchial affections. Many of the children are pale, have red eyes, often blind for weeks at a time, suffer from violent nausea, vomiting, coughs, colds, and rheumatism. When the glass is withdrawn from the fire, the children must often go into such heat that the boards on which they stand catch fire under their feet.

Pollution was still a problem – imagine window-cleaning the Crystal Palace! So in 1853 it was decided to move it from Hyde Park to Sydenham where the air was cleaner. The new palace was 50 per cent larger than the original. There were $16^1/_2$ miles of iron columns and 25 acres of glass. Ruskin, who lived nearby in Herne Hill, complained of the Crystal Palace 'for ever spoiling the view'.

The Crystal Palace after being moved to Sydenham, from a lithograph of 1854.

At the time there was talk of building new glass structures over streets in the city, turning them into vast arcades, or covering squares like Lincoln's Inn Fields and converting it into a 'vast glazed flower and water-garden' in the heart of London. But the *Illustrated London News* foresaw problems:

The smoke, however, would be the great drawback. A fortnight's muggy weather would strew the whole surface of the glass with more 'blacks' than there are in Africa, while nothing like the fine fresh air, which ought to breathe among the fruits and flowers of any gardens, winter or summer, could, we fear, be entrapped beneath the glass athwart the roofs and chimney-pots.

184

BEDDING SCHEMES

The Sydenham gardens which Paxton designed for the new location were intended to 'throw Versailles into insignificance'. They attracted tens of thousands of visitors each year and the bedding schemes – one year 50,000 scarlet pelargoniums were planted – had a considerable influence on gardening style. In 1854 *The Cottage Gardener* described the first year's bedding schemes, which included calceolarias, lobelias, petunias, verbenas, gaultherias, alyssums, nemophilas, salvias and heliotropes, interplanted with dwarf rhododendrons and azaleas. These bright plants originate from South America, North America, Asia, Africa. It is like a tribute from the world to a Britannia who ruled the waves, just as Victoria's funeral drew colourful tribute from the empire in the form of representatives from the colonies.

William Robinson, as might be expected, viewed the Sydenham gardens rather more critically:

> There are, from Versailles to Caserta, a great many ugly gardens in Europe, but at Sydenham we have the greatest modern example of the waste of enormous means in making hideous a fine piece of ground. This has been called a work of genius, but it is the fruit of a poor ambition to outdo another ugly extravagance – Versailles.

The gardens of Chatsworth also made a great impact on their visitors, as the editor of *The Gardener* noted in 1867:

> The parks and ground were swarming with holiday-makers, for it was one of England's great holidays, Whit-Monday. Here were pale-faced men and women from the cotton factories of Manchester, dark denizens of the Staffordshire potteries, and the sharp, active-looking mechanics of Leeds, Bradford, and Halifax, all brought hither on special trains, and, in the full heyday of an English holiday, rushing through the gorgeously-fitted-up rooms of the ducal mansion – admiring the conservatories, rockeries and fountains ...

The marrying of landed aristocrat, the Duke of Devonshire, and industrial entrepreneur, Joseph Paxton, illustrates the settlement of the mid-Victorian ruling class. The aristocracy gained from the rise in land values which came about due to the expansion of industry and urban development, and so they were prepared to vote for free trade.

It is also interesting to note how the more formal gardening style which Paxton introduced at Chatsworth, with its use of exotic bedding plants, spread to the seaside where it is still common today. In the same year in which the Crystal Palace was built, the Duke of Devonshire had Eastbourne developed as a holiday resort. It was situated at the end of a railway line and its formal gardens alongside the promenades were filled with bedding plants.

In the last quarter of the nineteenth century the bedding-out system began to decline. As James Douglas wrote in his *Hardy Florists' Flowers*, published in 1880: 'People are now getting tired of the monotony of dazzling masses of colour, and flowers are being valued more for their intrinsic merit.' But it had been an amazing phenomenon, linking different aspects of the industrial revolution and British imperialism: overcoming the enormous increase in pollution by using new technology in the form of glass and iron, and searching the four corners of the earth for exotic plants.

10

Women and Gardening

Usually the growth of greenstuff is checked by contact with a woman. Indeed, if she is also in the period of menstruation, she will kill the young produce merely by looking at it.

Democritus, fifth century BC.

In March and April, from morning to night,
In sowing and setting, good housewives delight;
To have in a garden, or other like plot,
To trim up their house, and to furnish their pot.

Thomas Tusser, 'Five Hundreth Points of Good
Husbandry' (1573)

Gardening, experimental philosophy, and literature, would afford women subjects to think of and matter for conversation, that in some degree would exercise their understandings.

Mary Wollstonecraft, *Vindication of the Rights of Woman* (1792)

A lady, with a small light spade may, by repeatedly digging over the same line, and taking out only a little earth at a time, succeed in doing all the digging that can be required in a small garden; and she will not only have the satisfaction of seeing the garden created, as it were, by her own hands, but she will find her health and spirits wonderfully improved by the exercise, and by the reviving smell of the fresh earth.

Jane Loudon, *Gardening for Ladies* (1840)

The history of gardening reveals the sexism present in most history. It is a story about men, written by men. Women are usually completely absent, or in a supporting role to men, or relegated to weeding. Admittedly there are the famous English female gardener/writers, Jane Loudon, Gertrude Jekyll, Vita Sackville-

West, but they are rather like the novelists Jane Austen, George Eliot and the Brontës, the exception which proves the rule.

The 1988 *Sunday Times* series 'The Making of the English Garden', refers to the 'men of the soil' and 'man manipulating nature', and claims to be a 'history not just of the garden itself but of man the gardener'. It talks about 'the earliest husbandmen' and 'the arrival of man the farmer, around 5000 BC'. Yet women were almost certainly the first gardeners. Edward Hyams, in *Soil and Civilisation*, concludes that 'the earliest agricultural communities were matriarchal and feminine in their social values' and 'women long remained in charge of their discovery of agriculture'.

The Australian historian, Geoffrey Blainey, in *Triumph of the Nomads*, dates the first gardens about 10,000 years ago, appearing simultaneously as far apart as Thailand, India, Jericho and Mexico: 'The first Garden of Eden was probably somewhere east of Suez or, less likely, somewhere north of Panama. In the next half century perhaps six or eight nations will, on the strength of archaeological research, lay claim to the site of that garden.'

Gardening in New Guinea began about the same time, but it did not spread to the continent of Australia, although gardens on Prince of Wales Island were visible from the mainland: 'There is a touch of drama about the way in which the world-wide advance of herds and gardens halted within sight of a strip of northern Australian coast.' Blainey concludes: 'Clearly the northern aboriginals must have preferred not to be gardeners. Perhaps more important, no outside conqueror arrived and forcibly imposed gardening and the new way of life upon them.'

PARADISE LOST

In *Paradise Lost*, despite the sexist roles described by Milton, the gardening in Eden is a joint venture:

> *our delightful task,*
> *To prune these growing plants, and tend these flowers.*

Nevertheless it is Eve who has to pick the fruit for the visiting angel Raphael and crush the grapes for his drink. She also realises, like many gardeners, that the work in the garden, 'their sweet gardening labour', seems continually to expand:

Adam, well may we labour still to dress
This garden, still to tend plant, herb, and flower,
Our pleasant task enjoin'd: but till more hands
Aid us, the work under our labour grows,
Luxurious by restraint; what we by day
Lop overgrown, or prune, or prop, or bind,
One night or two with wanton growth derides,
Tending to wild.

Apart from the idea of producing children, Eve's other solution is to work separately in order to stop Adam interrupting the gardening by gossiping:

Let us divide our labours: thou, where choice
Leads thee, or where most needs, whether to wind
The woodbine round this arbour, or direct
The clasping ivy where to climb; while I,
In yonder spring of roses intermix'd
With myrtle, find what to redress till noon:
For, while so near each other thus all day
Our task we choose, what wonder if so near
Looks intervene and smiles, or object new
Casual discourse draw on; which intermits
Our day's work, brought to little, though begun
Early, and the hour of supper comes unearn'd?

When they are finally expelled from the garden of Eden, Adam is speechless; later his main anxiety is being banished from the sight of God. Eve is more concerned about leaving the garden and is worried about who will look after it.

WOMEN'S WORK

Eve began a long line of women gardeners, as June Taboroff makes clear: 'The tradition of women who take care of gardens and lay vegetable beds is an ancient one. We find it in the Adonis gardens of classical Greece or in the Roman custom of women tending the hortus.'

The same was true of England in the Middle Ages. Writing in 1523, Anthony FitzHerbert, in *A new tract or treatyse most profytable for All Husbandmen*, confirms the woman's responsibility for the vegetable garden, including the weeding:

> And in the begynninge of Marche, or a lyttel afore, is tyme for a
> wyfe to make her garden, and to gette as many good sedes and
> herbes as she canne, and specilly suche as be good for the potte and
> to ete: and as ofte as nede shall requyre it must be weded, for else
> the wedes wyl overgrowe the herbes.

In 1577 Barnabe Googe, in *Foure Bookes of Husbandry*, also refers to
the garden as women's work: 'Herein were the olde husbandes

Two ladies gardening, from a Dutch painting of 1475.

very careful and used always to judge that where they founde the Garden out of order, the wyfe of the house (for unto her belonged the charge thereof) was no good huswyfe.'

In 1617 the first garden manual expressly written for women was published. This is William Lawson's *The Country House-Wife's Garden, Containing Rules for Hearbs and Seeds of Common Use, with Their Times and Seasons when to set and sow them*. It was very successful and ran to ten editions, the 1637 edition being the work of a woman printer. One suggestion in the book is to separate the garden into two sections, one for flowers and the other for vegetables:

> not that wee meane so perfect a distinction, that the Garden for flowers should bee without herbs good for the kitchen or the kitchin garden should want flowers nor on the contrary: but for the most part they would bee severed; first, because your Garden flowers shall suffer some disgrace, if among them you intermingle Onions, Parsnips etc: secondly, your Garden that is durable, must be of one forme: but that which is for your kitchin use, must yield daily roots, or other herbs, and suffer deformity.

A similar French book, *Le Jiardinier François qui enseigne à cultiver les arbres & herbes potageres*, published in 1651, is also addressed to women and was republished at least ten times. It is dedicated to women who are household managers and deals with all aspects of gardening: trees, shrubs, fruit, vegetables, herbs. Three hundred varieties of pear trees are listed. It indicates that women running large households had complex responsibilities, including that of organising the garden which was of great economic value.

Women today produce at least half the world's output of food, mostly in poor, agricultural countries where they grow, harvest and prepare virtually all the food consumed by their families. In Africa they perform 60 to 80 per cent of agricultural work. In Asia and Africa almost all women who are employed work in agriculture. In Mozambique, for example, 90 per cent of working women are engaged in the production of food, as Joni Seager and Ann Olson explain in their international atlas, *Women in the World*:

> Because much of women's agricultural work is done in or near the home, is small in scale, part-time or seasonal, it is considered unimportant by official agencies. As a result, women are often left out of economic development schemes. Women are at the bottom of the pay and power scales in agriculture.

THE DIVISION OF LABOUR

The concept of separate spheres of gardening for men and women is already expressed in Thomas Tusser's gardening books in the sixteenth century, *A Hundreth Good Pointes of Husbandrie*, published in 1557, and *Five Hundreth Points of Good Husbandry*, published in 1573. He indicates that the orchard and fruit lie within the man's province, and that flowers, plants for the kitchen, herbs and salad-ings come within the housewife's. Early in the next century, however, Gervase Markham describes women involved in the cherry harvest, carrying full baskets of cherries away on their heads.

William Lawson's recommendation in the seventeenth century to separate the useful plants from the decorative ones is signifi-cant. In the next century this was to culminate in the purely aesthetic landscape garden, with the kitchen garden banished from sight, whereas in the cottage garden vegetables and flowers were still often grown together.

The division of labour was to grow. Sir William Temple writes in *Upon the Gardens of Epicurus: or Gardening in the Year 1685*: 'I will not enter upon any account of flowers, having only pleased myself with seeing or smelling them, and not troubled myself with the care, which is more the ladies' part than the men's.' Fruit cultivation is the manly activity. Even in Campanella's utopian work *The City of the Sun*, published in Italy in 1623, the author has the men gathering fruit and the women working 'in the gardens near the city, gathering vegetables and herbs and performing other light duties'. Similarly Joseph Banks proposed originally to exclude the study of decorative plants from the activities of the Horticultural Society.

Vegetable gardening came to be seen as a male occupation. In *Lark Rise to Candleford*, Flora Thompson describes the division of labour in Oxfordshire during the 1880s:

> The women never worked in the vegetable gardens or on the allot-ments, even when they had their children off hand and had plenty of spare time, for there was a strict division of labour and that was 'men's work'. Victorian ideas, too, had penetrated to some extent, and any work outside the home was considered unwomanly. But even that code permitted a woman to cultivate a flower garden, and most of the houses had at least a narrow border beside the pathway.

192

As no money could be spared for seeds or plants, they had to depend upon roots and cuttings given by their neighbours, and there was little variety; but they grew all the sweet old-fashioned cottage garden flowers, pinks and sweet williams and love-in-a-mist, wallflowers and forget-me-nots in spring and hollyhocks and Michaelmas daisies in autumn.

The women also cultivated a 'herb corner, stocked with thyme and parsley for cooking, rosemary to flavour the home-made lard, lavender to scent the best clothes, and peppermint, pennyroyal, horehound, camomile, tansy, balm, and rue for physic'.

Flower gardening was meant to improve the female mind, as Louisa Johnson explains in her *Every Lady Her Own Flower Gardener* of 1839:

Flower-gardening has progressed rapidly; and the amusement of floriculture has become the dominant passion of the ladies of Great Britain. It is a passion most blessed in its effects, considered as an amusement or a benefit. Nothing humanizes and adorns the female mind more surely than a taste for ornamental gardening. It compels the reason to act, and the judgement to observe; it is favourable to meditation of the most serious kind; it exercises the fancy in harmless and elegant occupation, and braces the system by its healthful tendency.

According to Cobbett, in *The English Gardener*, published in 1829, there are *'moral* effects naturally attending a green-house', which prevent women from indulging in dangerous pursuits such as reading novels and gambling:

How much better, during the long and dreary winter, for daughters, and even sons, to assist, or attend, their mothers in a green-house, than to be seated with her at cards, or in the blubberings over a stupid novel, or at any other amusement that can possible be conceived! How much more innocent, more pleasant, more free from temptation to evil, this amusement, than any other? ... the taste is fixed at once and it remains to the exclusion of cards and dice to the end of life.

Today the same separation of tasks in the garden usually occurs. Men dig the vegetable patch and mow the lawn; women look after plants and weed. A survey, conducted in 1988 by the Garden Centre Association, illustrates this division. Men and women were asked who was responsible for specific tasks in the garden:

Table 10.1: The Division of Labour in the Garden, 1988

	Women (%)	Men (%)
Weeding	91	69
Looking after plants	88	54
Mowing the lawn	59	86
Vegetable patch	22	41
Planning and designing the garden	52	51

Source: The Garden Centre Association, 1988

WEEDING WOMEN

The earliest English records of women working as paid labourers in a garden are the entries in the fourteenth-century rolls of Ely Cathedral where women appear in the wages list for digging the vines and weeding. The number of historical references to weeding women is remarkable, and in the fourteenth century they were paid twopence halfpenny a day, only half the male gardener's wage. Even ladies would benefit from weeding, according to William Coles in *The Art of Simpling*, published in 1656: 'Gentlewomen, if the ground be not too wet, may doe themselves much good by kneeling upon a Cushion and weeding.'

In 1516 women were paid three pence a day for removing charlock, nettles, convolvulus, dodder, thistles, dandelions and groundsel from the gardens at Hampton Court. In 1696 the accounts for the Royal Gardens at Hampton Court show that the labour force consisted of about 60 men paid by the year. In addition there were ten casual men whose daily rate varied from two shillings to 1s. 6d. Women on casual rates were paid eight pence a day. Around the same period Celia Fiennes describes how at Woburn she saw 'a figure of stone resembling an old weeder woman', presumably meant as a birdscarer, which she thought was 'a real living body'. In the nineteenth century, whilst a jobbing gardener would earn about five or six shillings a day, his weeding women helpers would only get paid between eight and ten pence a day.

Writing in *The Victorian Kitchen Garden*, Jennifer Davies emphasises the male character of the country house garden:

Certainly there would have been no girl apprentices. If a woman were employed, she would probably have been a weeding woman, paid a pittance to spend hours on all fours scratching weeds out of the gravel paths with the spiked tips of leather gloves. This was in order that every path would be immaculate for the owner and his family and friends when they walked around on tours of inspection. Women might also have been given casual work, picking off caterpillars or hoeing, but it was a man's world and the god within it was not the master of the house but the head gardener.

Mrs Lawrence's garden in Drayton Green.

In the 1830s, in a 28-acre garden in Drayton Green to the west of London, Mrs Lawrence employed six gardeners 'with one or two women for collecting insects and dead leaves, and during the winter, three'. In the same period at Alton Towers in Staffordshire, Loudon observed that a number of women were 'constantly employed in weeding, sweeping, picking up dead leaves and insects, cutting off decayed flowers, and tying up straggling shoots'. Sometimes these women were 'put into Swiss dresses'.

In his garden at Selborne in Hampshire, the famous naturalist Gilbert White had assistance from many villagers. The men

195

helped planting trees, digging, hedge-cutting, shifting manure, but as Richard Mabey points out, the women weeded:

> Goody Hampton was employed as a 'weeding woman' in the summer months. She appears to have been a doughty worker, 'and indeed, excepting that she wears petticoats and now and then has a child, you would think her a man'. Less frequently, John Carpenter's wife also helped with the weeding.

Women Illustrators

Other delicate work, connected with gardening publications, has also been seen as female work. The prints in early nineteenth-century gardening books were coloured by women and children in assembly-line factory conditions, as described by Ray Desmond:

> An efficient organisation of labour was essential to cope with the vast quantities of prints that Ackerman and other publishers produced. The children and women engaged to do the colouring would sit around tables, usually each applying a single colour to each print, having before them a specimen coloured print as a guide. A master colourist would add the finishing touches to the better quality prints.

This tradition of women's and children's colouring work goes back a long way. In the sixteenth century Christophe Plantin of Antwerp employed women illuminators to colour by hand the botanical books he produced. His four daughters also helped him by reading the proofs of the gardening books which he published. They started this work when they were four or five years old and continued until they were twelve. In 1774 Salomon Schinz had wood-cuts for a herbal, published in Zürich, coloured by the children of an orphanage, which Agnes Arber calls 'an economical method of producing "editions de luxe", which was apparently not unusual in the eighteenth century'.

Similarly the work of many Indian and Chinese artists, often unacknowledged, was used to illustrate English botanical books, particularly after the establishment of the botanic garden of Calcutta in 1786. A famous Japanese artist called Kawaha Keiga was employed by Siebold for his *Flora Japonica* (1835–42), but no reference to him appears in the published volumes.

In 1790 Margaret Meen, from Bungay in Suffolk, began to

Flowering currant (Ribes sanguineum) *drawn by Augusta Withers, from* Transactions of the Horticultural Society, *Vol. VII, 1830.*

publish her botanical illustrations in a series called *Exotic Plants from the Royal Gardens at Kew*. Mary Delaney produced flower pictures made up of layers of tissue paper, using specimens from Kew and the Chelsea Physic Garden as her models. In the early nineteenth century the artist, Augusta Withers, did the 'excellent drawings' for the Fruit Committee of the Horticultural Society and illustrations for the *Pomological Magazine*. In 1871 Marianne North set out, aged 40 and alone, on her travels all round the world to paint flowers. Her collection of 848 oil paintings of plants and landscapes is housed in a special gallery at Kew.

INVISIBLE WOMEN

The absence of much reference to women involved in gardening is partly a reflection of their exclusion, partly a case of not being recorded. An example is to be seen in the official history of the Edinburgh Botanic Garden from 1670 to 1970. There is hardly a mention of a woman in the 300 pages. On page 222 we are told that in 1912 a post was 'temporarily filled by Bertha Chandler' and on page 261 that the Queen opened a new building in 1964 and planted a birch tree. At the same time a rare volume of paintings of Indian plants by Mrs James Cookson was

> specially purchased for the Library, and autographed by Her Majesty. Little is known about Mrs Cookson although her paintings show that she was a knowledgeable botanist and a very skilled artist. Thus the volume is not only an object of great beauty but is also of considerable scientific interest and value.

According to the authors, that is the sum total of female contribution to the Botanic Garden – a temporary job, an artist about whom little is known, and the Queen.

The book mentioned is actually entitled *Flowers Drawn and Painted after Nature in India* and was published in 1830. As Alice Coats notes in *The Book of Flowers*, Mrs Cookson was one of a number of women authors and illustrators in the nineteenth century. Some illustrated the work of others, occasionally a husband or brother, others illustrated their own books, for example Augusta Robley's *A Selection of Madeira Flowers* in 1845, Arabella Roupell's *Specimens of the Flora of South Africa by A Lady* in 1849, and Mrs Bury's two-volume *Selection of Hexandrian Plants* in 1831–4.

Mrs Cookson is a good example of the incomplete record of women's participation in gardening. There are enough similar examples of individuals to add to the impression that much of women's history is missing. Tantalising references to many women occur, usually a couple per book and only a few lines long.

In the eleventh century the nuns of Romsey cultivated flowering plants. The Abbess Hildegard (1098–1179), from Bingen in Germany, is reputed to have compiled a long list of plants known at the time. The list includes trees, herbs and vegetables, but also ornamental plants, such as the white lily, purple flag iris, rose and violet. A London ironmonger, Robert Parish of St Michael's, Queenhithe, in 1406 left £1 (equivalent to about £700 today) to Eleanour 'the woman who looks after my garden across the Thames', which was probably a commercial market garden. Gerard's wife helped him with his famous *Herbal* in 1597, her work consisting of some passages aimed specifically at women.

In the seventeenth century Mistress Bugg of Battersea raised a fine purple auricula and the garden of Mistress Tuggie at Westminster, which she ran after the death of her husband Ralph, was well known at the time. It was celebrated for the 'excellencie and varietie' of the 'Gilloflowers, Pinkes, and the like'.

On 4 April 1762 'Frances Harrison widow' was paid £14 4s 0d for 'removeing earth with her cart and horses' from Chatsworth, where 'Capability' Brown was redesigning the gardens for the fourth Duke of Devonshire. In 1786–7 there is an example of a woman's gardening wages being paid to her husband. In London's Temple gardens £2 2s was paid to 'Mr Elliott gardener, for his wife's keeping the seats in the garden clean'.

In the eighteenth century James Lee, who with Lewis Kennedy ran the Vineyard Nursery in Hammersmith, saw a beautiful fuchsia in the house of a sailor's wife who lived in Wapping, in East London. He offered eight guineas for the fuchsia and promised her two replacement plants. She reluctantly accepted the offer. Lee subsequently raised 300 cuttings and sold them at a guinea each.

In the same decade that Mary Wollstonecraft's *Vindication of the Rights of Woman* was published, two of the earliest gardening books written by women appeared: Mary Lawrance's *A Collection of Roses From Nature*, which she also illustrated, and Charlotte Murray's *The British Garden*, both published in 1799. Earlier, in 1737, Elizabeth Blackwell had written *A Curious Herbal* in order to raise money to get her husband out of a debtor's jail. In 1806 Henrietta Moriarty's *Viridarium: Coloured Plates of Greenhouse Plants* was published; in 1816 Maria Jackson wrote *The Florist's Manual*, dealing with the planting of beds with herbaceous plants and annuals; and in 1838 Catherine Gore's *The Rose Fancier's Manual* was published.

Dandelion (Taraxacum officinale) *engraved by Elizabeth Blackwell, from* A Curious Herbal, *1737.*

In Ireland Maria Edgeworth (1768–1849) wrote a book called *Practical Education* in collaboration with her father, in which gardening is recommended for children. As a girl, Maria had been given a garden-plot by her father and she became an avid plant collector, corresponding with William Hooker. Even at the age of 78 she was still planting roses. In 1883 Juliana Horatia Ewing also encouraged children to garden by writing a serial for them, called 'Mary's Meadow', in *Aunt Judy's Magazine*.

After the death of her father, Jane Austen designed the garden of their new house. Her mother, in her seventies, worked in the garden, dressed in a labourer's green smock. In the early nineteenth century Lady Amherst was botanising in India. She is the only woman included in Alice Coats's *The Quest for Plants, A History of the Horticultural Explorers*, sandwiched between accounts of the exploits of her husband, who was Governor-General of India.

Perhaps the most scandalous case of the disappearing woman is that of Miss Brailsford. Everyone has heard of Bramley's cooking apple, which first became well known when exhibited in London by Mr Merryweather in 1876. No one has heard of Mary Ann Brailsford, however, who actually raised it.

Henry Merryweather, who owned a nursery in Southwell in Nottinghamshire, obtained grafts of the tree in about 1856 from Matthew Bramley, the butcher, in whose garden it grew. Mr Bramley had bought the house and garden in Church Street about ten years earlier. Living in the same house previously was Miss Brailsford, who in 1809, when 18 years old, had sown some pips in a flower pot and planted the resulting seedling in her garden. It probably first fruited about ten years later. The woman who raised the tree has been forgotten, while the man who merely bought it has been remembered, as Miles Hadfield notes in *A History of British Gardening*: 'Mr Bramley, whose name is probably now borne by more apple trees than any other variety, was no more than a cipher in its production.'

In England plant lore was traditionally a female area of knowledge and was handed down from mother to daughter. Women looked after the herb garden and were expert in the medicinal use of plants. At the beginning of the seventeenth century Robert Burton in *Anatomy of Melancholy* claims that they were often better then the more educated doctors: 'Many an old wife or country woman doth often more good with a few known or common herbs, than our bombast physicians with all their prodigious, sumptious, far-fetched, rare, conjectural medicines.'

In his *Paradisus* of 1629 John Parkinson often refers to 'the names given by women to plants, indicating their role in handing down botanical knowledge. For example 'the speckled kinde (of Sweet John) is termed by our English Gentlewomen, for the most part, London Pride', or the common white daffodil with 'its pale whitish creame colour, tending somewhat neare unto the colour of a pale primrose hath caused our Countrey Gentlewomen to entitle it Primrose Peerlesse'.

THE EXCLUSION OF WOMEN

Despite the amount of gardening work done by women and the skills they possess, they are not normally regarded as experts. Garden centres and nurseries are usually run by men. *Practical Gardening* magazine, which sells 90,000 a month and has a readership of over 1.2 million, and *Amateur Gardening* which has a weekly sale of 85,000 copies, are both edited by men.

The Royal Horticultural Society had 14 vice-presidents in 1989, only one of whom was a woman; its council was composed of 14 men and only three women. In the RHS magazine *The Garden* there are often advertisements for gardeners to be accompanied by 'spouse to help in the house' or 'spouse to do some cooking/laundry', or 'must be willing to caretake with wife when butler on holiday'. It is never suggested that the gardener might be a woman.

The Thorpe Committee Inquiry into Allotments, which reported in 1969, found that only 3.2 per cent of allotment-holders were women, though Crouch and Ward provide evidence that women, and children too, have quite often worked on allotments. In 1986 in Tottenham, 8 per cent of plot-holders were women, while in the western part of the same borough, Haringey, the figure was 25 per cent. George Kay's study of allotments in Stoke-on-Trent, published in 1988, also shows that 8 per cent of plot-holders were women. But 46 per cent of the respondents to his survey said they have regular help in their allotments from members of their families. Kay concludes: 'Women, in fact, participate to some extent in the cultivation and management of about one-third of the allotments.'

A woman has only recently appeared on the BBC radio programme 'Gardeners' Question Time', and then in the company of three men, although the first popular gardening broadcaster was a woman, Marion Cran. She first went on the air in August 1923. Similarly the television programme 'Gardeners' World', with four to five million viewers in 1989, always used to be presented by men. It has had growing female representation in recent years, but always in a subsidiary role. The main academic journal on the history of gardening, *Garden History*, has a male honorary editor and all four editorial advisors are men.

Three of the first female gardeners at Kew in 1898, dressed in breeches as decreed after the earlier uniform of bloomers had been abandoned.

Women were not trained at horticultural college until 1891 when the first female students were admitted at Swanley. By 1896 there were 39, and in 1903 the college was given over completely to women students, numbering 63. In 1897 Mrs Earle wrote about the college:

Yesterday, I paid a visit to the Horticultural College at Swanley, with its branch for women students. It immediately struck me as quite possible that a new employment may be developed for women of small means out of the modern increased taste for gardening.

In 1910 the Women's Horticultural College at Studley in Warwickshire was founded. The Women's Farm and Garden Association was also founded at the turn of the century, with the aim of furthering the education and employment of women in agriculture and horticulture.

Female gardeners were allowed at Kew Gardens in 1895, but they were ridiculed in the press and laughed at by male passengers passing on buses. They had been instructed to wear clothing 'similar to that of the ordinary gardeners', which consisted of thick brown bloomers, woollen stockings and boots, tailored jackets, waistcoats and ties, and peaked caps. The director ordered the women to wear long macintoshes on their way to work to hide the bloomers.

JANE LOUDON

The most outstanding woman gardener of the first half of the nineteenth century was undoubtedly Jane Loudon (1807–58). Jane was a close friend of the novelist Mrs Gaskell and herself wrote a novel called *The Mummy*. This book was reviewed by John Loudon in the *Gardener's Magazine* in 1828. He thought at the time that it had been written by a man, but discovered his mistake when he met her. *The Mummy* is a 'romance of the twenty-second century', a precursor of science fiction. It is set in 2126 and predicts air travel, gas fires, coffee machines, overhead railways, electrical rain-making machines, inflatable beds, engines to milk cows, a plough drawn by a tractor, wireless and telephones. The futuristic London is described as a beautiful city with wonderful public gardens on each bank of the Thames.

They were married in 1830 and Jane almost literally became his right hand, for in 1825 John's arm had been amputated following a break which had been badly set. Her first job after their wedding was to transcribe, at her husband's dictation, the 1,150 pages of his *Encyclopaedia of Cottage, Farm and Villa Architecture and Furniture*. Between them they wrote a prodigious amount on gardening, being the first professional married couple devoted

204

full-time to writing about gardening. She learnt her botany and horticulture very rapidly and wrote particularly to involve women in the art and science of gardening. Her publications include the *Ladies' Magazine of Gardening* in 1841 which she hoped would 'prove useful to the class for which it was originally designed; that is, to all those who, though fond of flowers, are neither regular designers nor professional florists'.

Portrait of Jane Loudon (1807–58).

After John died in 1843, Jane reissued, revised and republished his writings and herself wrote extensively on botany, gardening and natural history. She completed some 20 books on gardening, mainly to make the subject and the activity accessible to women.

The Loudons wrote about gardening, but they were also both practical gardeners. Jane carried on gardening when she was pregnant with her daughter Agnes, and she would not have agreed with her contemporary, Louisa Johnson, who thought gardening might be taken up by single women 'as a distraction from the disappointments of life'.

They created their garden in Bayswater with their own labour, particularly Jane's. It was a quarter of an acre site in Porchester Terrace and was absolutely packed with specimens of 2,000 different kinds of plant species. The arboretum contained 60 different trees and shrubs, particularly roses and peonies, and in the lawn were over 300 species of bulbs.

Jane Loudon's Gardening for Ladies
first published in 1840.

VITA SACKVILLE-WEST

The most famous gardening woman of recent years is Vita
Sackville-West (1892–1962), an aristocrat by birth, and conserva-
tive in politics. She would have inherited the family estate at
Knole in Kent if she had not been a woman. The house at Knole
had 365 rooms and 52 staircases and had been occupied by
Cromwell's troops in 1642. Previously the estate had belonged to
Henry VIII who used it for hunting deer.

As a child Vita had a garden of her own at Knole 'because of the
tradition that every child must automatically love and cherish a
garden of its own', but she admitted that she did not like it much
as the 'weeds grow too fast and flowers too slowly'. She started
gardening as an adult, without any real horticultural knowledge,
in 1915 whilst living in Constantinople, and in 1917 went to see
Gertrude Jekyll's garden at Munstead. In 1930 she bought the
house and garden of seven acres just outside Sissinghurst in Kent,

Vita Sackville-West (1892–1962) in her garden
at Sissinghurst in Kent.

which was to become famous throughout the country after it was first opened to the public in 1938. It still attracts thousands of visitors every year: 13,200 in 1961; 47,100 in 1967; 91,584 in 1973; 137,921 in 1987.

Despite her aristocratic background and the fact that she employed several gardeners, Vita Sackville-West did garden herself, as she told a correspondent:

> May I assure the gentleman who writes to me (quite often) from a Priory in Sussex that I am not the armchair, library-fireside gardener he evidently suspects, 'never having performed any single act of gardening' myself, and that for the last forty years of my life I have broken my back, my finger-nails, and sometimes my heart, in the practical pursuit of my favourite occupation.

In 1946 she wrote, 'My back is worse. Think seriously about killing myself.' In the same year her husband found her propped against a lime tree 'and crying because she could do no gardening'.

Anne Scott-James writes: 'Sissinghurst garden was made by two people, the late Sir Harold Nicolson and his wife, Vita Sackville-West. He was the designer and she the plantsman and they

207

worked in perfect harmony.' It is a strange order to put them in, and Vita would have objected to being attached in this way, as she insisted on being a person in her own right. The work in the garden seems to have been done largely by Vita and the other gardeners, as Harold was regularly away. Also the two of them disagreed quite often over the garden, as Harold Nicolson notes in his diary on 30 September 1933: 'Try to measure our vista in kitchen garden prolonging the paved paths but come up against artichokes and V's indignation. Thereafter weed lawn sadly. We have a discussion about women's rights afterwards.'

On 29 December 1946 he writes:

> In the afternoon I moon about with Vita trying to convince her that planning is an element in gardening. I want to show her that the top of the moat-walk must be planted with forethought and design. She wishes just to jab in the things which she has left over. The tragedy of the romantic temperament is that it dislikes form so much that it ignores the effect of masses. She wants to put in stuff which 'will give a lovely red colour in autumn'. I wish to put in stuff which will furnish shape to the perspective. In the end we part, not as friends.

Vita's gardening style was derived from Gertrude Jekyll, particularly her taste in roses, though she was not so keen on Jekyll's herbaceous borders, and also from William Robinson whom she visited at Gravetye when he was nearly 90 years old. She copied his method of training roses to scramble up fruit trees. In 1933 she began giving gardening talks on the BBC every Friday evening, which were subsequently printed in the *Listener*. She argued in favour of 'straight determined lines' as the basis, broken by overhanging shrubs and straying plants: 'Too severe a formality is almost as repellant as the complete absence of it.' She recommended mass planting:

> I believe in exaggeration; I believe in big groups, big masses; I am sure that it is more effective to plant twelve tulips together than to split them into groups of six; more effective to concentrate all the delphiniums into one bed, than to dot them about at intervals of twos and threes.

In 1946 she began her weekly gardening articles in the *Observer* which were to make her more famous than any of her poetry, novels or biographical works. She continued these till 1961, the year before she died. A few years before her death Vita appointed her 'treasures', Pamela Schwerdt and Sibylle Kreutzberger, as head gardeners. They were friends and both highly qualified, holding diplomas from the Waterperry Horticultural College in Oxfordshire. When the National Trust took over Sissinghurst, they became the first professional women to take over an important National Trust garden.

SUFFRAGETTES ATTACK KEW GARDENS

The most violent clash between women and the gardening establishment took place at Kew just before the First World War. This was a period of increasing militancy in the Suffragette Movement. In 1912 secret arson began to be organised under the direction of Christabel Pankhurst. In January 1913 the Reform Bill was withdrawn by Asquith after the Women's Suffrage amendment had been declared out of order. The next month Mrs Pankhurst was accepting responsibility for every sort of destruction carried out by what the *Suffragette* was calling 'The Women's Revolution'. On 23 February she told a large public meeting in Cardiff: 'We have blown up Lloyd George's house at Walton Heath!' She was arrested next day and sentenced to three years' penal servitude.

Earlier in the month Kew Gardens had been attacked, as part of the general campaign, which included damaging flower-beds up and down the country. The glass in three orchid houses was smashed and the plants broken and torn up by the roots. The *Journal of Horticulture and Home Farmer* of 13 Feb 1913, was horrified:

> Kew has been marked out by the suffragettes as one of the scenes of their exploits. They smashed a quantity of glass in the orchid house, and, in a manner that one can scarcely accredit to sane adults, wantonly tried to destroy the plants. Rare and delicate plants, under bell-glasses, attracted the special venom of these feminists.

The report concludes on a happier note: 'Other better news from Kew is that the labourers have received an increase of 1s per week to their pay. Bravo!'

On 20 February at 3 am, the Refreshment Pavilion at Kew was seen to be on fire. The arboretum foreman, Mr Osborn, described the scene 20 minutes later: 'heard cracking noise, saw from bedroom window flames shooting up from Tea Pavilion, found impossible owing to flames to reach fire-hose hanging on Tea Pavilion'. Two women, discovered in the garden, were arrested by the police who had been stationed there since the previous incident.

The *Journal of Horticulture and Home Farmer* of 27 February 1913, again reports with outrage:

> For the second time within a fortnight female vandals have visited Kew Gardens with direful consequences. The picturesque tea pavilion was razed to the ground by fire. Happily the perpetrators were captured and are unlikely to resume their insane campaign for some time to come.

A young woman named Lilian Lenton was also arrested for complicity in burning down the pavilion. While being forcibly fed, the tube passed into the trachea and the food poured into her lungs. She was within minutes of dying of pleuro-pneumonia when she was released. For over a year she carried on her militant campaign, continually being arrested for arson, forcibly fed, released and then disappearing.

Rebecca West wrote about the incident in *The Clarion* of 28 February 1913, describing the forcible feeding as murder. The article was entitled 'The Mildness of Militancy, A Storm in a Tea-House' and in it she wonders why 'active young women should destroy beautiful flowers when the Albert Memorial still stands in Kensington Gardens and there is gunpowder in the land.' But she understands why the tea-house has been attacked,

> for I spent a little time of sleepy pleasure there one sunny day last summer. At the next table sat a dear old parson with silver hair and gold-rimmed spectacles, and a pale young curate. During the three-quarters of an hour I was there they talked with a delicate gravity and an air of profound culture about a correspondence in the *Spectator* about the decay of the subjunctive mood in modern English. The burning of the tea-house was an honest attempt to overcome the difficulty felt by reformers of getting in touch with people who are snowed under by decaying subjunctives.

She regrets the loss of the orchids, but calls the outburst of militancy 'legitimate tantrums': 'It says much for their self-control that there has been nothing worse than these quite discreet and controlled attacks on unimportant property.'

Sylvia Pankhurst was against the policy of secret arson:

I regarded this policy with grief and regret, believing it wholly mistaken and unnecessary, deeply deploring the life of furtive destruction it would impose upon the participators, and the harsh punishment it was preparing for them; for these unknown girls there would be no international telegrams; the mead of public sympathy would be attenuated.

But she did not repudiate it:

Though I deplored the new policy, I uttered no repudiation. To stop it was impossible; to attack it would but have caused another fissure in the movement. I would not add one word to the chorus condemning those courageous girls who trusted implicitly in the wisdom of the Union. I would not advocate secret militancy, I would take no part in it, but repudiation I would leave to others.

Sylvia's sister Adela worked alongside her in the Women's Social and Political Union, but she suffered an attack of pleurisy and completely lost her voice. Sylvia's description of how Adela took up gardening is an interesting commentary on women as gardeners at that time, and also points to the recurring theme of gardening as a retreat from political life:

Miserable at the prospect of inaction, and dependence upon others, she conceived the idea of becoming a gardener – perhaps the least suitable occupation she could have selected. The desire was a reaction from the knowledge that though a brilliant speaker, and one of the hardest workers in the movement, she was often regarded with more disapproval than approbation by Mrs Pankhurst and Christabel, and was the subject of a sharper criticism than the other organizers had to face. Mrs Pankhurst now offered to send her for a course at Studley Horticultural College, but exacted a promise that she would never speak in public again in this country. Having taken the course at Studley, Adela obtained a position as gardener, only to find that the woman gardener was expected to do the work of two men previously employed, and that the scientific culture of plants she was desirous to follow was under the circumstances of the place an impossible dream.

Adela eventually got round the promise made to her mother by going to Australia. She became an organiser of the Women's Party there, and later of the Australian Socialist Party.

The attack on Kew Gardens is one of the most famous incidents in the campaign for women's suffrage. It illustrates the political nature of gardening and its symbolic meaning, just like the

211

example of Kew's role in the British Empire. Destroying flower-beds and greenhouses seems insane, unless the gardens and the destruction of them by 'female vandals' are seen in terms of the power relations in society. Just as the orchid can symbolise extreme wealth, so a flower-bed can express the power of patri-archy in the political order. Women's exclusion from power in society has been mirrored by their position in gardening history.

11

Modern Gardening

About 25 years ago, when English gardening was mostly represented by the innate futilities of the 'bedding' system, with its wearisome repetitions and garish colouring, Mr William Robinson chose as his work in life to make better known the treasures that were lying neglected, and at the same time to overthrow the feeble follies of the 'bedding' system. It is mainly owing to his unremitting labours that a clear knowledge of the world of hardy-plant beauty is now placed within easy reach of all who care to acquire it, and that the 'bedding' mania is virtually dead.

Gertrude Jekyll, *The Idea of a Garden* (1896)

Formality is often essential to the plan of a garden but never to the arrangement of its flowers and shrubs, and to array these in rigid lines, circles, or patterns can only be ugly wherever it may be!

William Robinson, *The English Flower Garden* (1883)

The hardy herbaceous border is the best feature of the flower garden, though commonly regarded as the worst. When well made, well stocked, and well managed, it presents us with flowers in abundance during ten months out of twelve, and in the remaining two blank months offers some actual entertainment, and many agreeable hints of pleasures to come, to make ample reward for the comparatively small amount of labour its proper keeping will necessitate. Given a few trees and shrubs, a plot of grass, and comfortable walks, the three first essentials of a garden, a collection of hardy herbaceous plants is the fourth essential feature, and may be the last.

Shirley Hibberd, *The Amateur's Flower Garden* (1871)

'A Devonshire Cottage Garden', from William Robinson's
The English Flower Garden, *1883.*

Modern English gardening started with a woman, Gertrude Jekyll (1843–1932), and an Irishman, William Robinson (1838–1935). They led the movement against the rigidity of Victorian bedding-out. Both stressed informality in gardening style, Robinson promoting the wild garden, Jekyll reviving the cottage garden.

COTTAGE GARDENS

The cottage garden goes back centuries. In the Domesday Book in 1086 thousands of garths or yards were recorded. They varied from a few square yards to a couple of acres and were attached to peasant cottages and to town houses. In them were grown fruit, vegetables, herbs and flowers.

In the eighteenth century Defoe described cottage gardens in Surrey. 'Nothing can be more beautiful', he writes in his *Tour through the Whole Island of Great Britain* of 1724–6, than

> those villages filled with these houses, and the houses surrounded with gardens, walks, vistas, avenues, representing all the beauties of building and all the pleasures of planting: it is impossible to view these countries from any rising ground and not be ravish'd with the delightful prospect.

At the beginning of the nineteenth century Loudon writes:

> Almost every cottage in England has its appendant garden, larger or smaller, and slovenly or neatly managed, according to circumstances. In the best districts of England, the principal culinary vegetables, some salads, herbs, flowers, and fruits, are cultivated; and in the remote parts of Scotland, at least potatoes and borecoles are planted. Tradesmen and operative manufacturers, who have a permanent interest in their cottages, have generally the best cottage-gardens; and many of them, especially at Norwich, Manchester and Paisley, excel in the culture of florists' flowers.

Eleanour Rohde also acknowledges our debt to cottage gardeners. She makes it clear that bedding-out schemes were not the whole story in the nineteenth century, just as the eighteenth-century landscapes had not completely ousted earlier gardens. She remembers the contrasting styles when she was a child:

> The Victorian garden has been so persistently abused and its worst features, notably the geometric beds and ribbon borders, held up to such ridicule, that succeeding generations may perhaps imagine that this was the only type of garden made in those days. This, of course, is very far from the truth, for the old formal garden, although considerably modified, persisted until nearly the close of the last century. Those of us who were children in the late 'nineties, remember very well the two kinds – the dull gardens laid out with a magnificent display of bedding plants during the summer (and even

as a child one perceived dimly that between the owner and the garden there was a great gulf fixed) and the other delightful sort, so often associated in one's memories with cathedral and remote little country towns – gardens with mellowed walls where the broad, generous beds were full of fine old hardy plants and flowers with rich soft colours and delicious scents and hoary with traditions of centuries. Each garden had its characteristic atmosphere and the owner knew every tree and flower as a shepherd knows his sheep. It is to those gardeners and to cottagers that we owe the preservation of many treasures amongst the old herbaceous plants despised by the enthusiastic admirers of bedding-out plants.

THE HERBACEOUS BORDER

Shirley Hibberd heralded the nineteenth-century move away from bedding-out, with his emphasis on a 'collection of hardy herbaceous plants'. But Hibberd, who edited *The Floral World* in the 1860s, did provide his readers with information on the latest developments in bedding plants and was himself enthusiastic about their 'strikingly coloured foliage'. Nevertheless elsewhere in the magazine they are described as 'trashy', 'flimsy', and 'not worthy of a place in my garden'.

Hibberd objected to the bedding system only lasting for three months of the year: 'For the remaining nine months of the year it is a dreary blank.' He compares the production of bedding plants to a factory:

Yet for the sake of this temporary glory, ten thousand gardens, that would otherwise have been rich in interest, have been reduced to the condition of manufactories, and their summer show, as a proof to all observers of what the factory could produce, has been considered sufficient return.

He does give suggestions for extending the bedding season, but in the opening chapter of *The Amateur's Flower Garden*, first published in 1871, he states his preference:

A few simple borders, well stocked with mixed herbaceous plants, such as primulas, paeonies, lilies, phloxes, hollyhocks, and carnations, would, in many instances, afford more real pleasure and ever-changing interest than the most gorgeous display of bedding plants hemmed in between two glaring walls, or exposed on a great treeless, turfless place like the blazing fire at the mouth of a coal-pit.

216

In the magazine *The Floral World* of April 1864 Hibberd argues against the waste of time and money involved in the bedding system which had led to the 'deterioration of horticulture'. He advocates the herbaceous border and wants gardeners to

> restore to the neglected borders the noble clumps of fragrant white lilies, the patches of Christmas rose, winter aconite, double daisy, polyanthus, primula, Solomon's seal, Indian pink, potentilla, and the thousand other interesting subjects which make no blaze at any season, but are constantly presenting beautiful forms and cheerful colours.

Herbaceous border at Munstead Wood, photographed by Gertrude Jekyll in 1900.

The herbaceous border, however, was not new; it can be traced back to the Middle Ages. In 1829 Cobbett wrote of its continuing popularity:

> The fashion has for years been in favour of borders, wherein flowers of the greatest brilliancy are planted, so disposed as to form a regular series higher and higher as they approach the back part, or the middle of the border; and so selected as to insure a succession of blossom from the earliest months of spring until the coming of the frosts.

'NATURAL' GARDENING

In the previous century Joseph Addison, like Robinson, also advocated the wild garden, expressing a reaction against the formality
of the contemporary French style. In the *Spectator* of September
1712 he writes about his garden at Bilton Grange, near Rugby:

> I have several acres about my house, which I call my garden, and
> which a skilful gardener would not know what to call. It is a confu-
> sion of kitchen and parterre, orchard and flower-garden, which lie
> so mixed and interwoven with one another, that if a foreigner who
> had seen nothing of our country should be conveyed into my
> garden at his first landing, he would look upon it as a natural wilder-
> ness, and one of the uncultivated parts of our country. My flowers
> grow up in several parts of the garden in the greatest luxuriancy and
> profusion. I am so far from being fond of any particular one, by
> reason of its rarity, that if I meet with any one in a field which
> pleases me, I give it a place in my garden. By this means, when a
> stranger walks with me, he is surprised to see several large spots of
> ground covered with ten thousand different colours, and has often
> singled out flowers that he might have met with under a common
> hedge, in a field, or in a meadow, as some of the greatest beauties of
> the place.

Milton too, in the seventeenth century, praised the natural look
of God's garden:

> *Flowers worthy of Paradise, which not nice Art*
> *In beds and curious knots, but Nature boon,*
> *Pour'd forth profuse on hill, and dale, and plain.*

It is dangerously easy to see this concept of the natural garden
simply as a recurring theme, the inevitable swing of fashion. But
as Raymond Williams puts it in *The Country and the City*: 'We have
to be able to explain, in related terms, both the persistence *and*
the historicity of concepts.'

The eighteenth-century natural style was a public expression of
the power of the landed gentry in their country parks. The new
garden at the end of the nineteenth century was the private
suburban plot, which was also in marked contrast to the formal
shows in public parks and gardens. Hobsbawm traces the development of suburban middle-class housing from the garden suburbs
designed by architects like Norman Shaw in the 1870s to the
garden city of Ebenezer Howard in 1898:

The ideal middle-class house was no longer seen as part of a city street, a 'town house' or its substitute, an apartment in a large building fronting a city street and pretending to be a palace, but an urbanized or rather suburbanized country house ('villa' or even 'cottage') in a miniature park or garden, surrounded by greenery.

The growing number of nurseries and seed merchants made the buying of plants less expensive. Cheapness of printing and increased literacy in the nineteenth century enabled the amateur gardener to be informed by a vast range of gardening magazines. *Amateur Gardening*, which started in 1884 and was edited for the first three years by Shirley Hibberd, is still going strong today.

One way, however, in which the form of the landscape garden was revived at the end of the nineteenth century was through the creation of golf courses. Their undulating fairways and clumps of trees are remarkably reminiscent of the eighteenth-century landscape park. Before 1889, for instance, there were only two golf links in the whole of Yorkshire. Between 1890 and 1895 29 were opened in that county. One golf course, near Halesowen to the west of Birmingham, was created from William Shenstone's landscape garden, The Leasowes.

Golf courses were likewise meant to be exclusive, as Hobsbawm points out: 'The social potential of this game, played on large, expensively constructed and maintained pieces of real estate by members of clubs designed to exclude socially and financially unacceptable outsiders, struck the new middle classes like a sudden revelation.'

Both the landscape garden and the formal bedding schemes needed vast expenditure; the new suburban garden could be maintained by more modest means. The former required professional gardeners and hired hands; the latter ushered in the era of the amateur who could manage a garden in his or her spare time. In *The Ladies' Companion to the Flower Garden* Jane Loudon gives advice on employing gardeners and discusses the cost, but concludes:

> The great enjoyment of gardening, however, in my opinion, is only to be obtained by the amateur who gardens himself, and who understands the principles or reasons upon which each operation is founded; and, therefore, I should recommend all persons fond of gardening, and especially ladies, who have sufficient leisure, to manage their gardens themselves, with the assistance of a man to perform the more laborious operations.

Gardening was becoming a leisure activity and the invention of the lawn-mower helped the process by making possible an easily kept lawn.

LAWN-MOWERS

Edwin Beard Budding had invented the lawn-mower in 1830 and he claimed that, unlike scything, it did not produce any 'circular sears and inequalities and bare places'. His design was based on the rotary blades used in the cloth industry to produce an even pile on textiles. The original mower was made to be pushed from the rear, but had another handle at the front so that it could also be pulled by a second gardener in difficult areas. In 1833 John Loudon observed Mrs Lawrence's garden in Drayton Green, describing the lawn as 'one of the most beautifully kept we ever saw; and it is shaven with the mowing machine alone, with only the assistance of shears at the roots of the shrubs'.

In the 1844 edition of *The Ladies' Companion to the Flower Garden*, however, Jane Loudon comments that many gardeners are still prejudiced against the new mowing-machine, despite the fact that mowing with the scythe is 'the most laborious operation which falls to the lot of the working-gardener, and in large places there are generally a set of labourers, who are not gardeners, who are kept on purpose for it'. She argues for the lawn-mower, as it

> requires far less skill and exertion than the scythe, and answers perfectly where the surface of the soil to be mowed is perfectly smooth and firm, the grass of even quality, and the machine only used in dry weather. It is particularly adapted for amateurs, affording an excellent exercise to the arms and every part of the body.

Lawn-mowers eventually became very popular and were also used in the new public parks. Earlier the park lawns had been scythed and the grass used as fodder, just as in the landscape garden, or else sheep cropped the grass and manured it at the same time. In Australia kangaroos were used to crop the lawn of the Government House in Sydney.

In 1841 Alexander Shanks of Arbroath, in Scotland, registered a pony-drawn mower which also swept up the mowings. Queen Victoria was one of his first customers and his machines were used on the lawn at Balmoral. At the same time Samuelson of Banbury, in Oxfordshire, began to manufacture a mowing and rolling machine, also made to be pulled by a pony. Lawn-mowers drawn by a pony were first used in the Manchester and Salford parks in 1857.

*Advertisement from Shanks's catalogue for 1871, showing
pony-drawn mowers at use on the lawn at Balmoral.*

In his famous essay 'Of Gardens' (1625) Francis Bacon wrote: 'Nothing is more pleasant to the eye than green grass kept finely shorn.' William Robinson also thought that the lawn was 'the heart of the English garden', but he was not so keen on mowing: 'We want shaven carpets of grass here and there, but what nonsense it is to shave it as often as foolish men shave their faces! Who would not rather see the waving grass with countless flowers than a close surface without blossom?'

WILLIAM ROBINSON

William Robinson started his working life as a garden boy in Ireland. By the age of 21 he had become foreman in the gardens of Rev. Sir Hunt Henry Johnson-Walsh, in charge of a large range of hot houses full of exotic plants. He is presumed to have had a row with his employer and his manner of leaving was symbolic of his future gardening philosophy. On a night of severe frost in 1861 he is reputed to have let out the fires of the hot house boilers, leaving the plants to die, and then fled to Dublin. Similarly when in 1884, out of the profits of his publishing, he bought Gravetye Manor, the first thing he did was to do away with all the glass houses.

From Dublin he went to London where he was eventually put in charge of the herbaceous section of the Royal Botanic Society's garden in Regent's Park. He was also responsible for a small garden of English wild flowers and it was through collecting for this that he became familiar with the English countryside and the 'lovely cottage gardens' which were to be his inspiration. In *The English Flower Garden* he writes:

> Nothing is prettier than an English cottage garden, and they often teach lessons that 'great' gardeners should learn ... I often pass a small cottage garden in the Weald of Sussex never without a flower for nine months in the year. It is only a square patch, but the beauty of it is far more delightful than that of the large gardens near, and it is often pretty when they are bare.

Naturalised daffodils in William Robinson's garden
at Gravetye Manor, Sussex.

In 1870 he wrote *The Wild Garden* and in 1871 launched *The Garden: An Illustrated Weekly Journal of Horticulture In All Its Branches*. These were followed in 1879 by *Gardening*, later called *Gardening Illustrated*, which was a very successful magazine aimed at the suburban gardener, as was his main book *The English Flower Garden* of 1883. Robinson attacked 'pastry-work gardening', the formality associated with Paxton's Chatsworth and Crystal Palace, and the bedding schemes of Joseph Hooker at Kew Gardens: 'The genius of cretinism itself could hardly delight in anything more tasteless or ignoble than the absurd daubs of colour that every summer flare in the neighbourhood of nearly every country-house in Western Europe.' He did, however, respect Loudon, to whom he dedicated the first issue of *The Garden*.

In *The English Flower Garden*, which by 1898 had gone through six editions and further reprints, Robinson attacks the 'ugly, unnatural forms' which are produced by clipping trees:

In November 1891, in Hyde Park, I saw a man clipping Hollies at the 'Row' end of the Serpentine, and, asking him why it was done, he said that it was to 'keep them in shape', though to do him justice, he added that he thought it would be better to let them alone. Men who trim with shears or knife so fine a *tree* as the Holly are dead to beauty of form and cannot surely have seen how fine in form old Holly trees are.

In the same book, he writes: 'For the dismal state of flower-gardens in winter the extravagant practice of our public gardens is partly to blame. A walk by the flower beds in Hyde Park on Christmas Day, 1895, was not a very enlivening thing.' He goes on to describe the bare expanse of beds, with 'not one leaf, or shoot or plant, or bush in it from end to end; giants' graves and earth puddings – these and iron rails and the lines of planes behind'.

Against the bedding system, Robinson advocated natural groupings of plants, including ground-cover plants to avoid patches of bare soil: 'Have no patience with bare ground.' He encouraged the naturalised planting of bulbs in grass, which had started in England in the 1850s, though earlier in Scotland, and had become popular in the 1860s. In 1861 the seed firm of Barr and Sugden opened, to become renowned for its production of bulbs. In his garden at Gravetye Manor Robinson planted daffodils under the fruit trees and this combination seemed a novelty at the time, as did his idea of growing clematis up pear trees.

He makes it clear, however, that his ideas do not 'imply that the garden generally is to be a tangled wilderness'. Nor is he always against straight lines:

> Having plants in natural forms does not in the least prevent us from making a straight walk along a straight wall, or from having the necessary wall protection for our gardens. A straight line is often the most beautiful that can be used; but its use by no means implies that we are not to group our plants or bushes naturally alongside it.

His gardening style was popular for a number of reasons, as Miles Hadfield notes:

> His ideas of wild gardening were opportune. He came at a period when the host of hardy, self-reliant shrubs and plants from Western China were on their way; new gardens for a wealthy suburbia were being made in southern home counties – perfect homes for rhododendrons, magnolias, and so much that was now being introduced. And he arrived just prior to a period when labour costs were to rise and finally extinguish all possibilities of large gardens in the old manner. The Robinsonian tradition of gardening around the house is so well known that it need scarcely be described: wide, sweeping lawns, shapely beds filled with roses, shrubs, or hardy plants, and flowery creepers covering the walls. Always at the back of his mind was the image of a traditional English cottage garden.

Like John Loudon, Robinson also decried the state of the country's cemeteries. In *God's Acre Beautiful* in 1882 he supported cremation and wrote: 'The Cemetery of the future must not only be a garden in the best sense of the word, but the most beautiful and best cared-for of all gardens.'

GERTRUDE JEKYLL

Gertrude Jekyll met William Robinson around 1875 and began writing articles for his magazine *The Garden*, as did Ruskin, in 1872, and William Morris, who wrote 'The Art of the Future' in 1879. Robinson retired as editor in 1899 and Jekyll succeeded him for a few years as joint editor with E.T. Cook.

Jekyll came from a middle-class intellectual background and decided to become a professional artist. She travelled widely, particularly round the Mediterranean, knew Ruskin, and, after visiting William Morris in 1869, had a well-equipped workshop installed and became proficient in several crafts.

At the age of 25 Gertrude Jekyll made a garden at Wargrave Hill, when her family moved there in 1868, and she began then to introduce wild flowers into the borders. When her father died she planned a new garden for her mother in Surrey and in the 1880s began to design gardens, the first apparently for a factory worker from Rochdale who wanted his garden filled with as many plants as it could contain. At this time too she designed her own garden of 15 acres at Munstead Wood in Surrey and this was to be the basis of her writings: 'I have never written a line that was not accounted for by actual work and experience.'

Gertrude Jekyll (1843–1932) by William Nicholson, 1920.

Her inspiration was the cottage garden: 'I have learnt much from the little cottage gardens that help to make our English wayside the prettiest in the temperate world. One can hardly go into the smallest cottage garden without learning or observing something new.' It is important, however, to see her idealisation of the cottage garden in perspective, as Ronald King reminds us. He refers to Gertrude Jekyll's 'bourgeois fantasy' and says: 'She simply did not see the yard-cum-garden of the average cottager, with its chicken-house, rabbit-hutches and outdoor earth-closet.'

The cottage garden had survived in some form through the changes of the eighteenth-century landscape gardens and the

Victorian bedding-out schemes, both of which Gertrude Jekyll disliked because they had neglected the old garden flowers. Her application of cottage garden methods, however, was transformed both by the wealth of new plants available at this time and by her eye for colour and form. She designed planting in drifts rather than straight lines in her borders, although she was not totally opposed to the bedding system being used in the right context, for instance in parterres.

Ironically, some parterres at this time were being planted with herbaceous beds, such as the terrace garden at Blickling in Norfolk around 1872, with incongruous effect. At the same time the bedding system was finding its way into cottage gardens, as Mrs Loftie noted in 1879:

> Cottagers now try to fill their little plots with geraniums and calceolarias, which they are obliged to keep indoors at great inconvenience to themselves and loss of light to their rooms. Meantime my lady at the Court is hunting the nursery grounds for London Pride and gentianella to make edgings in her wilderness, and for the fair tall rockets, the cabbage roses, and the nodding columbines which her pensioners have discarded and thrown away.

Carpet bedding was still attracting the most attention in Hyde Park in 1904 when it was finally discontinued.

Garden informality, as anyone knows who has tried to create it, needs careful planning. Gertrude Jekyll writes in her book *Colour Schemes for the Flower Garden*:

> Those who do not know are apt to think that hardy flower gardening of the best kind is easy. It is not easy at all. It has taken me half a lifetime merely to find out what is best worth doing, and a good slice of another half to puzzle out ways of doing it.

Gertrude Jekyll became the first woman professionally to design gardens. She had commissions for 350 gardens in Britain, France, Switzerland, Yugoslavia and Hungary. One reason for her moving into gardening from her other artistic activities had been her failing eye-sight: 'When I was young I was hoping to be a painter, but, to my lifelong regret, I was obliged to abandon all hope of this, after a certain amount of art school work, on account of extreme and always progressive myopia.' Whe she died in 1932, William Robinson, at the age of 94 and crippled with arthritis for the previous 30 years, travelled to her funeral.

JOHN RUSKIN

Gertrude Jekyll was a contemporary of the French Impressionists and in *The English Garden* Fleming and Gore draw the connection: 'Her borders were like Impressionist water-colours, delicate and subtle, each plant placed as Seurat might have placed a spot of colour, not isolated but playing an important part in the whole composition.'

The artistic aspect of Jekyll's ideas is significant. John Ruskin, the most famous art critic of the nineteenth century, had continually attacked industrialism for its degradation of human beings and its neglect of art. He criticised manufacturers for their attention to 'novelties and gaudiness', their production for profit rather than use, and their lack of interest in design. The 'depressing and monotonous circumstances of English manufacturing life' made it impossible for workers to produce good design: 'It is impossible for them to have right ideas about colour, unless they see the lovely colours of nature unspoiled; impossible for them to supply beautiful incident and action in their ornament, unless they see beautiful incident and action in the world about them.'

This contrasts with the pre-industrial manufacture by Paisley weavers in the eighteenth century, when the skills of work and leisure could produce a creative interaction, as described by a local minister, Rev. W. Farrier:

> It is well known, that not only for the execution of the most delicate ornamental muslins, but also for the invention of patterns, the operative manufacturers of Paisley stand unrivalled. Their ingenuity is continually in exertion for new and pleasing elegancies, to diversify their fabrics. Now where such habits obtain, the rearing of beautiful flowers, which is an object very congenial to them, will easily be adopted and pursued as a favourite amusement. On the other hand, it seems highly probable that the rearing of flowers, by a re-action, must tend to improve the genius for invention in elegant muslins.

As early as 1837 Ruskin said, 'we must use the natural combination of flowers' when making a garden, and he echoes John Loudon's plans for green belts round London in order to keep it in touch with the countryside. He describes, in 'The Mystery of Life and its Arts' in 1868, a city as it might be:

> walled round, so that there may be no festering and wretched suburb anywhere, but clean and busy street within, and the open

country without, with a belt of beautiful garden and orchard round the walls, so that from any part of the city perfectly fresh air and grass, and sight of far horizon, might be reachable in a few minutes' walk.

It is a medieval image and, in looking back to the more organic society of the Middle Ages, Ruskin and the pre-Raphaelites were drawing partly on myth, partly on reality. The image of the cottage garden was used similarly, to indicate what 'natural' values had been lost and how they could be restored. The Arts and Crafts movement pointed to how art and industry could be reunited on a human scale. Likewise the cottage garden tradition was small-scale and linked the useful and the pleasurable.

John Sedding drew explicit connections between the two movements. He was a church architect and designed The Holy Trinity in Sloane Street, London, which Betjeman called 'the cathedral of the Arts and Crafts movement'. Sedding criticised Robinson's over-reaction against the artistic, but supported the harmony of beauty and utility. In *Garden-Craft Old and New*, published in 1891 after his death, he writes: 'The useful and the beautiful should be happily united, the kitchen and the flower-garden.'

THE MODERN GARDEN

Neither the 200-acre garden of Robinson, nor the 15-acre garden of Jekyll can be seen as exact models for the modern garden. The average size of the British garden is just over 2,000 square feet, or one twentieth of an acre. Nevertheless their style of gardening has been most influential. There are still gardens with only clipped grass and bedding schemes, but most gardens reflect a more varied approach, upholding the adage of Addison in 1712: 'I think there are as many kinds of gardening as of poetry.' They have shrubs and bulbs, herbaceous borders and climbers. Over 50 per cent of private gardens have a vegetable plot of some sort, compared to 40 per cent in the USA; one third of British gardens grow fruit.

The number of households in England and Wales having a garden was put at 66 per cent by Edward Hyams in 1970 and he calculated that there were nine million gardeners in England at that time. Anthony Huxley, using statistics from various sources in the mid-1970s, puts it at 80 per cent of households:

	%
Britain	80
Ireland	70
Holland	67
Denmark	63
USA	51
West Germany	49
France	45
Switzerland	30
Italy	15
Spain	7

Within England and Wales the figures vary across the regions. A survey in 1944 showed the split along the north/south divide:

	%
South-east	75
Wales	68
South	60
East	60
South-west	52
Outer London	47
Midlands	47
North Midlands	44
North	34
North-east	25
North-west	11

In 1986 a poll of 600 gardeners, conducted by *Practical Gardening*, showed that two thirds of them had gardens of less than 4,000 square feet, or one tenth of an acre. They spent an average of 16 hours a week working in the garden in summer, 13 in spring, eleven in autumn and five in winter. The favourite plant turned out to be the rose with over 13 per cent of the votes, followed by fuchsia and clematis, each with 7 per cent, then dahlia, delphinium, peony and rhododendron, lily, primula and pansy. In other words they include a mixture of shrubs and climbers, herbaceous perennials, tuberous and bulbous plants.

The most recent statistics show that 85 per cent of households have gardens and people spend an average of six to seven hours a week looking after them. The hours increase as the gardeners get older: under 25 – three hours; between 25 and 55 – five hours;

over 55 – nine hours. Statistics also show that 80 per cent of gardens have lawns and their average size is half that of the garden. Furthermore 85 per cent of gardens contain roses, the average number being eleven, and each year 35 million new roses are bought. Some 40 million packets of seed are sold every year and 75 per cent of households have at least one house-plant.

Many people belong to horticultural societies. There are about 2,500 such societies affiliated to the Royal Horticultural Society, which itself had 130,000 members in 1989. It does not compare, however, with the Soviet Union. In Byelorussia one in nine belongs to an amateur gardening society either concerned with horticulture or nature conservation.

GARDENING AND DISABILITIES

There has been some movement recently to make gardening more accessible to people with disabilities. This involves, for example, making safer paths, with tapping-rails, handrails, tactile junction indicators; constructing raised beds; providing braille labels, audio cassettes, embossed maps; and producing long-handled, light-weight tools. There are two demonstration gardens in London for people with disabilities run by the Disabled Living Foundation, in Battersea Park and at Syon Park. Another in Dulwich Park was begun in 1986, planned and in part built by people with disabilities. There is also one at the Royal Horticultural Society's gardens at Wisley, near Woking in Surrey.

Two similar developments in Liverpool and in the London borough of Southwark have been severely hit by the abolition of the Greater London Council and the Metropolitan Councils, and also by the government's policy of rate-capping which has threatened their very existence. In 1984 Victoria School, near Poole in Dorset, began to develop a garden suitable for use by children with disabilities. It covers an area of 120 feet by 50 feet and also enables the pupils to gain practical experience in the various processes of commercial horticulture.

Audrey Upton and Peter Thoday of the Department of Horticulture at Bath University have produced *A Bibliography of Horticulture and Out-Door Amenities for the Handicapped and Disadvantaged*, containing nearly 300 books and articles. There is also an illustrated book called *Landscape Design for Disabled People in Public Open Space* which deals with access, provision and design. The authors, Rowson and Thoday, argue against separate gardens for people with disabilities, and for 'integrated landscape provision'.

An organisation called 'Horticultural Therapy' in Frome, Somerset, which was established in 1978, has a comprehensive collection of printed material on gardening for people with disabilities. They produce a quarterly magazine called *Growth Point* which includes articles on subjects such as running a sheltered workshop in horticulture, planning a garden for children with special needs, how horticulture could be used by community-based services for people with mental health problems, advice for those with special needs seeking a job in horticulture.

Raised beds for people with disabilities at
Birmingham Botanical Gardens, 1989.

One issue of the magazine contains accounts of how people with disabilities have found gardening work. One man with celebral palsy, who was described as unemployable, became a full-time groundsman in the College of St Mark and St John in Plymouth. Another with epilepsy found work at Remploy's sheltered Horticultural Unit in Wisbech, Cambridgeshire.

A woman who became mentally ill in 1982 and was diagnosed as a manic depressive started work on a project run by Hammersmith and Fulham MIND. She did a two week basic skills gardening course at Gunnersbury Training Centre and then worked at the local Garden Centre on a month-long placement. Eventually she went on a two-days-a-week Hard Landscaping course for three months:

> Before the landscaping course, my colleagues and I completed a very informative three day Interview Techniques course where we were encouraged to participate and give our ideas. The tutor also explained what an equal opportunity employer was. At present the ratio of men and women in the gardening team is about 50/50. The chargehands and supervisor are women, and I have found it very helpful having this positive role model of experienced women gardeners.

In her book *The Garden and the Handicapped Child*, Patricia Elliott argues that people with disabilities are often given repetitive jobs which do not make full use of their abilities. Also recent technical innovations have operated against them: 'The introduction of sophisticated machinery for spraying, hedge-cutting, leaf-sweeping and other jobs has reduced the number of jobs in public parks.'

Several local authorities, such as Leeds and Sheffield, provide sheltered employment. Liverpool has groups of people with

Water plants in a raised ornamental pond, from Patricia Elliott's The Garden and the Handicapped Child, *illustrated by Brenda Naylor and Elizabeth Watkins, 1978.*

epilepsy working under the constant care of someone trained in first aid, and with rest room facilities close by. The Brighton parks department offers sheltered work to a group of people with physical disabilities, providing them with special facilities such as raised beds.

A number of colleges provide residential courses designed to suit individual needs, for example Queen Elizabeth's College in Leatherhead:

> Suitable students can go on to the college gardening courses which lead to qualifications of the Royal Horticultural Society (RHS). In the past, students suffering from epilepsy (stabilised by drugs), schizophrenia, spastic hemiplegia, brachial plexus lesions and partial sight have been successful. Some students have taken jobs in parks, nurseries, school grounds, private estates and a few in botanical gardens.

The Advisory Committee for Blind Gardeners, working with the support of the South Regional Association for the Blind, has produced guidelines to be borne in mind when designing gardens. They make it clear that they do not support the idea of gardens exclusively for people with visual impairment, but say that 'all gardens should be designed with the enjoyment of everyone alike in mind'. Attached to the guidelines is a list of fragrant plants recommended by the Royal Horticultural Society.

There is a directory of scented gardens and gardens suitable for people with disabilities. This has been prepared at Manchester Polytechnic for the Royal National Institute for the Blind and lists over a 100 parks and gardens throughout the country. In the introduction the author writes:

> Public gardens do not necessarily need to possess elaborate facilities to be enjoyable for visually handicapped visitors. What seems to be important, however, is that access for every type of visitor should be as safe and as unproblematic as possible i.e. paths should be flat and even, clear of obstacles and, in addition, adequate shelter and seats should be provided. Another vital ingredient of any garden is that its plants should be accessible to touch and smell without the need to perform any perilous gymnastic feats. Most of the gardens included within this directory possess raised plant-beds and/or 'wall gardens' in which flowers and shrubs grow at waist height, therefore enabling both visually handicapped and wheelchair-bound people to get within easy reach.

Helen Keller, who was both blind and deaf, gives a remarkable account of her enjoyment of a garden:

> Sometimes I rose at dawn and stole into the garden while the heavy dew lay on the grass and flowers. Few know what joy it is to feel the roses pressing softly into the hand, or the beautiful motion of the lilies as they sway in the morning breeze. Sometimes I caught an insect in the flower I was plucking, and I felt the faint noise of a pair of wings rubbed together in a sudden terror, as the little creature became aware of a pressure from without. Another favourite haunt of mine was the orchard, where the fruit ripened early in July. The large, downy peaches would reach themselves into my hand, and as the joyous breezes flew about the trees the apples tumbled at my feet. Oh, the delight with which I gathered up the fruit in my pinafore, pressed my face against the smooth cheeks of the apples, still warm from the sun, and skipped back to the house!

Gardening has often been used as therapy for the ill and injured. An occupational therapy textbook of 1944 describes horticultural programmes being used as treatment at a miners' rehabilitation centre. In 1974 a national survey showed that 43 per cent of occupational therapy departments used gardening. In 1988 the Royal Society for Nature Conservation organised a campaign to develop wildlife gardens close to hospitals. Their publications show how to plan, fund and maintain such gardens.

Mary Chaplin, in *Gardening for the Physically Handicapped and Elderly*, illustrates the use of gardening in rehabilitation units and occupational therapy departments of hospitals:

> Gardening can give a wide range of exercise for the various limbs. The fingers are used in pricking out seedlings; hoeing gives arm exercise and helps hands to regain their gripping power, at the same time helping a firm stance to be maintained. A hedge cut with shears brings arm movement as well as correct co-ordination, sweeping leaves brings a wide shoulder movement, while picking runner beans can be a bending or a stretching exercise according to where the bean pods are growing on the plants.

Gardening for people with disabilities and gardening as therapy are not just examples of using the garden as a haven from the outside world. They are a way of integrating people in society through productive work and also a method of healing people through creative activity.

12

Politics, Language and Education

Who are our jailors? I say scholars.

Nicholas Culpeper, *A Directory for Midwives* (1651)

Newton was as incomprehensible to the average mechanic as Thomas Aquinas. Knowledge was no longer shut up in the Latin Bible, which priestly scholars had to interpret; it was increasingly shut up in the technical vocabulary of the sciences which the new specialists had to interpret.

Christopher Hill, *The World Turned Upside Down* (1972)

The most current and authoritative names are apt to be founded on some unclean or debasing association, so that to interpret them is to defile the reader's mind.

John Ruskin (1819–1900)

If you want real highbrow talk, commend me to three experts talking about auriculas. Bloomsbury is nothing to it. I couldn't understand half they said.

Vita Sackville-West (1938)

I lay no claim either to literary ability, or to botanical knowledge, or even to knowing the best practical methods of cultivation; but I have lived among outdoor flowers for many years, and have not spared myself in the way of actual labour, and have come to be on closely intimate and friendly terms with a great many growing things, and have acquired certain instincts which, though not clearly defined, are of the nature of useful knowledge.

Gertrude Jekyll, *Wood and Garden* (1899)

235

Gardening is often seen as being above politics and only ideological in relationship to style and taste. But the possession of a garden, and its size and location, are political issues, as are the origins and classification of plants. The language of gardening and its place in our educational system are ideological, and developments in horticulture and botany illustrate economic and political forces at work.

Botany and Medicine

In the Middle Ages botany and medicine were closely linked, so horticulture was for healing, as well as for food and beauty. So too in the sixteenth and seventeenth centuries. In Padua the curator of the botanic garden was the professor of pharmacology. In Paris the 'Jardin du Roi', also known as the 'Jardin Royal des Plantes Médicinales', was superintended by the king's physician. In London John Evelyn saw his garden as a medical garden, where he could obtain the remedies needed for his family and for the neighbourhood.

As scientific thought in the West developed, the two disciplines of botany and medicine grew apart. In 1760 John Hope was appointed to the joint professorships of botany and medicine in Edinburgh University, where he taught medicine in the winter and botany in the summer. But in 1768 he arranged for the appointment of a separate professor of medicine while he concentrated on botany, using the botanic garden to illustrate his teaching. The connection between botany and medicine, however, did not disappear entirely. Most of the collectors sent out to India, for instance, began as surgeons of the East India Company, and until recently the study of botany was a compulsory part of training in medical schools.

The study of botany became centred on the herbarium, as microscopes were developed and dried specimens brought back from abroad. Plants were seen as essentially static rather than dynamic, as William Stearn explains in *Botanical Latin*:

> Down to the eighteenth century botanists knew their plants mostly in a living state, as organisms shooting up from the root, bursting into leaf and flower, giving birth to the fruit; they wrote in this way of the plant's development because thus it happened under their eyes. Their plants grew in gardens around them or were observed in

the wild, which meant that the number available was limited. The elimination of the verb from technical descriptions was symptomatic of a different technique, that of studying by means of herbarium specimens from distant lands, which could not be examined when alive. The herbarium worker usually sees an individual plant only at the stage of development it had reached when gathered and dried for the herbarium.

The collection and classification of plants in the nineteenth century helped Darwin develop his theory of evolution. Then at the end of the century, in the 1880s, the same period as the new gardening style of Jekyll and Robinson, came the shift to the new botany from the continent which, according to Fletcher and Brown, 'shifted the emphasis from the study of the dead plant to the living; from the herbarium to the laboratory and garden; from the external morphology to structure, function, development, and life history of both flowering and non-flowering plants'.

THE CHELSEA PHYSIC GARDEN

There has often been a conflict between established academic centres and the development of science. In Pisa, however, the two were closely linked. The University of Pisa in the sixteenth century was one of the leading universities of its time, particularly the medical faculty with its reputation for botanical learning. In 1543 the botanic garden in Pisa was established by the new professor of botany, Luca Ghini, who became its first director.

In London, by contrast, the Chelsea Physic Garden, founded in 1673 by the Society of Apothecaries, was not associated with a university. This corresponds with other scientific advances in the seventeenth century, in physics, chemistry, mathematics, astronomy and navigation, for example, which were taking place in London, not the academic centres of Oxford and Cambridge. It is described by Christopher Hill as 'the work of merchants and craftsmen, not of dons'.

The Chelsea Physic Garden in the eighteenth century became the most richly stocked botanic garden in the world. In 1748 the Swedish botanist Peter Kalm visited it and described it in his diary as 'one of the largest collections of all rare foreign plants, so that it is said in that respect to rival the botanic gardens of both Paris and Leyden'. The 3,600 dried specimens of plants which were

237

grown there between 1722 and 1795 are now in the British Museum.

An example, connected with this garden, of the continuing link between botany and medicine is the Madagascan or rosy periwinkle. In the middle of the eighteenth century seeds of this plant were sent from the Jardin des Plantes in Paris to Philip Miller, curator of the Chelsea Physic Garden. It is not a true periwinkle, or *vinca*, and is now called *Catharanthus roseus*. Over 60 alkaloids have been isolated from the plant, some being used for attacking cancer. As Stearn comments: 'No single plant in modern times except Cannabis has received more intensive biochemical enquiry than this periwinkle emanating from the Chelsea Physic Garden.'

A gardener working in the Chelsea Physic Garden which has now been restored and is open to the public.

MEDICAL PRACTITIONERS

Botany and medicine were not the only subjects linked in the sixteenth century. Music, for example, was in the faculty of mathematics. Disciplines were not as separate as they later became and there was a constant fertilisation between different spheres of knowledge. William Gilbert (1540–1603), who was President of the College of Physicians, was expert in the science of navigation, astronomy, philosophy, chemistry and botany. His friend Richard Hakluyt was knowledgeable in biology, anthropology and mathematics, as well as chemistry and botany.

Nevertheless the actual practice of medicine was segregated, being organised into three groups. The physicians had to be university graduates, as their knowledge was theoretical, based on tradition, and they disliked it being made available in English. Only physicians were licensed to administer internal medicines. The surgeons, on the other hand, had to serve a seven-year apprenticeship and were limited to manual operations. Surgery was looked down on by physicians as a menial craft. Apothecaries underwent apprenticeship too and their job was to prepare the medicines, although often they also dispensed them to the poor.

Two other groups of medical practitioners, usually neglected in the history of medicine, were women healers, often called herbwomen or wise women, and midwives. In *A Directory for Midwives*, published in 1651, Culpeper praised the 'knowledge, skil, care and industry' needed by the midwife to 'perform her office'.

Witches hanging, from a contemporary pamphlet on the third Chelmsford witch trial in 1589.

In the Middle Ages women healers organised themselves in groups as pharmacists, cultivating healing herbs and exchanging their knowledge. Thousands upon thousands were burnt at the stake as witches from the fourteenth to the seventeenth centuries because they were seen as a threat to the male authority of Church, state and medical profession. Their methods were empirical, relying on trial and error, rather than the metaphysical theories of the Church. Many of the herbal remedies developed by witches still have their place in modern pharmacology, as Barbara Ehrenreich and Deirdre English show:

> They had pain-killers, digestive aids and anti-inflammatory agents. They used ergot for the pain of labor at a time when the Church held that pain in labor was the Lord's just punishment for Eve's original sin. Ergot derivatives are the principal drugs used today to hasten labor and aid in the recovery from childbirth. Belladonna – still used today as an anti-spasmodic – was used by the witch-healers to inhibit uterine contractions when miscarriage threatened. Digitalis, still an important drug in treating heart ailments, is said to have been discovered by an English witch.

In more recent times herb-women continued to practise their skills, for example those women in the eighteenth century who

Purple foxglove (Digitalis purpurea), *painted by G.D. Ehret (1710–70).*

taught Joseph Banks his early botanical knowledge. In the nine-teenth century too, in her novel *Mary Barton*, Mrs Gaskell describes Alice Wilson: 'She had been out all day in the fields gathering wild herbs and medicines, for in addition to her invaluable qualities as a sick nurse and her worldly occupation as a washer woman, she added considerable knowledge of hedge and field simples.'

The Civil War

The male profession split during the Civil War, the College of Physicians siding with the king, while the surgeons and apothe-caries tended to join with parliament. One reason given at the time for Cromwell's victory was that he had the best surgeons on his side to treat the wounded.

Frontispiece to Gerard's Herbal *of 1597.*

It is against this background that the famous herbals were written: in 1597, most of it copied from foreign botanists, by John Gerard, who was a surgeon; in 1640 by John Parkinson, an apoth-ecary; and in 1652 by Nicholas Culpeper, also an apothecary. They helped establish British medicine and botany as amongst the best in Europe at the time, after Leyden and Padua. It was typical of much of the scientific work of the time that it was carried out by practitioners rather than academics in the universities.

Miles Hadfield maintains that during this period probably the

> most outstanding gardeners and botanists were Royalists. Some
> retired from the English political scene either to France or Holland,
> where they became well acquainted with the horticultural and
> aesthetic developments in those countries. Others retreated to their
> country houses and consoled themselves in their gardens. There
> were also many outstanding horticulturalists who carried the label
> of Roundhead.

This reference to Roundhead horticulturalists has often been disputed. Julia Berrall writes of the many gardens that were 'ruined during the eleven-year Commonwealth' and says that 'they were much too pleasurable for the moral scruples of the Puritans'. May Woods and Arete Warren in their book *Glass Houses* also argue: 'To the Puritan Roundheads, fanciful schemes for embellishing their properties would have verged on immorality; they preferred to invest in trade.'

This view perpetuates the mistaken notion that the Puritans were not interested in gardening, but in fact there were many supporters of the Commonwealth who were enthusiastic gardeners and botanists. Gladys Taylor says of London's Temple gardens that 'care was taken of the gardens during the Commonwealth, but with the Restoration came a period of neglect'. Similarly Loudon acknowledges Oliver Cromwell's interest in gardening: 'Cromwell was a great promoter of agriculture and the useful branches of gardening, and his soldiers introduced improvements whenever they rested any time in a place.'

The parliamentary general and Yorkshireman, John Lambert (1619–84), was a keen gardener and amateur botanist. In 1657, when he refused to take the oath of allegiance to Cromwell, he retired to study botany in his garden in Wimbledon which was noted for its tulips. His love of tulips is satirised in a pack of cards produced during the Commonwealth. The eight of hearts has a full length portrait of him holding a tulip in his right hand, with the caption underneath: 'Lambert Kt. of ye Golden Tulip'. He remained a captive after the Restoration until his death in 1684.

Thomas Willisel was a soldier under General Lambert. While in the army he was taken out by local botanists looking for plants and became a keen botanist. He taught himself Latin so that he could understand the science, though previously 'all the profession he had was to make pegges for shoes and all his cloathes on his back not worth 10 groats'. He went on to collect natural history specimens from all over Britain for the Royal Society.

RALPH AUSTEN

Ralph Austen, the radical Oxford horticulturalist, may have fought in the parliamentary army. He was certainly involved in the purge of Oxford University, following the siege of 1646, which ejected royalists and replaced them with Puritan academics. Austen, born around 1612, came from a yeoman family in Leek, Staffordshire and was related to the parliamentary leader, Henry Ireton. He had no university education and no official status, but he became a successful nurseryman, publishing his *Treatise of Fruit-Trees* in 1653. In it he gives a vivid account of the pleasures of the orchard and how it appeals to all five senses.

In many ways this book anticipates John Evelyn's *Sylva*, of 1664, though Evelyn never mentions Austen. James Turner concludes that 'only political bias can explain this omission'. Evelyn's main concern is to stress the need to increase the supply of timber for the navy, although in 1656 Austen had already begun planting timber trees on a large scale to meet the threatened shortage.

The use of oak in ship-building determined the way in which the trees were planted and so affected the appearance of the English landscape. The oaks were widely spaced to encourage their branches to spread and so produce their characteristic sharp angles. These could then be used to provide brackets of great strength to hold the ship firm in heavy seas and under fire.

Austen was a self-taught scientist and a practical gardener. He would not accept any author's advice until he had tried it out for himself. Even Bacon, whose scientific method he admired, is challenged and disproved in *Observations upon some part of Sir Francis Bacon's Naturall History*, which was published in 1658. Austen read the classical and modern texts on gardening, but more importantly he practised the subject, as he puts it, 'endeavouring to find out things of use and profit, by Practise and Experience, that I might speake upon better and surer grounds than some others who have written upon this Subject.'

He wanted to see a massive nationalised programme of fruit-tree plantation, supplied by his nurseries and guided by his text-books: 'I know from what I now doe yearly, that my selfe with two workemen to helpe me might prepare Twenty thousand Plants

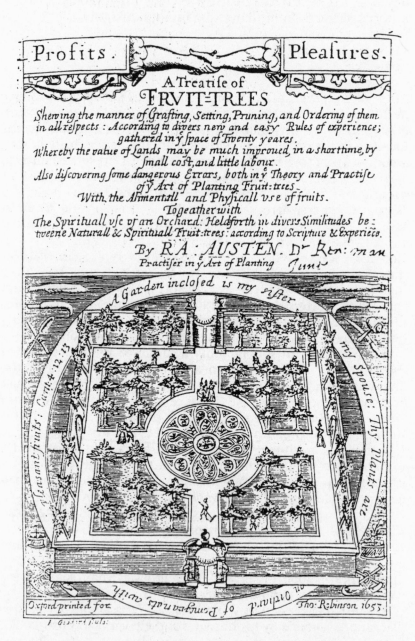

Title-page of Austen's book, engraved by John Goddard.

yearly at least: and those being sould at the Common Rates of 12d a peece amount to £1000.' The government never adopted his scheme, but many orchards were planted locally. He produced many varieties of fruit trees and developed all the necessary skills of grafting, pruning and manuring.

Hartlib, like Austen, wanted fruit trees planted everywhere. In 1652 he produced *A Designe for Plentie, by an Universall Planting of Fruit Trees*. Every waste piece of ground was to be covered with apples, pears, quinces and walnuts 'for the relief of the poor, the benefit of the rich, and the delight of all'. Similarly John Taverner, writing as early as 1600, suggested that all the hedgerows in England should be planted with fruit trees. He adds that those picking the fruit to satisfy their own hunger should go unpunished, and only be dealt with as thieves if they carry the fruit away.

James Turner discusses Austen's place in the development of horticulture during this period:

> The English Revolution saw a great upsurge of interest in horticulture; Cromwell himself, Austen notes, 'had a disposition to (and would often be speaking of) matters of Husbandry'. The publications and correspondence of Samuel Hartlib greatly stimulated this interest, but Austen took the initiative to publicise his own work, and found enthusiastic supporters among Oxford friends he knew before he began to correspond with Hartlib – the vice-chancellor, medical dons and lawyers, puritan preachers and leading officers from the Civil War military government.

Christopher Hill has argued that it is no coincidence that many of the early scientists were Protestants:

> The sharp division in Protestant theology between natural and supernatural knowledge helped to establish the independence of the former. Some (though by no means all) English Protestants denied the association between sin and disease traditionally favoured by the Catholic Church, and became champions of more scientific and hygienic methods.

He quotes the example of the botanist Thomas Penney who was the first Englishman to anticipate Bacon's insistence on the collection of data before theorising. Penney was censured by the Archbishop of Canterbury as 'ill-affected towards the establishment'.

The same point could be made about the founders of German botany – Brunfels, Bock, Fuchs and Cordus – a group of herbalists working in the first half of the sixteenth century. They were all Lutherans and published their work in German as well as Latin. Jerome Bock, who was a Lutheran pastor, also practised medicine and studied botany. He observed plants at first hand, rather than relying on classical authorities, and so proved Dioscorides wrong, and the country people right, about the existence of fern seed.

Leonhart Fuchs, a professor of medicine, was indignant at the ignorance of herbs displayed by medical men:

> Is it to be wondered at that kings and princes do not at all regard the pursuit of the investigation of plants, when even the physicians of our time so shrink from it that it is scarcely possible to find one among a hundred who has an accurate knowledge of even so many as a few plants?

Nicholas Culpeper

Nicholas Culpeper (1616–54) was another of those who upheld 'Doctors Reason and Experience against Dr. Tradition'. He fought on the Parliamentary side, was wounded at Newbury in 1643, and supported the execution of the king: 'God gave Tyrants in his Wrath, and will take them away in his Displeasure.' Quite prepared when necessary to challenge the highest authorities, such as Galen and Dioscorides, he also attacked the monopoly of the Royal College of Physicians: 'The Papists and the College of Physicians will not suffer divinity and physic to be printed in our mother tongue, both upon one and the same ground.'

Culpeper knew Latin and Greek, but wanted knowledge made available in English. In 1649 he translated the Pharmacopoeia of the Royal College of Physicians without gaining their permission. In his preface he toasted the Commonwealth, called for the 'liberty of the subject', and castigated the 'proud, insulting, domineering doctors, whose wits were born above 500 years before themselves'.

Gerrard Winstanley the Digger, one of the most radical thinkers of the time, also attacked the reliance on classical texts and demanded first-hand experience: 'Everyone who speaks of any herb, plant, art, or nature of mankind is required to speak nothing by imagination, but what he hath found out by his own industry and observation in trial.' He supported the sort of education

246

carried out at Gresham College in London where lectures were free, in English, accompanied by practical demonstrations and followed by discussion. He wanted Gresham-type lectures on natural history to replace the Sunday sermon in every parish.

Winstanley and Culpeper were no doubt the kind of people King Charles I had in mind when, as a prisoner in Carisbrooke Castle, he complained:

> *The Marigold observes the Sun*
> *More than my Subjects me have done.*

Engraving of Nicholas Culpeper (1616–54)
by Thomas Cross, 1649.

Culpeper was maligned by royalists as an atheist, drunkard, lecher and poisoner, and now suffers something of the reputation of a quack. He believed in astrology, but then so did William Harvey, who discovered the circulation of the blood, and so did one of the physicians to Charles II, John Archer, who in his *Compendius Herbal* of 1673 gave full astrological directions for the gathering of herbs to be used as medicines.

One of the few people to reject astrology was William Fulke, an outspoken Puritan and one of the founders of scientific meteorology in England. In 1566 he attacked Thomas Hyll for his reliance on astrology to determine when to sow seeds:

Good days to sowe and plante, I thinke be when the earth is moderately moystened, and gentilly warmed with the heat of the sonne ... As for the sygne or constellation ... it is as much healpe unto the sedes as it was ease for the Camell whenne the Flye leapt of from his backe.

Nevertheless astrology was an important attempt at the time to interpret nature by materialist rather than just metaphysical means. In *Religion and the Decline of Magic*, Keith Thomas writes: 'Astrology was probably the most ambitious attempt ever made to reduce the baffling diversity of human affairs to some sort of intelligible order.' The eminent mathematician John Dee was an astrologer; Bacon thought there was a core of physical knowledge in alchemy, magic and astrology which was worthy of scientific examination; and Newton was as interested in alchemy and biblical prophecies as in mathematics and physics.

As F.N.L. Poynter has argued, Culpeper had

a far greater influence on medical practice in England between 1650 and 1750 than either Harvey or Sydenham [the founder of modern clinical medicine]. His writings reflect faithfully the orthodox medicine of his own time, and his translations of the leading European medical writers of his age gave to English doctors for the first time a comprehensive body of medical literature in their own tongue which represented the best contemporary authorities.

Even an enemy said in 1664 that 'Mr Culpeper hath been, by the ignorant, more highly esteemed than both Hippocrates and Galen'.

He was particularly concerned to give medical help to the poor. A biography published in 1659, a few years after his death, recorded:

To the poor he prescribed cheap but wholesome Medicines, not removing, as many in our times do, the Consumption out of their bodies into their purses; not sending them to the East Indies for Drugs, when they may fetch better out of their own Gardens.

After the Restoration many royalist gardeners returned from France with Charles II. One of these was Robert Morison (1620–83) who was appointed in 1669 as the first professor of botany at Oxford University. These returning exiles help to explain the emergence of the French formal style of gardening at this time, just as a Dutch influence was felt after 1688 with the arrival of William and Mary.

Many of the gardens of this period are described by Celia Fiennes in her diary. She was the daughter of a colonel in Cromwell's army and in 1698 travelled 3,000 miles, the length and breadth of the country, on a white horse. She admired the new gardening that had been taking place, the cut-work hedges and dwarfed trees, box labyrinths and avenues of conifers, florists' flowers and exotics in pots.

PLANT SEXUALITY

A sexual revolution accompanied the political revolution of seventeenth-century England. Free love and nudity with the Ranters, free choice in marriage proposed by Winstanley, freedom of divorce advocated by Milton and Mrs Attaway, were all widely discussed, though as Winstanley pointed out, it was freedom mainly for men, as in the 1960s.

There was also a sexual revolution in the world of plants. The sexual reproduction of palm trees had been known since the days of Theophrastus in Aristotle's Botanic Garden, but it was considered exceptional. In the seventeenth century several botanists were putting forward the stunning proposition that flowers had a sex life. John Ray, the son of a Braintree blacksmith, who became a famous naturalist and lecturer in mathematics, Greek and Latin at Cambridge, speculated on the sexuality of plants, and in 1682 Nehemiah Grew announced to the Royal Society the likelihood of plant sex.

The development of magnifying glasses provided the possibility of closer observation of plants and in 1694 the German botanist Camerarius, director of the botanic garden in Tübingen, published his proof of plant sexuality, based on experiments which he had carried out on the castor oil plant. He explicitly related the plant's sexual organs to those of human beings, thus giving them a 'nobler name'. William Stearn describes this discovery as 'revolutionary at the time and among the most important in the whole history of botany'.

At the same time parts of the flower were being distinguished more specifically and given names. In 1649 Fabio Colonna suggested that the word *petalum*, from the Greek meaning a leaf, be used to indicate the floral leaves of a plant as opposed to its

Engraving of a castor oil plant by James Sowerby (1757–1822).

ordinary leaves. In 1682 John Ray adopted the word and it was translated into many modern languages. It is strange to think that the word petal, with all its connotations, was unknown to Shakespeare.

The discovery of floral organs led to Linnaeus's system of plant classification, based on the male parts, the anthers. It also produced the inevitable anthropomorphism, likening plants to humans, as in Linnaeus's undergraduate dissertation: 'Yes, love comes even to plants, males and females; even the hermaphrodites hold their nuptials, showing by their sexual organs which are males, which are hermaphrodites.' He went on to describe the petals as 'precious bed-curtains' concealing the lovers in their marriage bed. One group of plants he called Monardia which had only 'one husband in marriage', whereas in the Polyandria 'twenty males or more lay in the same bed with the female'.

Ruskin was horrified by 'these obscene processes and prurient apparitions'. One of his followers, Forbes Watson, in his book *Flowers and Gardens*, attacked hybridisation as being against the work of God. He also thought that bedding-out was evil, as it only showed the plant at one stage of its life. The botanist Johann Siegesbock could not believe in the sexual promiscuity of plants: 'God never would have allowed such odious vice as that several males should possess one wife in common.' Mary Wollstonecraft quotes a writer who objected to women studying the subject because instruction in the 'modern system of botany' could not be consistent with 'female delicacy'.

HYBRIDISATION

The discovery of plant sexuality led to hybridisation, the deliberate act of making a cross between two parent plants by taking pollen from the plant selected as the male parent and transferring it to the stigma of the female parent. As early as 2000 BC, however, the Chinese had already hybridised chrysanthemums, camellias and roses. The first Englishman to experiment seriously with hybridisation was probably Thomas Fairchild (1667–1729) who crossed a sweet william with a carnation. He owned a nursery in Hoxton, east London, and wrote a book called *The City Gardener* in 1722. Already at this time he discusses the rapid increase in smoke pollution and makes suggestions for planting town squares and other public places.

At the end of the eighteenth century ships of the East India Company brought back perpetual-flowering roses from the Chinese nurseries near Canton. These were crossed with native once-flowering roses to become the ancestors of most modern roses. In the 1790s William Rollisson hybridised Cape heaths at his nursery in south London and in the 1820s William Herbert worked with amaryllis and gladiolus. By 1883 Shirley Hibberd could claim in the *Gardener's Magazine* that 'the hybridist who has thoroughly mastered the art may predetermine, with almost mathematical exactitude, what it is in his power to produce'.

In July 1899 The Royal Horticultural Society held its first International Hybridisation Conference, attended by practical plant breeders and scientists. In 1900 Mendel's famous paper, originally published in 1865, was rediscovered by the Dutch botanist Hugo de Vries. He sent it to the scientist William Bateson, who had been studying hybridisation by means of statistics. At the third International Conference on Hybridisation in 1906 the term 'genetics' was born.

The creation of new plants has entered our mythology. Is it possible to create a blue rose or a pink daffodil? The search to produce a black tulip was turned into a novel by Dumas. At the height of the tulip mania in the seventeenth century the equivalent of £2,000 in today's currency was offered for a pair of rare bulbs, and as late as 1854 tulips such as 'Duchess of Cambridge' were being sold at 100 guineas. A red delphinium and a green rose were finally achieved in 1988. It now seems possible to make a blue chrysanthemum through a form of micropropagation called protoplast fusion, crossing the chrysanthemum with a blue aster.

LANGUAGE

The plain style of language, understood and written by merchants and artisans in the seventeenth century, formed the basis of the new scientific language. After the Restoration, the Royal Society, which had grown out of Gresham College and the group of educational reformers which included Hartlib and Comenius, undertook the task of developing this language. Nevertheless the passion of popular language was missing from the Royal Society's prose. The defeated revolution was still seen as a danger: ' "Enthusiasm" was taboo.' Christopher Hill, in his book on Bunyan, goes on to talk of Roger L'Estrange, Charles II's censor, who wanted to suppress 'the great masters of the popular style' because they 'speak plain and strike home to the capacity and humours of the multitude'.

John Locke, who was interested in botany and owned a herbarium, argued in 1690 for simplicity and consistency in order to 'convey the knowledge of things'. He proposed a system of classification and wanted 'words standing for things that are known and distinguished by their outward shapes' to be illustrated by drawings: 'A vocabulary made after this fashion would perhaps, with more ease, and in less time, teach the signification of many terms than all the large and laborious comments of learned critics.'

Paradoxically this rationalisation of the language, as well as marking the beginning of the division between the arts and sciences, eventually developed into the academic botanical Latin which few people understand and which contrasts so vividly with the common language used for flowers and plants. It led in the nineteenth century to a reaction against Latin names for plants.

William Robinson accepted a Latin name in its right place, but preferred to use English names:

> It is best to speak of things growing about our doors in our own tongue, and the practice of using in conversation long Latin names, a growth of our own century, has done infinite harm to gardening in shutting out people who have a heart for a garden, but none for the Latin of the gardener. There is no more need to speak of the plants in our gardens by their Latin names than to speak of the dove or the rabbit by Latin names.

Ruskin also objected to the use of Latin words, mainly because of their sexual connotations.

Up to the eighteenth century Latin was still used for academic, diplomatic, ecclesiastical and legal affairs in Europe. It was also often used in private correspondence and in conversation. In 1735–6, when Linnaeus visited Germany, Holland, France and England, he talked mainly in Latin. Even in the nineteenth century, Elias Magnus Fries, the founder of modern mycology (the study of fungi) was only allowed to speak to his father in Latin when he was a boy. He therefore came to learn Latin before being able to speak his native Swedish.

Plant description up until this time was often vivid and referred to many aspects of plant use, but there was no universal system. Theophrastus (370–c. 285 BC), who inherited Aristotle's botanic garden in Athens, describes plants in relationship to their beauty, economic use or other peculiarities, using current Greek words. In his description of the sacred lotus, *Nelumbo nucifera*, he compares the thickness of the stalk to that of a man's finger, its air passages to a honeycomb, the size of its leaf-blade to that of a Thessalian hat, the size of its flower to that of a large poppy, its colour to a rose's, its receptacle to a round wasp's nest and its fruits to beans. Similarly Aztec botanical science used words to classify plants in various ways, according to habitat, method of growth, shape, form, fragrance and the effects they had on people when eaten.

CARL LINNAEUS AND PLANT CLASSIFICATION

The Swedish botanist, Carl Linnaeus (1707–78), devised the modern system of plant classification. It uses medieval and Renaissance Latin, not the classical form, and has been expanded with new words derived from both Latin and Greek. The classifica-

Japanese woodcut of a sacred lotus (Nelumba nucifera).

tion of horticultural plants is now governed by the 'International Code of Nomenclature for Cultivated Plants'. It uses Linnaeus's binomial system which he originally published in 1737 – the first name for the genus or group of plants, the second for the species within that group. A third name can be given to a subspecies, variety or cultivar. According to William Stearn, Linnaeus developed his curt style of writing and his classification system basically as a 'paper-saving device in a country where paper was often in short supply'.

An example of the importance of correct plant classification comes from New Zealand where a species of St John's Wort had spread as a weed on arable land. It was identified simply as *Hypericum perforatum*, so an insect, bred at great expense in Britain, which was known to destroy the fruits of this plant, was used to try to prevent its further distribution by seed dispersal. The insects refused to do their job and, when the plant was finally examined in the herbarium, it was discovered to be a Mediterranean form of the species known as *Hypericum perforatum* variety *angustifolium* which was inhabited by a different insect. When the appropriate insect was bred and shipped to New Zealand, it succeeded in controlling the spread of the weed.

There is no doubt as to the value of a systematic international language. I have been to botanic gardens as far apart as Iceland

and Brazil and been able to read the labels on the plants. At the same time it is also an example of linguistic imperialism. It is clearly far more difficult for Chinese or Japanese people, for example, to learn botanical Latin than for Europeans. As Rousseau observed in *Letters on the Elements of Botany Addressed to a Lady*, the language also puts many people off the study of botany.

EXPLORERS AND THE LANGUAGE OF PLANTS

The fact that this language developed at a time of European expansion and colonialism means that many of the botanical Latin words given to plants come from the names of European men. Usually they were scientists or men of the church. Sometimes they were both, like Rev. Adam Buddle (1660–1715) the botanist after whom buddleia is named; or Georg Joseph Kamel (1661–1706) a pharmacist and Jesuit priest who spent his life as a missionary in the Philippines and gave his name to camellia; or Father Armand David (1826–1900), a zoologist who went to China as a missionary in 1862, from whom *Clematis armandii* got its name.

In the seventeenth century the Bishop of London, Henry Compton, had jurisdiction over the Anglican Church in North America. He sent out missionaries who had botanical training, to preach and also to collect plants. One of these was the Reverend John Banister who botanised in the West Indies and Virginia. Between 1678 and 1692 he sent back to Compton around 340 species of plants. They were kept in greenhouses in the bishop's garden at Fulham Palace.

Often the botanical explorers were just doing a commercial job. Kerria is named after William Kerr (died 1814) who was sent out to China as a collector from Kew; and *Pieris forrestii* after George Forrest (1873–1932) who was sent out by Bees nursery and who introduced the plant into this country from China, along with 300 new rhododendron species.

Needless to say, most of these plants had names and uses in their region of origin, before being taken back to Europe. For instance a whole species of Australian plants has been named after Joseph Banks. These banksias have bottle-brush type flowers which are full of nectar. The nectar was eaten by the Aborigines and used to sweeten water. Sometimes the honey was extracted by rolling the flower in the hands and then licking off the nectar that was stuck to the hands. The seed cones of the plants were used as hair brushes.

The official names of plants usually indicate the dominance of a particular culture. In Europe the derivations are usually Latin or Greek. So the Latin name *aquilegia* comes from *aquila*, an eagle, and its English name columbine from the Latin word *columba*, a dove, both meanings reflecting the shape of the flowers. The words *Fritillaria meleagris* mean dice-box and guinea-fowl, and indicate the design of the snake's-head fritillary. *Galanthus*, or snowdrop, is derived from the Greek *gala*, meaning milk, and *anthus*, a flower. *Calendula*, or marigold, comes from the Latin for the first day of the month, as the flower blooms nearly every month of the year.

Nevertheless most of our flowers have a variety of regional names. The viola or pansy, for instance, has some 60 different names in English. Some plant names have Anglo-Saxon origins, such as hollyhock which comes from the word *hoc* meaning mallow, and foxglove deriving from *foxes-gleow* which was a musical instrument in the shape of an arch with different sized bells hanging from it.

There is also an Arabic influence. Saffron, for which it takes 4,300 blossoms of *Crocus sativus* to produce one ounce, comes from *sahafaran*, and *alchemilla*, or lady's mantle, from *alkemelych*. Drops of moisture from the *alchemilla* were used in preparing the Philosopher's Stone. The Damask rose was brought to England from Damascus during the crusades in the thirteenth century.

GARDENING AND EDUCATION

There has often been a tension between social classes in the study of horticulture and botany, which is connected with language and education, as illustrated by Culpeper. The amateur aristocrat, Joseph Banks, despite his poor Oxbridge education, had the money and contacts to extend his knowledge of the field. John Loudon, the professional gardening expert, had the education and cultural know-how to further his career. But many working-class people developed their knowledge and expertise in a very different context.

The Coventry weaver, Joseph Gutteridge, had to make his own microscope to observe pollination and taught himself herbal medicine. Thomas Edward, whose father was a weaver in Fife, started work at the age of six in a tobacco factory and was apprenticed as a shoemaker at eleven. He accumulated a vast knowledge of Scottish plants from observing them in the wild and collecting them. In different circumstances each of them could have been as celebrated as Joseph Banks and John Loudon.

Lancashire textile workers in the 1850s were said to grow better specimens of flowers than anyone in the land. In *Hardy Florists' Flowers*, James Douglas describes how these workers grew polyanthuses, which were originally created by crossing a wild primrose with a cowslip. He discusses whether Darwin or the Lancashire weavers were responsible for recent discoveries:

> It has been supposed by some of our leading scientific men, that Mr. Darwin was the first to recognize the relative uses of the pin-eyed and thrum or moss-eyed Polyanthuses. That Mr. Darwin did make some discoveries on his own account I can fully believe, but it is equally certain that the Lancashire silk hand-loom weavers – of which old David Jackson, of Middleton, may be instanced as a type – knew the practical value of them, probably before most of us who are now alive saw light. These old and patient workers had a high standard (which had been agreed upon by mutual consent), to work up to; and if they raised any that did not come up to that, they were rejected.

The florists' flowers (tulip, auricula, carnation, pink, anemone, ranunculus, hyacinth, polyanthus) went out of fashion during the bedding-out period, when '5,000 Calceolarias, 5,000 Verbenas, 5,000 Zonal Pelargoniums, etc., were required in one establishment'. As Douglas goes on to say: 'With the strain upon the gardener to supply such quantities of plants, and the amount of space required under glass for their development, no wonder that the old florists' flowers went to the wall.'

Florists' flowers were closely connected with the working class. They were called 'mechanics' flowers' and often looked down on by other classes. Orchids, on the other hand, which could at one time fetch 1,000 guineas each, had an even clearer class connotation.

D.H. Lawrence, after attacking a woman's attitude to flowers, writes of the miner's appreciation of the flowers in his garden:

> Most of the so-called love of flowers to-day is merely this reaching out of possession and egoism: something I've *got*; something that

embellishes *me*. Yet I've seen many a collier stand in his back garden looking down at a flower with that odd, remote sort of contemplation which shows a *real* awareness of the presence of beauty. It would not even be admiration, or joy, or delight, or any of those things which so often have a root in the possessive instinct. It would be a sort of contemplation: which shows the incipient artist.

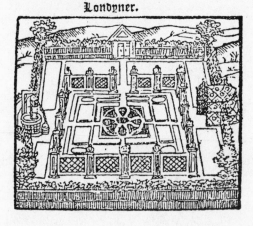

Title page of Thomas Hyll's book, 1563. There was an earlier edition, probably published in 1558.

In *The Old English Gardening Books*, Eleanour Sinclair Rohde praises the writers of Tudor and early Stuart gardening manuals for their knowledge of plants 'gained from a lifetime of close communion with flowers'. She stresses that 'with a few notable exceptions they were the works, not of scholars, but of unlearned men'. Thomas Hyll, for example, who produced the first gardening book printed in England in 1563, speaks of his 'rudeness of pen' and says he has never 'tasted of the learned laake but rather always rudely taught'. His book is for 'the simple and vnlettered' and 'to please the common sort, for whose onelye sake, I haue taken these paines and haue published this Booke'.

Neither has illiteracy necessarily been a bar to expertise in gardening. Edward Hyams was 'filled with admiration' for the 'illiterate and erudite botanists' he met in Java who were employed by the National Biological Institute: 'They have an astonishing and perfectly reliable memory for the names of plants, retaining many hundreds and always able to identify them correctly.' In the same way the Walbiri of the Australian Western Desert were familiar with 103 different species of flora, all of which were used for food, medicinal, technological or ceremonial purposes.

With the growth of state education in nineteenth-century England, however, qualifications were beginning to be required to become a gardener, as John Loudon observed in his *Gardener's Magazine* of 1836:

> The most remarkable circumstance which had occurred during the past year was the decision of the Horticultural Society of London to admit no young men into the garden as journeymen who had not some school education, and to recommend no one from their gardens for situations as head gardeners who had not been regularly examined in scientific knowledge and received a certificate stating their degree of proficiency.

Loudon agreed with educating gardeners: 'We would, therefore, strongly recommend every young man who has entered on the profession of gardening, to be most assiduous in his endeavours to add to his stock of knowledge, from books, from observation, and from personal intercourse with eminent gardeners.' Accumulation of facts was not enough: 'The mind must be exercised on these facts, so as to generalise on them, and make them its own; to trace them up to principles of general application; and thus to be enabled to apply them in unforeseen cases.' The education of gardeners was eventually put on a formal basis with the establishment of the National Diploma of Horticulture in 1913.

Even Vita Sackville-West was worried about her lack of formal education and felt unqualified when it came to gardening. In

1956 she wrote: 'I am taking a correspondence course in Horticulture. I shall have to fill in a weekly examination paper and send it up for correction.' The course was run by Mr Ibbett from Dawlish in Devon and was advertised as suitable for 'preliminary training', useful for students not ready to take the RHS senior examination.

HORTICULTURE IN SCHOOL

In today's schools horticulture or gardening is hardly part of the national curriculum. In his presidential address to the annual general meeting of the Royal Horticultural Society in 1989, Robin Herbert said:

> Plant sciences, together with the principles and practices of horticulture, provide a nucleus of relevant life skills. With increased leisure time, much of which is spent in horticulturally related pursuits, it is to be regretted that these subjects tend not to be included within the framework of the National Curriculum for secondary schools, and we deplore the demise of Rural Science. Plants and their use would form an ideal optional study area within the new syllabuses.

Where horticulture does appear in the school syllabus, it is usually for the bottom streams whose pupils are meant to be good with their hands. Horticulture is taught in a number of Midlands schools, preparing pupils for GCSE. It is based on a rural science course, integrating physics, chemistry, biology and maths, and is both theoretical and practical. One of its aims is to appreciate the 'social, economic, ethical and cultural implications in horticultural practices'.

An example of horticulture being taught in a primary school comes from Wootton, near Woodstock in Oxfordshire, where some of the children cultivate a 20 foot by 18 foot vegetable plot. They have also twinned with a village school in Thailand and when this school lost its first crop through drought, the Oxfordshire children sold their surplus produce to finance them to buy seed for another crop. The children garden every Tuesday afternoon and are in regular correspondence with their Thai counterparts, exchanging tapes, letters and photographs, learning what they grow as well as how they live. The scheme has spread and a number of local schools are now twinned with schools in Thailand.

These examples, however, are exceptions in our educational system. Compare Holland where they spend £1 million a year on school gardens just in the city of Amsterdam. In this country nature study has usually had sexist connotations of being cissy, and botany is rarely taken as an exam subject. Sometimes it is subsumed under biology which is the subject with the third highest number of exam entrants at age 16, after maths and English. Two thirds of these entrants are girls, for biology is seen as a 'soft' science.

It is clear from the place of horticulture in our education system that it is not seen as a high status academic subject. Yet the roots of the subject in botany and medicine indicate its importance in our cultural history. Gardening has not only led to crucial discoveries in medicine, but also to hybridisation and the theory of evolution. Above all, for millions of people, it is a subject that unites theory and practice, and combines the aesthetic and the scientific.

13

Utopia

I know a little garden close
Set thick with lily and red rose
Where I would wander if I might
From dewy dawn to dewy night,
And have one with me wandering.
William Morris, 'The Life and Death of Jason' (1867)

The little garden is crowded with a medley of old-fashioned
herbs and flowers, planted long ago, when the garden was
the only druggist's shop within reach, and allowed to grow
in scrambling and wild luxuriance – roses, lavender, sage,
balm (for tea), rosemary, pinks and wallflowers, onions and
jessamine, in most republican and indiscriminate order.
Elizabeth Gaskell, *Mary Barton* (1848)

Beauty, and use, and beauty once again
Link up my scattered heart, and shape a scheme
Commensurate with a frustrated dream.
Vita Sackville-West, 'Sissinghurst' (1930)

The garden was one of those old-fashioned paradises which
hardly exist any longer except as memories of our child-
hood: no finical separation between flower and kitchen-
garden there; no monotony of enjoyment for one sense to the
exclusion of another; but a charming paradisiacal mingling
of all that was pleasant to the eye and good for food.
George Eliot, *Scenes of Clerical Life* (1858)

Paradise, and groves
Elysian, Fortunate Fields – like those of old
Sought in the Atlantic Main – why should they be
A history only of departed things,
Or a mere fiction of what never was?
William Wordsworth, 'The Recluse' (1806)

The Garden of Eden and Paradise are religious utopias, common to Judaism, Christianity and Islam. The word 'utopia' comes from the Greek, meaning nowhere or a place that does not exist. The place may not exist but the yearning is real. Marx describes religion as the opium of the people but he also calls it the 'heart of a heartless world'. Gardening often serves a similar purpose as consolation and escape from the world. At the same time, like the church, gardens and gardening are often the expression of power and oppression in the world.

The most obvious exercise of this power is through enclosure and eviction, and through the harsh manual labour often involved in gardening. A less obvious but equally telling example is the ownership of dovecotes. Until the seventeenth century doves were kept for food, particularly for the winter. Hartlib, writing in the middle of the seventeenth century, estimated that there were 26,000 dovecotes in England, each holding at least 500 pairs of birds. As Eleanour Rohde comments: 'The old dovecotes that remain are now amongst the most picturesque buildings in the country, but in past centuries they must have been regarded with scant favour by the humble folk whose crops they pillaged.'

The garden as an integrated part of a free and equal society is utopian, it does not exist. Nevertheless there has been a continuing tradition which has presented a vision of such gardens and has tried, however partially, to realise it: women healers and radical apothecaries, Winstanley and the Diggers, the movement for free public parks, Jane and John Loudon, cottage gardeners and florists' societies, land cooperatives and the allotment movement, garden cities, the Greens and the ecology movement. The hallmarks of this tradition are the attempts to integrate beauty and use, town and country, work and leisure, public and private, academic and popular, mental and manual labour.

OWNERSHIP AND CONTROL

The main stumbling-block to realising what Winstanley calls the 'free enjoyment of the earth' is the continual ownership of the land by a few rich people and also the colonial conquest of other people's lands. The patriotic poet Michael Drayton (1563-1631) even had the effrontery to locate his paradise in an American colony, without thought of the native Americans who already lived there. In 'To the Virginian Voyage' he praises the new colony:

> *Virginia,*
> *Earth's only paradise.*
>
> *Where nature hath in store*
> *Fowl, venison, and fish,*
> *And the fruitfull'st soil*
> *Without your toil*
> *Three harvests more,*
> *All greater than you wish.*

Arriving in Virginia people were struck by the great forests growing right down to the shore. In 1650 E.W. Gent described the variety of trees:

> Nor is the present wildernesse of it without a particular beauty, being all over a naturall Grove of Oakes, Pines, Cedars, Cipresse, Mulberry, Chestnut, Laurell, Sassafras, Cherry, Plum-trees and Vines, all of so delectable an aspect, that the melanchollyest eye in the World cannot look upon it without contentment, nor content himselfe without admiration.

There were 'large and delicious' strawberries growing beneath the trees, an abundance of deer and wild turkeys weighing up to 50 lbs.

Nevertheless many of the early colonists died of disease or starvation. The Virginia Company published broadsheets and pamphlets describing the place in glowing terms in order to encourage settlers. Drayton's poem can be seen to serve a similar function. Likewise Thomas Hariot in his *Briefe and True Report of the New Found Land of Virginia*, published in 1588, described the land as a pastoral paradise.

Thomas More, though a wealthy man himself, recognised this exploitation in his *Utopia* of 1516. He deplored the ruinous enclosures carried out by noblemen and gentlemen, abbots and holy men, to replace people with sheep and to create parks for the owners. In his utopia, property is 'exiled and banished' and all things held in common. The utopians value their gardens highly. They combine pleasure and use, cooperation and friendly rivalry:

> They set great store by their gardens. In them they have vineyards, all manner of fruit, herbs and flowers, so pleasant, so well furnished, and so finely kept, that I never saw thing more fruitful nor better trimmed in any place. Their study and diligence herein cometh not

264

only of pleasure, but also of certain strife and contention that is between street and street, concerning the trimming, husbanding and furnishing of their gardens, every man for his own part. And verily you shall not lightly find in all the city anything that is more commodious, either for the profit of the citizens, or for pleasure. And therefore it may seem that the first founder of the city minded nothing so much as he did these gardens.

More's own garden by the Thames in Chelsea was famous in his day and was described by the playwright John Heywood: 'Wonderfully charming, both from the advantages of its site and also for its own beauty; it was crowned with almost perpetual verdure; it had flowering shrubs, and the branches of fruit trees interwoven in so beautiful a manner that it appeared like a tapestry woven by Nature herself.' Thomas More expected his servants to 'occupy their leisure with gardening, music or books'.

COMMON OWNERSHIP

John Bunyan, in *Pilgrim's Progress*, attacked the enclosures taking place in the middle of the seventeenth century. He presents the issue in the confrontation between the pilgrims and the giants. Mr Great-heart asserts a right of way against Giant Grim who has blocked the road by enclosure. Giant Despair accuses the pilgrims: 'You have this night trespassed on me by trampling and lying on my grounds', and he leads them off to his dungeon.

By comparison, in the Celestial City pilgrims have houses of their own and access to orchards and vineyards. In Bunyan's utopia, lands and their produce are 'rent-free' and 'common for all the pilgrims'. Similarly in 'the Holy City', 'plums and figs and grapes and apples will be open to every passenger, in common and free for all'.

Gerrard Winstanley, Bunyan's contemporary, was made unemployed in the clothing trade and became a hired labourer herding cows. He had more pressing need for change than Thomas More and was more revolutionary than Bunyan. He told the lords of the manor:

The power of enclosing land and owning property was brought into the creation by your ancestors by the sword; which first did murder their fellow creatures, men, and after plunder or steal away their land, and left this land successively to you, their children. And

265

John Parkinson's Paradisus *of 1629. The title is a pun on the author's name, 'Paradisi in Sole' being Latin for 'park in sun'.*

therefore, though you did not kill or thieve, yet you hold that cursed thing in your hand by the power of the sword.

Taking part in the English Revolution, he was more concerned with the earthly nature of paradise than a distant utopia: 'Why may not we have our heaven here (that is, a comfortable livelihood in the earth) and heaven hereafter too?'

In a chapter on education, Winstanley lists husbandry as the first of 'five fountains from whence all arts and sciences have their influence'. After the preparation of the land, the 'second branch of husbandry is gardening, how to plant, graft and set all sort of fruit trees, and how to order the ground for flowers, herbs and roots for pleasure, food or medicinal'. He argues for common ownership and cooperation: 'If every one did but quietly enjoy the earth for food and raiment, there would be no wars, prisons nor gallows.'

Two and a half centuries later, in his essay 'A Factory as It Might Be', William Morris put a similar case for 'skilled cooperative gardening for beauty's sake, which beauty would by no means exclude the raising of useful produce for the sake of livelihood'. His model factory

> stands amidst gardens as beautiful (climate apart) as those of Alcinous, since there is no need of stinting it of ground, profit rents being a thing of the past, and the labour on such gardens is like enough to be purely voluntary, as it is not easy to see the day when 75 out of every 100 people will not take delight in the pleasantest and most innocent of all occupations, and our working people will assuredly want open-air relaxation from their factory work. Even now, as I am told, the Nottinghamshire factory hands could give many a hint to professional gardeners in spite of all the drawbacks of a great manufacturing town.

Like Winstanley, Morris goes on to claim that this ideal is not impossible, given a change from private to collective ownership:

> Impossible! I hear an anti-socialist say. My friend, please to remember that most factories sustain today large handsome gardens, and not seldom parks and woods of many acres in extent; with due appurtenances of highly-paid Scotch professional gardeners, wood reeves, bailiffs, gamekeepers, and the like, the whole being managed in the most wasteful way conceivable; *only* the said gardens, etc., are, say, twenty miles away from the factory, *out of the smoke*, and are kept up for *one member of the factory only*, the sleeping partner to wit ...

As Christopher Hill says: 'The symbolism of the garden has almost as great a significance for Winstanley as for Marvell or Milton. Eden is mankind. In Eden is fought out the conflict between Reason on the one hand and covetous imagination on the other.' Winstanley sees the connection between the expulsion from Eden and the Norman Conquest. He considers the earth 'a common treasury of livelihood to whole mankind' and calculates that 'if the waste land of England were manured by her children, it would become in a few years the richest, the strongest and most flourishing in the world'.

The same argument is presented by Aaron in George Eliot's novel *Silas Marner*, first published in 1861:

> There's never a garden in all the parish but what there's endless waste in it for want o' somebody as could use everything up. It's what I think to myself sometimes, as there need nobody run short o' victuals if the land was made the most on, and there was never a morsel but what could find its way to a mouth. It sets one thinking o' that – gardening does.

He goes on to suggest how he could bring some lavender from the Red House for Eppie's garden: 'I can bring you slips of anything; I'm forced to cut no end of 'em when I'm gardening, and throw 'em away mostly.'

COOPERATION AND ALLOTMENTS

Cooperation amongst gardeners is not utopian, but a long established tradition. Gardening lends itself to the exchange of plants and seeds. It is easy to collect seeds from the garden to give to others, to divide plants and at the same time benefit those remaining, to take cuttings at no expense, to share the produce of the garden. In the sixteenth century Tusser shows how women were accustomed to displaying such neighbourliness:

> *Good huswifes in Sommer will save their owne seedes*
> *against the next yere, as occasion needs.*
> *One seede for another, to make an exchange*
> *with fellowlie neighbourhood seemeth not strange.*

In the seventeenth century Ralph Austen likewise encourages generosity: 'Oh how sweet and pleasant is the fruit of those trees which a man hath planted and ordered with his owne hand, to gather it and largely and freely to bestow and distribute it among his kindred and friends.' He also sees this as the best way of defending an orchard:

> Above all, let those that have much fruit spare a part to them that have but little or none of their own, and be no niggards but liberate to their neighbours; and this bounty will bring a double blessing, first from God, to increase the fruits; secondly from men, not to diminish them.

In the 1890s Durham and Northumberland miners put forward a programme of land nationalisation, following earlier attempts at establishing communes by Owenites and Chartists. Their manifesto included 'the great ideal of living in perfect harmony in cooperative communities, each seeking the good of all and all seeking the good of each, broadly based upon the land'.

Allotments have traditionally been a centre of cooperative activity. They were introduced into urban areas such as Birmingham in the early eighteenth century, but were mainly developed at the beginning of the nineteenth century as an attempt to compensate people for the loss of their land through enclosure. In 1819 an Act of Parliament was passed permitting parishes to acquire land to provide plots for the poor to grow vegetables and 'for the promotion of industry among the poor'. The 1845 Enclosure Act provided for the allotment of part of the enclosed land as 'field gardens' for the labouring poor, and for recreation. In 1908 the Allotment Act made it obligatory for all local councils to provide allotments, and this still stands under the 1950 Allotments Act.

They were basically a paternalistic project to provide for the poor and to reduce the poor rate. Allotments were also meant to stop the labourers drinking, as Reverend H. Munn illustrates in a circular he sent to his allotment tenants: 'They are intended to improve the conditions of the labourers and their families, giving them employment in the summer evenings, increasing their supply of food, and withdrawing them from the influence of the public-house.' A similar point is made in *The Penny Magazine* of 1845: 'The objective of making these allotments is moral rather than economic; the cultivation of a few flowers is a pleasing occupation and has a tendency to keep a man at home and from the ale house.' The Report of the Parliamentary Committee on the Labouring Poor of 1843 also makes this objective clear: 'The possession of an allotment has been the means of reclaiming the criminal, reforming the dissolute, and of changing their whole moral character and conduct.'

From a radical political perspective, allotments and gardens could be seen as a palliative, preventing workers from engaging in

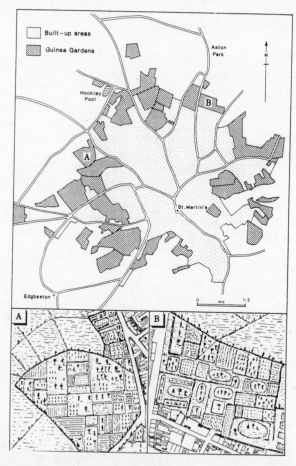

A plan of the 'guinea gardens' in Birmingham, 1824–5, from The Thorpe Report *of 1969. These allotments, with an annual rent of a guinea, began in the eighteenth century and were largely used by members of the lower middle class.*

political struggle. In Disraeli's novel *Sybil*, published in 1845, Field the Chartist says of Trafford the factory owner: 'He is a most inveterate Capitalist and would divert the minds of the people from the Five Points by allotting them gardens and giving them baths.' Bishop Hatton, ridiculed by Disraeli as a drunken supporter of the Charter, adds: 'We will have no more gardens in England; everything shall be open.'

Many farmers objected to allotments for fear of losing their labourers. The Report of the Poor Law Commission in 1834 presents their argument: 'We can do little or nothing to prevent pauperism; the farmers will have it: they prefer that the labourers should be slaves; they object to their having gardens, saying: The more they work for themselves, the less they work for us.' Taking account of this view, the 1843 Report on the Labouring Poor declared that, since the allotment should not become an inducement for the holder to neglect his usual work, it 'should be of no greater extent than can be cultivated during the leisure moments of the family'.

On the other hand allotments also provided the opportunity for cooperation, self-help and survival. A struggle was necessary to gain the rights in the various acts, and is still necessary today to protect those rights. In November 1988, after the Labour Party had won a ward by-election in Nottingham, John Peck, the only communist on the council, found himself holding the balance of power. He said he would ensure a Labour administration took over, but on condition that they supported his motion to 'stop industry bulldozing 300 allotments'.

During the two world wars allotments became essential to the war effort. In the First World War they rose from about half a million in 1913 to one and a half million by the end of the war. In the Second World War numbers nearly doubled from about 815,000 in England and Wales in 1939 to about 1,500,000 in 1945, when 4,000 local societies were affiliated to the National Society of Allotment and Leisure Gardeners. In 1988 the number of affiliations stood at only 1,378 representing 100,341 members, but in the same year the allotment movement was seen to be growing again for the first time since the Second World War. In that year there were about half a million allotment holders. They have to be ever vigilant, however, for even on statutory, protected sites allotments are continually under threat. In 1987 the National Society was approached by over 60 local societies objecting to proposed changes of land use which threatened their allotments.

MENTAL AND MANUAL LABOUR

The division between those who own gardens and those who work in them has often been in evidence. So too has the split between those who do the mental work of planning and design and those who carry out the manual labour of digging and planting, pruning and weeding. Abolition of this division of labour has sometimes been attempted in revolutionary periods.

William Dell, an army chaplain in the New Model Army, wanted to see universities or colleges set up in every city in the country, through which students could work their way whilst still living at home. He had a vision of schools and universities where both intellectual and manual labour would be combined. This idea was behind Marx's proposals for polytechnic education and was also incorporated into the educational programme of the Paris Commune. Similarly in Cuba, the schools in the country combine the theory and practice of gardening.

In Thomas Hardy's *The Return of the Native*, Clym Yeobright wants to alter the class division between intellectual and physical labour: 'He wished to raise the class at the expense of individuals rather than individuals at the expense of the class.' This leads him to leave fashionable Paris and instead cut furze on the Wessex heath while preparing to become a teacher: 'The monotony of his occupation soothed him, and was in itself a pleasure.' It seems strange that monotonous manual work can be soothing and pleasurable, for when it is alienated wage labour which people are obliged to do, it is usually deadening. But gardeners who voluntarily sweat over their gardens, even doing weeding, know that the activity can be fulfilling. If planning, execution, and appreciating the result are all done by the same people, the alienation can disappear.

Wordsworth wrote a poem called 'To the Spade of a Friend'. It was 'composed while we were labouring in his pleasure-ground'. Here again labour and pleasure are seen as united:

> *Thou art a tool of honour in my hands;*
> *I press thee, through the yielding soil, with pride.*

As well as bridging the division of labour, gardening can also unite the academic and the popular. Most gardeners are self-taught or have learnt from other gardeners, not from an educational institution. At the same time gardening is an opening into many relevant academic worlds which can be seen to have practical and theoretical purpose, for example botany, anthropology, linguistics, sociology, history, chemistry, literature, politics, ecology, art, architecture – to name but a few. It is unfortunate that the last two, art and architecture, have sometimes dominated the history of gardening, with their high cultural veneer proving often very exclusive.

Work and Leisure

Gardening also provides a link between the separate spheres of work and leisure. These are so distinct in our culture that it seems strange that people should enjoy work and want to prolong it. A survey in 1948 showed that Aborigines in Arnhem Land collected food every day, whereas if they wished they could have collected enough yams or fish to last for several days. This was because they enjoyed the food expeditions as they were social outings in which much time was spent in talking and resting. Margaret McArthur, observing the women, saw no sign that they disliked their work, no sign that the walking and digging and carrying was seen as 'either monotonous or as drudgery'.

A similar combination of work and pleasure is recorded in James Douglas's *Hardy Florists' Flowers*. In his introduction to the book, Francis Horner looks back to the early part of the nineteenth century:

> There yet stands many an old house, deeply embedded in a town, that used to have its garden – oftentimes a florist's. Here, for instance, is the very window – curiously long and lightsome – at which a handloom weaver worked behind his loom, able to watch his flowers as closely as his work – his labour and his pleasure intermingled, interwoven as intimately as his silken threads. But the mill may have supplanted his patient hand-machine, and brickwork swallowed up his garden.

Cobbett would have sympathised with this view. Since childhood he had enjoyed the hard work of making a garden:

> From my infancy, from the age of six years, when I climbed up the side of a steep sand-rock, and there scooped me out a plot four feet square to make me a garden, and the soil for which I carried up in

273

the bosom of my little blue smock-frock (or hunting shirt), I have never lost one particle of my passion for these healthy and rational and heart-cheering pursuits, in which every day presents something new, in which the spirits are never suffered to flag and in which industry, skill and care are sure to meet with their due reward. I have never, for any eight months together, during my whole life, been without a garden.

He said of gardening: 'There is no part of the business which first or last I have not performed with my own hands.' Cobbett also managed to combine a love of gardening with an enthusiasm for radical political campaigning.

The challenge and hard work in making a garden, as well as delight in the results, are nowhere better expressed than by Gervase Markham in 1613. In *The English Husbandman* he argues that gardens are easy to make where the soil is rich and fertile, as in the south of England, but up in the Peak District it is a different matter:

> When I behoulde upon a barraine, dry and deserted earth, such as the Peake-hills, where a man may behould snow all summer, or on the East-mores, whose best hearbage is nothing but mosse, and iron stone, in such a place, I say, to behoulde a delicate, rich, and fruitful garden, it shewes great worthiness in the owner, and infinite Art and industry in the workeman, and makes us both admire and love the begetters of such excellencies.

A contemporary of Markham's, and possibly a friend, as their books were often published bound together, was William Lawson, a Yorkshireman. In *A New Orchard and Garden*, published in 1618, he writes specifically for 'North Countryfolk' and the first chapter is entitled 'Of the Gardener, and his Wages'. Lawson concludes: 'If you bee not able, nor willing to hyre a gardner, keepe your profites to your selfe, but then you must take all the paines.' But later on he vividly expresses the joy in gardening:

> For it is not to be doubted: but as God hath given man things profitable: so hath he allowed him honest comfort, delight and recreation in all the works of his hands. Nay, all his labours under the Sunne without this are troubles, and vexation of minde: for what is greedy gaine without delight? but moyling, and turmoyling in slavery? But comfortable delight, with content, is the good of everything, and the patterne of heaven. And who can deny, but the principall end of an Orchard is the honest delight of one wearied with the worke of his lawful calling? The very works of, and in an Orchard and Garden, are better than the ease and rest of and from other labours.

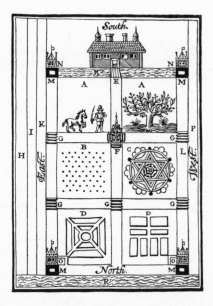

Lawson's plan of a garden from A New Orchard and Garden, *1618. Squares A and B are for fruit trees, C is a knot garden, and D is the kitchen garden.*

USE AND BEAUTY

As a tenant farmer at Tew Lodge in Oxfordshire from 1808 to 1811, Loudon wished the farm to be practical and profitable, but also wanted gardens and picturesque scenery to be included in the agricultural landscape. He argued against Humphrey Repton, the famous landscape gardener of the late eighteenth century, who maintained that it was ridiculous to try to achieve visual harmony between the profitable working farm and the landscape park. For Loudon, tilling the land should beautify it, not disfigure it. The farmer should be a landscape gardener, and labour should be invested with beauty.

Like Vita Sackville-West over a century later, Loudon came to believe that beauty and use ought to be united: 'To unite the agreeable with the useful is an object common to all the departments of gardening.' As John Parkinson put it in the 1620s: 'Herbs are for use and delight.' And Celia Fiennes liked to see 'ornament

275

and use' combined, when 'dwarfe fruit trees and flowers and greenes in all shapes' were intermixed with her favourite strawberries.

Loudon's Tew Lodge Farm was also an educational experiment where agricultural students could learn about rural affairs, gardening, planting, architecture, political economy and statistics. Loudon led field trips to other farms and landscape gardens and gave lectures on the site, sometimes under a spreading oak or in the shelter of a hedge – occasionally even on horseback. Tew Lodge Farm was in effect England's first agricultural college.

Gardening is clearly not free from the cash-nexus, but it can well illustrate the possibility of combining beauty with use, rather than with exchange value and profit. Cobbett wrote in *The American Gardener* in 1821: 'For my part, as a thing to keep and not to sell; as a thing, the *possession* of which is to give me pleasure, I hesitate not a moment to prefer the plant of a fine carnation, to a gold watch set with diamonds.'

In Marge Piercy's utopian novel *Woman on the Edge of Time* this combination of use and beauty is symbolised in the mixing of

Carnations and pinks from Lyte's A Nievve Herball *of 1578.*

vegetables and flowers and the integration of the gardens with·the buildings: 'Small gardens ran right among the clumps of buildings, vegetables and flowers intermixed, tomato plants growing with rosebushes and onions, pansies and bean plants. Some were planted in open borders and some were surrounded by a thin shimmery fence like spiderweb.'

Young and old work together in the gardens, combining intellectual and manual work:

In one of the spiderweb gardens an old man with a bush of white hair and a gnarled face, arms like driftwood scoured by salt and wind, was picking peas into a basket and weeding into another, with two kids of nine or ten working on either side.

'How come they aren't in school?' she asked. 'Is school out already for the summer?'

'That *is* school,' Luciente said, drawing Connie nearer to them.

'This one is lamb's-quarters, no?' one kid was asking.

'Can you eat it?'

'Fasure.'

'Look at the shape of the pea flowers. Most legumes have irregular flowers with five petals – see, the two lower ones join in a keel, like the keel on the fishing boats. The two at the sides are like spread wings. Then you have one on top. Most legumes have leaves like these.'

'Alternate. Compound. With these twisty things that hold on?'

'Tendrils. Some have thorns instead. After we're done weeding, we'll look for a tree that's evolved in a typical legume way, that has thorns a couple of inches long.' His fingers showed the size.

As they strolled on, she said, 'But they can't possibly learn as much that way as they would in a classroom with a book!'

'They can read. We all read by four or so,' Jackrabbit said. 'But who wants to grow up with a head full of facts in boxes? We never leave school and go to work. We're always working, always studying. We think, what person thinks person knows has to be tried out all the time. Placed against what people need. We care a lot *how* things are done.'

The idea of 'producing' a public garden, not just 'consuming' it, was behind the setting up in May 1987 of the Culpeper Community Garden in Islington, in the centre of London. Its intention was to provide 'local people who were without a garden, with an opportunity to work together collectively, or individually by way of having their own plots, to create a public garden under community management'.

277

Pollution and Conservation

Since the Clean Air Acts of 1956 and 1968, pollution in the garden has come not so much from smoke as from lead and certain pesticides, such as diazinon and calomel, or mercurous chloride, which are still used, despite being officially banned in EEC countries. Lead pollution has been aggravated by the slow introduction of unleaded petrol, only one per cent of total sales in 1988, though the percentage increased sharply in 1989 with the sudden rise in green consciousness. Also transport policies, for instance stopping local authorites charging cheap bus fares, have led to more traffic on the roads.

In 1989 all land in inner London was contaminated by lead, coming mainly from vehicle exhaust-pipes. In some areas levels were ten times higher than the government guidelines, according to a London Scientific Services survey of 20 London boroughs. This led Southwark Environmental Health Department to write to all its 800 allotment holders warning that lead levels were so high that they should think carefully about the kinds of foodstuffs they grow. Popular allotment crops like lettuces, cabbages and blackberries contained up to seven times the government's accepted levels for lead and were unfit for human consumption.

Another common form of pollution is that of litter and graffiti. Philips Park and Queen's Park, in run-down areas of north

Philips Park, Manchester, 1989.

Manchester, are full of graffiti, some of it racist. Along with Peel Park, now situated next to Salford University, they contain disused games areas, such as the bowling green, and swings with the swings missing. Next to the once famous flower-beds in Philips Park stands a burnt out wreck of a car. There has also been a proposal to disband the park police, with the consequent threat to the safety of women and children.

Comparing the public squalor of the Manchester parks with the private affluence exuding from the Birmingham Botanical Gardens makes a stunning commentary on the Thatcherite enterprise culture of the 1980s.

Awareness of environmental pollution has led to a growing ecological movement concerned with conservation. In 1981 the London Wildlife Trust was founded and has become a major force for nature conservation in London. It has been responsible for the creation or protection of over 30 nature reserves across the capital. At the back of King's Cross Station, the trust runs Camley Street Natural Park, two acres of open space which includes a large pond, marshland, young woodland, scrub and wildflower meadow. They provide a natural environment for birds, bees, butterflies, frogs and toads, as well as a rich variety of plant life. Over 150 species of flowering plants have been found in the park. They include broomrape, now rare in the countryside, hairy buttercup and American bur-marigold, all of which have arrived independently in the park.

There are facilities for school groups and the visiting area also contains changing displays and visiting exhibitions. Over 5,000 inner-city children use the park each year and there have also been visitors from Russia, East and West Germany, Italy, Malaysia, South Korea, the USA and Canada. The whole park is threatened, however, by the massive King's Cross development which is taking place.

Similarly in Hackney, in East London, the London Wildlife Trust works to protect wild plants and animals and to promote visits to areas like Victoria Park, which is described as

a large park with many mature trees and shrubs. The older trees provide nesting sites for tawny owls and great spotted woodpeckers. Kestrels may occasionally be seen hunting for small mammals in the grassland and on summer evenings bats fly over the lakes feeding on moths and other insects.

Internationally one of the key conservation issues is the practice of digging up and exporting bulbs from the wild. *Gardening from Which?* in September 1989 claimed that in the previous ten years Turkey exported 20 million cyclamen, 71 million anemone corms and 111 million aconites. Unlike the sixteenth-century Turkish trade in cultivated species, these bulbs were largely collected from the wild. The answer, according to the magazine, is for suppliers to grow their own bulbs or buy from wholesalers who do.

THE GARDEN CITY

The split between town and country, which became so acute in the nineteenth century, has often been represented as a contrast between sophistication and simple-mindedness, between progress and backwardness. Or the country is seen as natural and innocent, the city as artificial and corrupt; the country as the past, the city as the future. Many utopias, or dystopias, are projections of urban trends, for example the science fiction of H.G. Wells or George Orwell's *1984*.

To counter the urban nightmare of industrial capitalism, the idea of the garden city was developed. Between the wars, Alfred Salter, Labour MP for Bermondsey in south London, campaigned for every working-class house to have a garden, a demand which was disastrously forgotten in the 1960s when so many high-rise flats were built. As Crouch and Ward point out:

> The majority of the houses built in the twenty years between the wars, both by local authorities and by speculative builders, were laid out to the formula of 'twelve to the acre' which had been 'woven into the law' by the Garden City architect Raymond Unwin, whose convictions dominated the Tudor Walters Report of 1918. This was a lower density than that of the bye-law housing typical of the period between 1875 and 1914, and was certainly lower than that of almost all the housing built, whether publicly or privately, after the Second World War. It was deliberately intended to meet most families' gardening ambitions, and it did.

The idea of the garden city goes back at least to the seventeenth century when John Evelyn wanted London to be surrounded with plots of 30 to 40 acres, bordered with 'such shrubs as yield the most fragrant and odoriferous flowers'. He includes honeysuckle, jasmine, roses, lavender, rosemary, pinks, carnations, primroses, violets, lilies, daffodils and many others, along with a list of herbs. The air would be 'perpetually fanned' from all these fragrant shrubs and flowers, and 'the whole City would be sensible of the sweet and ravishing varieties of the perfumes'.

In the early eighteenth century Thomas Fairchild commented on the popularity of gardens in London: 'I find that almost every Body will have something of a Garden at any rate.' His book *The City Gardener* was written to help those living in cities to 'delight themselves in Gardening'. He describes some of the plants flowering in London courtyards: lilac, jasmine, lilies, pinks, daisies, French marigolds, angelica, scarlet lychnis and wallflowers. Flowering currants grew in tavern-yards and even 'on the tops of the houses amidst the Chimneys'. Balconies were adorned with apple trees grown in large pots.

Children collecting chestnuts in Kensal Green Cemetery, 1989.

In the more devastated urban setting of the nineteenth century, John Loudon tried to plan a gardening environment for the city, including public parks and garden cemeteries. Kensal Green Cemetery is still used today for burials and also as a public park. When I visited it in the autumn of 1989, a group of children were collecting chestnuts to play conkers. They were also observing the headstones and new graves, discussing death and satanism. A girl told me she would not want to bury her mother there as it was a 'bit too tatty'. Earlier in the year these children had picked raspberries in the cemetery near the banks of the canal. Loudon would surely have approved, just as he would have liked the cemetery near the centre of Sheffield which is now used as a public garden.

A Sheffield cemetery now used as a public park.

In 1829 Loudon published a plan for concentric green belts in London, as an alternative to the random speculative building being carried out on the outskirts of the city. He argued for a representative municipal body for London with power to plan the city and its suburbs. The idea came from his visit to Bavaria where a government commission had powers to improve public buildings, gardens and forests. Such a body was eventually created in 1889, the London County Council, later the Greater London Council, only to be abolished by the Conservative government nearly a century later in 1986.

Marx and Engels thought that the housing problem could never be solved while 'modern big cities' existed, and that only socialism could restore 'the intimate connection between industrial and agricultural production'. Engels writes of socialism 'abolishing the contrast between town and country, which has been brought to its extreme point by present-day capitalist society'. Ruskin too envisaged cities ringed by gardens.

In 1893 Robert Blatchford, under the influence of William Morris rather than Marx or Engels, put forward his vision of socialism in *Merrie England*, a book which sold nearly a million copies. Like Engels he attacked the 'forty thousand houses unfit for inhabitation' in Manchester: 'The houses are ugly and mean. The streets are too narrow. There are no gardens. There are no trees.' All towns had a 'deficiency of common-land, of open spaces'. So he argued for public parks and 'public gardens for recreation and music and refreshment', all free of charge. His utopia is one of 'towns rebuilt with wide streets, with detached houses, with gardens and fountains and avenues of trees'.

Blatchford uses images of flowers and fruit to indicate the state of the country and what people could be like:

> The question is whether human nature is bad. We must begin by asking under what circumstances? Will a peach tree bear peaches? Yes, if planted in good soil and against a south wall. Will a rose tree flourish in England? Not if you set it in an ash-heap and exclude the light and air. Is a river a beautiful and a wholesome thing? Yes, when it is fed by the mountain streams, washed by the autumn rains, and runs over a pebbly bed, between grassy meadows, decked with water lilies, fringed with flowering rushes, shaded by stately trees; but not when it is polluted by city sewers, stained by the refuse of filthy dye vats and chemical works.

In 1898 Ebenezer Howard's *Tomorrow; a Peaceful Path to Social Reform* was published, to be reissued in 1902 with a change of title as *Garden Cities of Tomorrow*. The garden city movement was born. In 1903 the land was bought for a registered company, First Garden City Limited, and the building of Letchworth began. Howard was influenced by Ruskin and Robert Owen and he envisaged new towns of 30,000 inhabitants: 'Town and country *must be married*, and out of this joyous union will spring a new hope, a new life, a new civilisation.'

In this century Edward Hyams puts a convincing argument against high-density housing by showing that 'garden activity declines in proportion to the density of housing' and that 'cottage and suburban and council house gardens are not less but more efficient food producers than farms or market gardens'. He refers to a survey carried out in 1956 by Wye College, the agricultural and horticultural college of London University, which indicated that the output of food from an acre of land covered with houses and small gardens at the usual working-class housing estate

283

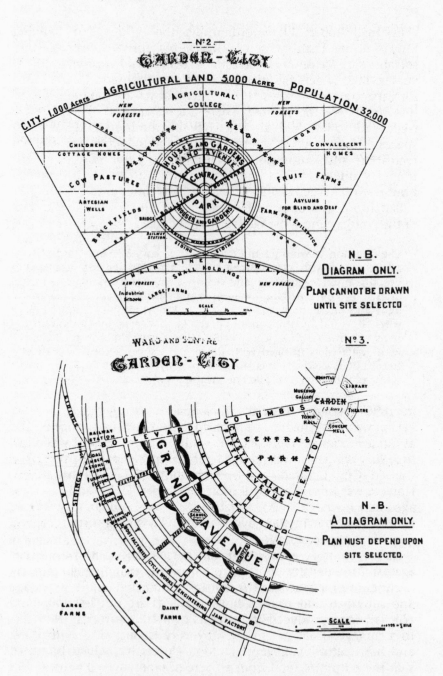

Ebenezer Howard's designs for a garden city, 1898.

density, is almost equal to that from an acre of the best farmland entirely given over to the plough, and better than that from an acre of average quality farmland. In 1944, when everyone was encouraged to grow vegetables, 10 per cent of all the food produced in Britain came from people's gardens and allotments. In 1963 in the USSR, 50 per cent of the country's vegetables came from private plots, though they consisted of only 4 per cent of the total arable land. In 1985 the state had a register of over 5 million allotment-holders, producing each year over a million tons of fruit and vegetables.

CLOUSDEN HILL

In 1895 the Clousden Hill Free Communist and Cooperative Colony was set up just outside Newcastle upon Tyne by a small international group of anarchist communists. The idea was similar to that of the Chartist land colonies of the 1840s, organised by people like Feargus O'Connor. The Clousden Hill colonists were influenced by William Morris and the Russian anarchist Kropotkin who maintained that vineyards could be constructed in Durham heated by local coal. He also wanted to 'grow oranges and lemons and bananas as well as tomatoes, just to prove how wonderfully full of colour we could make the coal-mining areas if only we gave the miners full opportunity to use the coal they bring up from the depths'.

Following Kropotkin's advice, the members of the Clousden Hill Colony built greenhouses and used modern fertilisers. Work was voluntary and, as Kropotkin had predicted, hard. They often worked an average of 19 hours a day, including Sundays. Four acres were intensively cultivated, growing peas, cauliflowers, cabbages, celery and carrots. There were 120 apple trees, 25 cherry trees, 2,000 berry and currant bushes, and a quarter of an acre of strawberries. Flowers were also grown, as Nigel Todd recounts in his book *Roses and Revolutionists*: 'Flowers were extremely popular, with large sales of chrysanthemums, orchids (grown by a Colonist from Brussels), and roses were the "speciality of the Colony which had 3–4,000 rose trees."'

By 1898 conflicting political views were beginning to lead to the break up of the Colony. Jim Connell, however, writing in the *Labour Leader*, sums up his impressions after a visit in 1897:

285

I came away feeling how much more enjoyable and healthy is a life led among plants and flowers than the long-drawn-out agony of those who suffer in the mill or the mine There is talk of starting other colonies, to be run on the same lines in the Midlands and the South. If these come to anything, many of us may yet enjoy the romance of rose culture and the poetry of potatoe planting.

The site at Clousden Hill is still being used for allotments.

WILLIAM MORRIS

Clousden Hill was dependent on the financial help received from sympathisers. One of the groups that sent money was the Hammersmith Socialist Society, to which William Morris belonged. Morris put forward his idea of utopia in *News From Nowhere*, but he is no utopian, in the sense in which Engels uses the word, but a revolutionary socialist. In England he observes that the 'cottage-gardens are bright with flowers', but sees through the 'pretty sight' of the 'hayfield' to the exploitation behind it, which is very similar to that of the cities. However in an article entitled 'Under an Elm-Tree; or Thoughts in the Countryside', published in *Commonweal* in 1889, he writes of what it could be like if the land were worked cooperatively:

> Suppose the haymakers were friends working for friends on land which was theirs, as many as were needed, with leisure and hope ahead of them instead of hopeless toil and anxiety, need their useful labour for themselves and their neighbours cripple and disfigure them?

When Morris signed his membership card of the Democratic Federation, he wrote one word on it, 'Designer', which for him referred to both mental and manual processes. He wanted to maintain the unity of the design process, between drawing-board and loom, and create a workshop where work would be enjoyable. The patterns he designed for fabrics and wallpapers nearly all contain flowers: 'I must have unmistakable suggestions of gardens and fields, and strange trees, boughs, and tendrils.'

In *News From Nowhere* Morris attacks the division of labour. His Yorkshire weaver alternates weaving and mathematics with being a boatman ferrying people across the river. Work is pleasure, especially the 'pleasantest of all work – cultivating the earth'. Schools are abolished and learning comes from activity and experience. The difference between town and country grows less and less. Manchester has disappeared.

The most striking contrast is in London. In his poem 'Earthly Paradise', written in 1870, Morris has already seen an image of a different city:

And dream of London, small, and white, and clean,
The clear Thames bordered by its gardens green.

William Morris (1834–96), photographed by Abel Lewis, 1880.

In *News From Nowhere* he describes the 'squalor' of London in the nineteenth century with its 'hideous hovels'. It is 'ugly' and 'shabby', a 'sordid loathsome place'. Instead of the 'sweet scents' of the countryside 'one gets an extra smell of dirt'. After the revolution, all the pollution has gone, including the 'grimy sootiness which I was used to on every London building more than a year old'. The noise has also disappeared: 'The soap-works with their smoke-vomiting chimneys were gone; the engineer's works gone;

the lead-works gone; and no sound of riveting and hammering came down the west wind from Thorneycroft's.' In their place are countless trees and gardens. London has been changed into a series of small towns and villages. There is a continuous stretch of woodland from Kensington, through Paddington, Notting Hill, Primrose Hill, Kingsland, Stoke Newington and Clapton to Epping Forest, near where Morris was born in Walthamstow. The woods are made up of oaks, sweet chestnuts, planes and sycamores.

A similar scheme was envisaged by Abercrombie in his 1944 proposals for 24 green wedges to bring the green belt into London. He planned, for example, to join up Primrose Hill to Hampstead Heath and Mill Hill.

Epping Forest played an important part in Morris's vision. As a boy he knew every yard of it, with its pollarded hornbeams and holly thickets. In a letter to the *Daily Chronicle* in 1895 he expresses concern at the suggestion that it may be turned into a landscape garden or a golf course. He attacks the committee of experts formed to sit in judgement on Epping Forest:

> An 'expert' may be a very dangerous person, because he is likely to narrow his views to the particular business (usually a commercial one) which he represents. In this case, for instance, we do not want to be under the thumb of either a wood bailiff, whose business is to grow timber for the market, or of a botanist whose business is to collect specimens for a botanical garden; or of a landscape gardener whose business is to vulgarize a garden or landscape to the utmost extent that his patron's purse will allow of.

In utopia England is a garden. London has gardens down to the river's edge with flowers 'blooming luxuriantly, and sending delicious waves of summer scent over the eddying stream'. Each house is surrounded by a 'teeming garden', 'carefully cultivated and running over with flowers'. The garden trees are all fruit trees, 'except for a bay here and there, and occasional groups of limes'.

In the heart of London, the Houses of Parliament are now called Dung Market and are used as a 'storage place for manure'. And Trafalgar Square, where in 1887 Morris was present on 'Bloody Sunday', has been transformed. He describes what it was like that November day with the police guarding it against the demonstration of the unemployed, and how it has changed:

A strange sensation came over me; I shut my eyes to keep out the sight of the sun glittering on this fair abode of gardens, and for a moment there passed before them a phantasmagoria of another day. A great space surrounded by tall ugly houses, with an ugly church at the corner and a nondescript ugly cupolaed building at my back; the roadway thronged with a sweltering and excited crowd, dominated by omnibuses crowded with spectators. In the midst a paved befountained square, populated only be a few men dressed in blue, and a good many singularly ugly bronze images (one on top of a tall column). The said square guarded up to the edge of the roadway by a fourfold line of big men clad in blue, and across the southern roadway the helmets of a band of horse-soldiers, dead white in the greyness of the chilly November afternoon –

I opened my eyes to the sunlight again and looked round me, and cried out among the whispering trees and odorous blossoms, 'Trafalgar Square!'

Afterword

Unbounded freedom ruled the wandering scene;
No fence of ownership crept in between
To hide the prospect from the gazing eye;
Its only bondage was the circling sky.

John Clare (1793–1864) 'The Moors'

To see a World in a Grain of Sand
And a Heaven in a Wild Flower,
Hold Infinity in the palm of your hand
And Eternity in an hour.

William Blake (1757–1827) 'Auguries of Innocence'

Many books on the history of gardening contain ideological premises which are not made explicit, and the authors rarely take issue with other writers in the same field. It is as if a consensus existed on the main topics. One purpose of this book has been to open up areas for discussion, to write from an explicit political position and to see where others stand in the political spectrum. The obvious example is that of the plant hunters, who are everywhere portrayed as the heroes of the garden story, but here have been shown in a different light. Each chapter in the book has dealt with such issues, which are politically controversial.

Much garden history concentrates on style and fashion. It looks at gardens throughout the ages and notes how they change, rarely linking these changes to political and economic events. Where connections are made, it is usually to the world of art and architecture. This is a very limited approach and confines garden history to the high cultural field of aesthetics.

Social historians hardly ever mention gardens or gardening, and garden historians have little to say generally about politics. A visit to Kew makes it clear that it is impossible to separate the many aspects of gardening history and exclude some from study. Kew Gardens are a microcosm of the many issues contained in this book. The lay-out of the gardens in the eighteenth century reflected the new landscape style, based on enclosure and owner-ship by the wealthy in the land. Directors of Kew sent out collectors to all corners of the world and made the gardens the centre of economic botany. When the gates were opened to the public, millions flocked there to enjoy the gardens. In 1895 women gardeners were first employed there and in 1913 suffra-gettes attacked the orchid houses and burnt down the tea pavilion. No one discipline can encompass such a wide variety of themes.

An aim of this book has been to try to show the connections between political, economic and social history and the history of gardening. The whole area of economic botany, for example, is thought by some to have nothing to do with garden history. Yet it should be apparent from the chapters on Banks, Fortune and Hooker that world-wide botanical exploration, geared to commer-cial exploitation and connected with the spread of the British Empire, is a crucial element in the development of our gardening culture.

In the same way the labour expended in creating gardens cannot be treated as peripheral, with the odd footnote here and there. It is fundamental, but it has largely been neglected. Far more emphasis has been put on design and ownership, with little discussion of the division of labour between mental and manual work. The main focus of garden history has also been on famous private gardens, with scant reference to public parks and town planning.

A visit to Mexico would seem the last place to excite an interest in English gardening. But the amazing accounts of Aztec gardening which were taken back to Spain provide the link with Europe, and within Europe the Arab influence helps explain the earlier diffusion of horticultural knowledge. No insular history of English gardening will suffice. Similarly Captain Cook's journey round the world is taught regularly in schools, usually omitting both its military aim and also its horticultural results.

This book is based on a love of gardening. It would have been difficult to follow all these stories if I had not myself dug and planted, pruned and weeded, harvested and consumed, sat and enjoyed a garden. This is one thing all gardening writers seem to share. But can gardening be seen as so separate from the rest of

COCOXOCHITL.

Aztec dahlia from Inventory of the Medicinal Resources of
New Spain *by Francisco Hernandez.*

our lives? It is this question that has led to these many avenues of inquiry and to the argument of this book.

The meanings of gardening in our culture are many and varied. There is no intention here to limit these by imposing one rigid interpretation, nor to undermine people's enjoyment of gardening. Rather it is a question of setting gardening in its social and political context, anchoring it in the real world, and enhancing an understanding of its history so that it can be more fully enjoyed.

Bibliography

Allan, Mea, *The Hookers of Kew 1785–1911* (Joseph 1967)
——, *Plants That Changed Our Gardens* (David & Charles 1974)
Amherst, Alicia (Evelyn Cecil), *A History of Gardening in England* (Quaritch 1895)
——, *London Parks and Gardens* (Archibald Constable 1907)
Anon, *The Language of Flowers* (Frederick Warne c.1880)
Arber, Agnes, *Herbals* (Cambridge University Press 1912)
Arens, W., *The Man-Eating Myth* (Oxford University Press, New York 1979)
Astell, Mary, *A Serious Proposal to the Ladies* (printed for R. Wilkin 1694; in ed.
    Bridget Hill, *The First English Feminist*, Gower/Maurice Temple Smith 1986)
Austen, Ralph, *A Treatise of Fruit-Trees* (for T. Robinson, Oxford 1653)
——, *Observations upon some part of Sir Francis Bacon's Naturall History* (H. Hall for T.
    Robinson, Oxford 1658)
Ballard, Phillada, *An Oasis of Delight, The History of The Birmingham Botanical
    Gardens* (Duckworth 1983)
Batey, Mavis, 'The Way to View Rousham by Kent's Gardener', *Garden History* , vol.
    11, no. 2 (1983)
Berrall, Julia S., *The Garden: An Illustrated History from Egypt to the Present Day*
    (Thames & Hudson 1966)
Blackwell, Elizabeth, *A Curious Herbal* (Samuel Harding 1737)
Blainey, Geoffrey, *Triumph of the Nomads* (Macmillan 1975)
Blatchford, Robert, *Merrie England* (Clarion Press 1893; Journeyman edn 1976)
Boccaccio, Giovanni, *The Decameron* (1350; Penguin edn 1972)
Boniface, Priscilla (ed.), *In Search of English Gardens* (Lennard Publishing 1987)
Bourdillon, Hilary, *Women as Healers* (Cambridge University Press 1988)
Bower, F.O., *Joseph Dalton Hooker* (SPCK 1919)
Boys, Philip, 'Saying it with Flowers', *Guardian* (21 May 1988)
Brecht, Bertolt, *Gesammelte Gedichte* (Suhrkamp 1976; *Poems 1913–1956*, Methuen
    edn 1976)
Brockway, Lucile H., *Science and Colonial Expansion: the Role of the British Royal
    Botanic Gardens* (Academic Press 1979)
Broome, Richard, *Aboriginal Australians* (George Allen & Unwin 1982)
Brown, Jane, *Vita's Other World* (Viking Penguin 1985)
Bunyan, John, *Pilgrim's Progress* (1678; Penguin edn 1965)
Bury, Mrs Edward, *A Selection of Hexandrian Plants* (R. Havell 1831–4)
Cameron, Hector Charles, *Sir Joseph Banks K.B., P.R.S., the Autocrat of the
    Philosophers* (Batchworth 1952)
Campanella, Thomas, *The City of the Sun* (1623; Journeyman edn 1981)
Carter, Tom, *The Victorian Garden* (Bell & Hyman 1984)
Chancellor, E. Beresford, *The Pleasure Haunts of London* (Constable 1925)

Chaplin, Mary, *Gardening for the Physically Handicapped and Elderly* (Batsford 1978)

Clare, John, *The Poems of John Clare* (J. M. Dent & Sons 1935)

Clark, Frank, 'Nineteenth-century Public Parks from 1830', *Garden History*, vol. 1, no. 3 (1973)

Cloet, Audrey and Underhill, Chris, *Gardening is for Everyone* (Souvenir Press 1982)

Coats, Alice M., *Flowers and Their Histories* (A. & C. Black Ltd. 1956)

——, *The Quest for Plants, A History of the Horticultural Explorers* (Studio Vista 1969)

——, *The Book of Flowers* (Phaidon 1973)

Coats, Peter, *Flowers in History* (Weidenfeld and Nicolson 1970)

Cobbett, William, *The American Gardener* (New York 1819; C. Clement, London 1821)

——, *Advice to Young Men* (printed by B. Bensley, Andover, published by the Author, London 1829)

——, *The English Gardener* (published by the Author, Andover 1829; Oxford University Press edn 1980)

——, *Rural Rides* (William Cobbett, London 1830; Penguin edn 1967)

Colburn, Nigel, 'A Singular Man: W. T. Stearn', *The Garden: Journal of the Royal Horticultural Society*, vol. 114, part 4 (1989)

Cole, Nathan, *The Royal Parks and Gardens of London* (Journal of Horticulture Office, London 1877)

Coles, William, *The Art of Simpling* (J.G. for Nath. Brook, London 1656)

Conway, Hazel, 'The Manchester/Salford Parks: Their Design and Development', *Journal of Garden History*, vol. 5, no. 3 (1977)

Cookson, Mrs, *Flowers Drawn and Painted After Nature in India* (1830)

Coombes, Allen J., *Dictionary of Plant Names* (Collingridge Books 1985)

Cowan, J.M., 'Cinchona in the Empire', *Empire Forestry Journal*, vol. 8, no. 1 (1929)

Cowell, Fiona, 'Richard Woods (?1716–93): A Preliminary Account', *Garden History*, vol. 15, no. 2 (1987)

Cowen, David L., 'The Boston Editions of Nicholas Culpeper', *Journal of the History of Medicine*, vol. 11 (1956)

Cowley, Abraham, *The Works of Mr Abraham Cowley* (ed. Thomas Sprat, J.M. for Henry Herringman, London 1668; Clarendon Press edn of Poetry and Prose 1949)

Creel, J. Randal, 'The Lost Beauty of Texcotzingo', *Garden Journal* (October 1972)

Crouch, David and Ward, Colin, *The Allotment: Its Landscape and Culture* (Faber & Faber 1988)

Culpeper, Nicholas, *A Directory for Midwives* (printed by Peter Cole, London 1651)

Curl, James Stevens, 'The Architecture and Planning of the Nineteenth-century Cemetery', *Garden History*, vol. 3, no. 3 (1975)

——, 'Spas and Pleasure Gardens of London, from the Seventeenth to the Nineteenth Centuries', *Garden History*, vol. 7, no. 2 (1979)

——, 'John Claudius Loudon and the Garden Cemetery Movement', *Garden History*, vol. 11, no. 2 (1983)

Darley, Gillian, *Villages of Vision* (Architectural Press 1975)

Davies, Andrew, *The People's Guide to London (Central and West End)* (Journeyman 1984)

Davies, Jennifer, *The Victorian Kitchen Garden* (BBC Books 1987)

de Beauvoir, Simone, *The Second Sex* (1949; English edition: Jonathan Cape 1953)

de Bray, Lys, *Manual of Old-Fashioned Shrubs* (Oxford Illustrated Press 1986)

Defoe, Daniel, *Tour through the Whole Island of Great Britain* (G. Strahan, etc., London 1724–6; Penguin edn 1971)

Delamer, E.S., The *Kitchen Garden* (Routledge 1855)

Desmond, Ray, 'Victorian Gardening Magazines', *Garden History*, vol. 5, no. 3 (1977)

Devonshire, Duchess of, *The Garden at Chatsworth* (Derbyshire Countryside 1987)

Dickens, Charles, *Appeal to Fallen Women* (1846)

——, 'Address to the Gardeners' Benevolent Institution' (14 June 1852; in Hammerton, J. A., *The Dickens Companion*, vol. XVIII, The Educational Book Co. Ltd 1910)

——, 'Home for Homeless Women', *Household Words* (23 April 1853)

Disraeli, Benjamin, *Sybil* (Henry Colburn 1845; Penguin edn 1967)

Dodge, Bertha S., *It Started in Eden: How the Plant-Hunters and the Plants They Found Changed the Course of History* (McGraw-Hill 1979)

Douglas, James, *Hardy Florists' Flowers* (William Cate 1880)

Duthie, Ruth E., 'Some Notes on William Robinson', *Garden History*, vol. 2, no. 3 (1974)

——, 'Florists' Societies and Feasts after 1750', *Garden History*, vol. 12, no. 1 (1984)

Dutton, Ralph, *The English Garden* (Batsford 1937)

Edgeworth, Maria and Richard Lovell, *Practical Education* (London 1798)

Ehrenreich, Barbara and English, Deirdre, *Witches, Midwives and Nurses: A History of Women Healers* (Compendium 1974)

Eliot, George, *Silas Marner* (William Blackwood & Sons 1861; Penguin edn 1967)

Elliott, Brent, *Victorian Gardens* (Batsford 1986)

——, 'Behind Barbed Wire', *The Garden: Journal of the Royal Horticultural Society*, vol. 113, part 11 (1988)

Elliott, Patricia, *The Garden and the Handicapped Child* (Disabled Living Foundation 1978)

Engels, Frederick, *The Conditions of the Working Class in England* (1845; Panther edn 1969)

Etlin, Richard A., 'Père Lachaise and the Garden Cemetery', *Journal of Garden History*, vol. 4, no. 3 (1984)

Evelyn, John, *The Diary of John Evelyn* (1641–1706; Clarendon Press edn 1955)

——, *Fumifugium: or The Inconveniencie of the aer and smoak of London dissipated* (Gabriel Bedel & Thomas Collins, London 1661)

Fairchild, Thomas, *The City Gardener* (T. Woodward, London 1722)

Fein, Albert, 'Victoria Park: Its Origins and History', *East London Papers*, vol. V, no. 2 (1962)

Fielding, Henry, *Joseph Andrews* (A. Millar, London 1742; Penguin edn 1977)

FitzHerbert, Anthony, *A new tracte or treatyse most profytable for All Husbandmen* (Rycharde Pynson, London 1523)

Fleet, Kathleen, *A Manual for Blind Gardeners* (RNIB 1978)

Fleming, Laurence and Gore, Alan, *The English Garden* (Michael Joseph 1979)

Fletcher, Harold R. and Brown, William H., *The Royal Botanic Garden Edinburgh 1670–1970* (HMSO 1970)

Fortune, Robert, *Three Years' Wanderings in the Northern Provinces of China* (John Murray 1847)

——, *A Journey to the Tea Countries of China* (John Murray 1852)

Gavin, Hector, *Sanitary Ramblings: Sketches and Illustrations of Bethnal Green* (J. Churchill, London 1848; Frank Cass & Co. Ltd edn 1971)

Glendinning, Victoria, *Vita* (Weidenfeld & Nicolson 1983)

Glenny, George, *Glenny's Garden Almanac* (Houlston & Stoneman 1848 and 1849)

Googe, Barnabe, *Foure Bookes of Husbandry* (translated and increased from the book by Conrad Heresbach, Printed by R. Watkins 1577)

Gore, Catherine G. F., *The Rose Fancier's Manual* (Henry Colburn, London 1838)

Gorer, Richard, *The Flower Garden in England* (Batsford 1975)

Gosse, P.H., *Wanderings through the Conservatories at Kew* (Society for Promoting Christian Knowledge 1856)

295

BIBLIOGRAPHY

Hadfield, Miles, *A History of British Gardening* (Hutchinson 1960)
Hadfield, Miles and John, *Gardens of Delight* (Cassell 1964)
Hagedorn, Rosemary, *Therapeutic Horticulture* (Winslow Press 1987)
Hall, Mrs S. C., 'A Day at Chatsworth', *The Art-Journal* (1851)
Hampton, Christopher (ed.), *A Radical Reader* (Penguin 1984)
Hardy, Thomas, *The Return of the Native* (Smith, Elder & Co., London 1878; Penguin edn 1978)
Hartlib, Samuel, *A Design for Plentie* (Printed for R. Wodenothe, London 1652)
Harvey, John H., 'Gardening Books and Plant Lists of Moorish Spain', *Garden History*, vol. 3, no. 2 (1975)
——, 'Turkey as a Source of Garden Plants', *Garden History*, vol. 4, no. 3 (1976)
——, *Medieval Gardens* (Batsford 1981)
——, 'The First English Garden Book', *Garden History*, vol. 13, no. 2 (1985)
——, 'Henry Daniel: A Scientific Gardener of the Fourteenth Century', *Garden History*, vol. 15, no. 2 (1987)
Hawkins, Roy, *Green London* (Sidgwick & Jackson 1987)
Hellyer, Arthur, 'Edgbastion's Bastion', *Country Life*, vol. 182 (November 1988)
Hepper, F. Nigel (ed.), *Plant Hunting for Kew* (HMSO 1989)
Hessayon, David, *The Armchair Book of the Garden* (pbi Publications 1986)
Hibberd, Shirley, *The Amateur's Flower Garden* (Groombridge & Sons 1871; Croom Helm edn 1986)
Hibbert, Christopher, *The English, A Social History 1066–1945* (Paladin 1988)
Hill, Christopher, *Intellectual Origins of the English Revolution* (Oxford University Press 1965)
—— (ed.), *Winstanley: The Law of Freedom and Other Writings* (Penguin 1973)
——, *The World Turned Upside Down* (Maurice Temple Smith 1972)
——, *A Turbulent, Seditious, and Factious People: John Bunyan and his Church 1628–1688* (Oxford University Press 1989)
Hobhouse, Henry, *Seeds of Change* (Sidgwick & Jackson 1985)
Hobsbawm, E. J., *Industry and Empire* (Penguin 1969)
——, *The Age of Empire* (Weidenfeld & Nicolson 1987)
Hooker, Joseph Dalton, *Himalayan Journals* (John Murray 1854)
Hopf, Alice L., 'From the New World', *Garden Journal* (December 1974)
Howard, Ebenezer, *Tomorrow; a Peaceful Path to Social Reform* (Swan Sonnenschein & Co., London 1898)
——, *Garden Cities of Tomorrow* (Swan Sonnenschein & Co., London 1902; Faber edn 1951)
Hunt, Leigh, *Autobiography* (Smith, Elder & Co., London 1850; Cresset Press edn 1949)
Huxley, Anthony J., *An Illustrated History of Gardening* (Paddington 1978)
——, *The Penguin Encyclopedia of Gardening* (Penguin 1983)
Huxley, Leonard, *Life and Letters of Sir Joseph Dalton Hooker* (John Murray 1918)
Hyams, Edward, *Great Botanical Gardens of the World* (Nelson 1969)
——, *Soil and Civilisation* (John Murray 1976)
——, *English Cottage Gardens* (Penguin 1987)
Idris, S. M. Mohamed, *Malaysian Consumers and Development* (Consumer Association of Penang 1986)
Ingrams, Richard (ed.), *Cobbett's Country Book* (David & Charles n.d.)
Jackson, Maria E., *The Florist's Manual* (Henry Colburn, London 1816)
Jacques, David and van der Horst, Arend Jan, *The Gardens of William and Mary* (Christopher Helm 1988)
Jekyll, Gertrude, 'The Idea of a Garden', *The Guardian* (1896)
——, *Wood and Garden* (Longmans 1899)

——, *Colour Schemes for the Flower Garden* (George Newnes 1908; Antique Collectors' Club edn 1982)

Johnson, George W., *A History of English Gardening* (Baldwin & Cradock, and Longman & Co. 1829)

Johnson, Louisa, *Every Lady Her Own Flower Gardener* (W. S. Orr & Co., London 1839)

Josselyn, John, *New England's Rarities Discovered* (G. Widdowes 1672)

Kay, George, *Allotment Gardens in Stoke-on-Trent* (Department of Geography and Recreation Studies, North Staffordshire Polytechnic 1988)

Keller, Helen, *The Story of My Life* (Collier Macmillan 1982)

King, Ronald, *The Quest for Paradise* (Whittet/Windward 1979)

Larwood, Jacob, *The Story of the London Parks* (Chatto & Windus 1881)

Lawrance, Mary, *A Collection of Roses from Nature* (Miss Lawrance, London 1799)

Lawrence, D. H., *Selected Essays* (Penguin 1950)

Lawson, William, *The Country House-wife's Garden* (printed for R. Jackson, London 1623)

——, *A New Orchard and Garden* (R. Aesop for R. Jackson, London 1618)

Leiper, Glenn, *Muturoo Plant Use by Australian Aboriginal People* (Eagleby South State School 1984)

Leith-Ross, Prudence, *The John Tradescants* (Peter Owen 1984)

Lemmon, Kenneth, *The Golden Age of Plant Hunters* (Phoenix 1968)

Lewis, Gwilym, *Postcards from Kew* (HMSO 1989)

Lipp, Frank J., 'A Heritage Destroyed: The Lost Gardens of Ancient Mexico', *Garden Journal* (December 1976)

Littlefield, Susan and Schinz, Marina, *Visions of Paradise* (Thames & Hudson 1985)

Lord, George de F., 'From Contemplation to Action: Marvell's Poetical Career', *Philological Quarterly*, vol. XLVI (1967)

Loudon, Jane, *Gardening for Ladies* (London 1840)

——, *The Ladies' Companion to the Flower Garden* (London 1841; William Smith 1844)

Loudon, John, *An Encyclopaedia of Gardening* (Longman 1822)

——, *An Encyclopaedia of Cottage, Farm, and Villa Architecture and Furniture* (Longman 1836)

Lyte, Charles, *Sir Joseph Banks* (David & Charles 1980)

Mabey, Richard, *Gilbert White* (Hutchinson 1986)

——, *The Complete New Herbal* (Elm Tree Books 1988)

——, *The Flowering of Kew* (Century Hutchinson 1988)

Mack, Maynard, *The Garden and the City* (University of Toronto Press 1969)

McLean, Teresa, *Medieval English Gardens* (Collins 1981)

MacLeod, Dawn, *Down to Earth Women* (Blackwood 1982)

Marcus, Jane (ed.), *The Young Rebecca: Writings of Rebecca West 1911–17* (Virago 1983)

Markham, Gervase, *The English Husbandman* (T. S. for J. Browne, London 1613–15)

Marvell, Andrew, *The Works of Andrew Marvell* (ed. Thomas Cooke, E. Curll, London 1726; *The Complete Poems* Penguin edn 1972)

Marx, Karl, *The German Ideology* (1846; Lawrence & Wishart edn 1938)

Mason, William, *The English Garden* (R. Horsfield, London 1772)

Massingham, Betty, 'William Robinson', *Garden History*, vol. 6, no. 1 (1978)

Mavor, Elizabeth, *The Ladies of Llangollen* (Michael Joseph 1971)

Milton, John, *Paradise Lost* (1667; Longmans edn 1968)

More, Thomas, *Utopia* (Louvain 1516; Penguin edn 1965)

Moriarty, Henrietta M., *Viridarium: Coloured Plates of Greenhouse Plants* (London 1806)

Morris, William, 'Under an Elm-Tree: or Thoughts in the Countryside', *Commonweal* (6 July 1889)

——, *The Collected Works of William Morris*, ed. May Morris (Longmans, Green, & Co., 1910–15)

——, *News From Nowhere* (Roberts Bros, Boston, Mass. 1890; Routledge & Kegan Paul edn 1970)

Morton, A. L. (ed.), *Political Writings of William Morris* (Lawrence & Wishart 1973)

——, *A People's History of England* (Lawrence & Wishart 1976)

Müllenbrock, Heinz-Joachim, 'The "Englishness" of the English Landscape Garden and the Genetic Role of Literature: a Reassessment', *Journal of Garden History*, vol. 8, no. 4 (1988)

Murray, Charlotte, *The British Garden* (Bath 1799)

O'Brian, Patrick, *Joseph Banks: a Life* (Collins Harvill 1987)

Olmsted, Frederick Law, *Walks and Talks of an American Farmer in England* (New York 1852)

Pankhurst, Sylvia, *The Suffragette Movement* (Longmans & Co. 1931; Virago edn 1977)

Parkinson, John, *Paradisi in Sole, Paradisus Terrestris* (H.Lownes & R. Young, London 1629; Methuen edn. 1904)

——, *Theatrum Botanicum* (T. Cotes 1640)

Penny, N. B., 'The Commercial Garden Necropolis of the Early Nineteenth Century and its Critics', *Garden History*, vol. 2, no. 3 (1974)

Pepys, Samuel, *The Diary of Samuel Pepys* (4 September 1666; ed. Robert Latham and William Matthews, G. Bell & Sons edn vol. VII 1972)

Pettigrew, W. W., *Municipal Parks* (Journal of Parks Administration, London 1937)

Piercy, Marge, *Woman on the Edge of Time* (Women's Press 1979)

Poulsen, Charles, *Victoria Park* (Journeyman 1976)

Poynter, F. N. L., 'Nicholas Culpeper and His Books', *Journal of the History of Medicine*, vol. 17 (1962)

Prescott, William H., *History of the Conquest of Mexico* (Routledge 1843)

Prest, John, *The Garden of Eden* (Yale University Press 1981)

Price, Uvedale, *An Essay on the Picturesque* (London, Hereford 1794–8)

Pugh, Simon, *Garden–Nature–Language* (Manchester University Press 1988)

Rackham, Oliver, *The History of the Countryside* (J. M. Dent 1986)

Robinson, William, *The Wild Garden* (John Murray 1870)

——, *God's Acre Beautiful* (The 'Garden' Office, London 1880)

——, *The English Flower Garden* (John Murray 1883)

Robley, Augusta J., *A Selection of Madeira Flowers* (Reeve Brothers 1845)

Rohde, Eleanour Sinclair, *The Old English Gardening Books* (Martin Hopkinson 1924)

——, *The Story of the Garden* (The Medici Society 1932)

——, *Shakespeare's Wild Flowers* (The Medici Society 1935)

Rolt, L. T. C., *Victorian Engineering* (Allen Lane 1970)

Roupell, Arabella Elizabeth, *Specimens of the Flora of South Africa by a Lady* (London 1849)

Rousseau, Jean Jacques, *Julie: ou La Nouvelle Héloïse* (Amsterdam 1761; Pennsylvania State University Press edn 1987))

——, *Émile* (Amsterdam 1762; Heinemann edn 1956)

——, *Letters on the Elements of Botany Addressed to a Lady* (Translated by Thomas Martyn, London 1785)

Rowbotham, Sheila, *Women, Resistance and Revolution* (Penguin 1972)

——, *Hidden from History* (Pluto 1973)

Rowson, N. J. and Thoday, P. R., *Landscape Design for Disabled People in Public Open Space* (University of Bath 1985)

Ruskin, John, 'The Mysteries of Life and Its Arts', Lecture in Dublin 1868, added to *Sesame and Lilies* in 1871; in John D. Rosenberg (ed.), *The Genius of John Ruskin* (George Allen & Unwin 1963)

——, *The Works of John Ruskin* (ed. E.T. Cook and Alexander Wedderburn, George Allen 1903–12)

Sackville-West, Vita, *The Land* (Heinemann 1926)

——, *Sissinghurst* (Hogarth Press 1931)

——, *The Garden* (Michael Joseph 1946)

Sanecki, Kay N., *Old Garden Tools* (Shire Publications 1979)

Scharf, Aaron, *Art and Industry* (Open University 1971)

Schuyler, David, 'The Evolution of the Anglo-American Rural Cemetery', *Journal of Garden History*, vol. 4, no. 3 (1984)

Scott-James, Anne, *Sissinghurst* (Michael Joseph 1975)

—— and Lancaster, Osbert, *The Pleasure Garden* (John Murray 1977)

Scourse, Nicolette, *The Victorians and Their Flowers* (Croom Helm 1983)

Seager, Joni and Olsen, Ann, *Women in the World* (Pan 1986)

Sedding, John Dando, *Garden-Craft Old and New* (Kegan Paul, Trench, Trübner & Co. 1891)

Sexby, J. J., *The Municipal Parks, Gardens, and Open Spaces of London* (Elliot Stock 1898)

Shenstone, William, 'Unconnected Thoughts on Gardening', *The Works in Verse and Prose of William Shenstone* (G. Faulkner, Dublin 1764)

Shoard, Marion, *This Land is Our Land* (Paladin 1987)

Simo, Melanie L., 'John Claudius Loudon: On Planning and Design for the Garden Metropolis', *Garden History*, vol. 9, no. 2 (1981)

——, *Loudon and the Landscape* (Yale University Press 1988)

Smiles, Samuel, *Self Help* (London 1859; Sphere Books edn 1968)

Smith, Charles H.J., *Parks and Pleasure Grounds* (Reeve & Co. 1852)

Smith, Edward, *The Life of Sir Joseph Banks* (John Lane 1911)

Stearn, William T., 'The Chelsea Physic Garden', *Garden History*, vol. 3, no. 2 (1975)

——, *Botanical Latin* (David & Charles 1983)

Stow, John, *Survey of London* (J. Wolfe 1598; Dent edn 1956)

Strang, John, *Necropolis Glasguensis* (Atkinson, Glasgow 1831)

Stuart, David, *The Garden Triumphant: A Victorian Legacy* (Viking Penguin 1988)

Taboroff, June, '"Wife, unto Thy Garden": The First Gardening Books For Women', *Garden History*, vol. 11, no. 1 (1983) ·

Taverner, John, *Certaine Experiments Concerning Fish and Fruite* (printed by R. Field for W. Ponsonby 1600)

Taylor, Geoffrey, *Some Nineteenth Century Gardeners* (Skeffington 1951)

——, *The Victorian Flower Garden* (Skeffington 1952)

Taylor, Gladys, *Old London Gardens* (Batsford 1953)

Temple, William, *Upon the Garden of Epicurus* (1685; in *Miscellanea Part II*, London 1690)

Thacker, Christopher, *The History of Gardens* (Croom Helm 1979)

Thomas, Keith V., *Religion and the Decline in Magic* (Weidenfeld & Nicolson 1971)

Thompson, E.P., *The Making of the English Working Class* (Penguin 1968)

——, *Whigs and Hunters* (Allen Lane 1975)

——, *William Morris: Romantic to Revolutionary* (Merlin 1977)

Thompson, Flora, *Lark Rise to Candleford* (Oxford University Press 1945)

Tipping, H. Avray, *English Gardens* (Country Life 1925)

Todd, Nigel, *Roses and Revolutionists* (People's Publications 1986)

Tomei, Paolo Emilio and del Prete, Carlo, 'The Botanical Garden of the University of Pisa', *The Herbarist*, vol. 49 (1983)

299

Trautmann, Joanne, *The Jessamy Brides: The Friendship of Virginia Woolf and V. Sackville-West* (Pennsylvania State University 1973)

Turner, James, 'Ralph Austen, an Oxford Horticulturalist of the Seventeenth Century', *Garden History*, vol. 6, no. 2 (1978)

Turner, T. H. D., 'John Claudius Loudon and the Inception of the Public Park', *Landscape Design* (November 1982)

Turrill, W. B., *The Royal Botanic Gardens, Kew* (Herbert Jenkins 1959)

——, *Joseph Dalton Hooker* (Nelson 1963)

Tusser, Thomas, *A Hundreth Good Pointes of Husbandrie* (printed by R. Tottel, London 1557)

——, *Five Hundreth Points of Good Husbandry* (printed by Richard Tottill, London 1573)

Tweedie, Mrs Alec, *Hyde Park, Its History and Romance* (Eveleigh Nash 1908)

Upton, Audrey J. and Thoday, Peter R., *A Bibliography of Horticulture and Out-Door Amenities for the Handicapped and Disadvantaged* (Department of Horticulture, University of Bath 1980)

Voltaire, *Candide* (1758; Penguin edn 1947)

Ward, F. Kingdon, *The Romance of Plant Hunting* (Edward Arnold 1924)

Waters, Michael, *The Garden in Victorian Literature* (Scolar Press 1988)

Watson, Forbes, *Flowers and Gardens* (London 1872)

Wells, H. G., *Short History of the World* (Cassell & Co. 1922; Penguin edn 1970)

Whately, Thomas, *Observations on Modern Gardening* (T. Payne, London 1770)

White, Gilbert, *The Natural History of Selbourne* (B. White & Son, London 1789; Penguin edn 1977)

Whitaker, Ben and Browne, Kenneth, *Parks for People* (Winchester Press 1971)

White, John Talbot, *Country London* (Routledge & Kegan Paul 1984)

Williams, Raymond, *The Country and the City* (Chatto & Windus 1973)

——, *Culture and Society* (Penguin 1961)

Wilson, Ernest H., *China, Mother of Gardens* (The Stratford Company, Boston 1929)

Wollstonecraft, Mary, *Vindication of the Rights of Woman* (London 1792; Penguin edn 1975)

Woodbridge, Kenneth, 'Henry Hoare's Paradise', *The Art Bulletin*, vol. XLVII (1965)

Woods, May and Warren, Arete Swartz, *Glass Houses* (Rizzoli 1988)

Wright, Richardson, *The Story of Gardening* (George Routledge 1934)

Wroth, Warwick, *The London Pleasure Gardens of the Eighteenth Century* (Macmillan 1896)

Acknowledgements

The Bodleian Library, Oxford

Douce Prints a.24 *Britannia Illustrata* 1709. Badminton drawn by Leonard Knyff and engraved by Joannes Kip.

N.2288 b.6 *The Illustrated London News* 21 Dec 1850. Page 473 Top 'Frozen Out Gardeners' drawn by Foster.

N.2288 b.6 *The Illustrated London News* 17 Nov 1849. Page 328 'The Gigantic Water-Lily'.

Vet. A2. c8 *Theatrum Botanicum, The Theater of Plantes* by John Parkinson 1640. 'The Title Page'.

Antiq. Ce. 1629.1 *Paradisi in Sole, Paradisus Terrestris* by John Parkinson 1629. 'Illustrated Title Page'.

Royal Botanic Gardens, Kew

Antilles Cotton, water colour attributed to Margaret Meen.

The Rhododendrons of Sikkim Himalaya by Joseph Hooker, 1849. Rhodo-dendron edgeworthii: lithograph by W.H. Fitch from a drawing by Joseph Hooker.

The *Illustrated London News*, August 1859. Engraving of the Palm House, Kew Gardens.

Photograph of Sir Joseph and Lady Hooker, 30 June 1907.

Female Gardeners at Kew Gardens in 1898.

National Portrait Gallery, London

John Clare by William Hilton, 1820.

Lancelot 'Capability' Brown by Nathaniel Dance, *c.*1770.

Joseph Banks by Joshua Reynolds, 1772–3.

Gertrude Jekyll by William Nicholson, 1920.

William Morris photographed by Abel Lewis, 1880.

The Royal Horticultural Society, London

Philips Park, Manchester, 1913.

Transactions of the Horticultural Society, Vol. VII, 1830. Flowering Currant drawn by Augusta Withers.

A Curious Herbal by Elizabeth Blackwell, 1737. Dandelion engraved by Elizabeth Blackwell.

Carpet Bedding at Kew Gardens, 1870.

ACKNOWLEDGEMENTS

Institute of Agricultural History and Museum of English Rural Life, University of Reading
Lawn Mowers at Balmoral, from Shanks's catalogue for 1871.

Victoria & Albert Museum, London
E3947–1900 Crystal Palace, Sydenham: General View of Fountains and Grounds. Lithograph of 1854.

The Mansell Collection Limited, London
William Cobbett, engraving by F. Bartolozzi after J.R. Smith.

The William Morris Gallery, Walthamstow, London
Edward Burne-Jones: Frontispiece drawing for the first edition of William Morris's *A Dream of John Ball*, 1888.

Devonshire Collection, Chatsworth
Gardeners in front of the Lily House, Chatsworth. Reproduced by permission of the Chatsworth Settlement Trustees.

The Medici Society Limited, London
Eleanour Sinclair Rohde (1881–1950).

British Library, London
MS 20698 f17 Two Ladies Gardening, 1475.

Steve Bell
1789 IF... Cartoon, 3 March 1988.

Index

Note: Illustrations are given *italic* page numbers. Only those plants with illustrations or significant references are listed, and modern authors cited are not included. The chapter headings are not indexed.

Aalsmeer flower market 3
accommodation for gardeners 48–9
Adam 25–6, 189
Addison, Joseph 218
Adelard of Bath 64
Africa: exploration of 94
agriculture 26, 172; and garden cities 283, 285; improvements in 40; women in 188, 191
Allotment Act (1908) 269
allotments 269–71; in Birmingham *270*; as compensation for emparking 37; as cooperative activity 269; development 269–71; as form of escape 9; and lead pollution 278; statistics 271; value in wartime 271, 285; women's work in 202
Allotments Act (1950) 269
Alton Towers 195
Amateur Gardening 219
America: cactus *76*; Indians 58; plants from 95, 170, 173; United States of 55, 56, *see also* Virginia
Amherst, Alicia 170, 175
Amherst, Lady 201
Anatomy Act (1832) 137
anemone japonica 99, 100
animals, in landscaped gardens 36, 40
Anne, Queen of England 31
Arabic language: origin of plant names 256

Arabs: botanical theory 73; influence on English gardening 64–5, 172; medieval gardens 63–4
Arts and Crafts Movement 228
Assyria 27
astrology in botany 247–8
auriculas 52, 53
Austen, Jane 201
Austen, Ralph 19–20, 243–6, *244*; cooperation between neighbours 269
Australia: Aborigines 26, 86, 90, 139, 259; Aborigines collecting food 273; Botany Bay 86; Cook's voyage to 82–6; discovery 86; kangaroos as lawn-mowers 220; no early gardens in 188; settlement of 86– 90; sheep introduced into 81; Walbiri tribe 259
Aztecs 3, 67–78, *68, 69*; botanic gardens 70–3; commoners' gardens 74–5; concept of heaven 27; dahlia 75, 77, *292*; description of plants 253; royal gardens 69–70, 73; Texcotzingo gardens 28, 49–50, *see also* Mexico

Babylon: Hanging Gardens of 24, 28
Bacon, Francis 243, 245, 248
Badminton, Glos 32–3, *33*
Baghdad 63
Bagnigge Wells gardens 145
Balmoral Castle: lawn-mowers at 220, *221*
banana: grown under glass 181–2
Banister, Rev John 255
Banks, Joseph 80–1, *91*, 256; 'banksia' species 255; with Cook to Australia 3, 82–6, 90–2; and creation of

British Empire 94–5; division of labour between sexes 192; early knowledge 241; and Kew Gardens 93–5; President of The Royal Society 92–3; proposes cinchona transfer 119; and settlement of Australia 86–90
banksia species 87, *88*, 255–6
Bateson, William 251
Battersea Park: garden for disabled 230
Beaulieu Abbey, Hants 50
bedding-out system: attacked by Robinson 223; in cottage gardens 226; decline 186, 216; development *171*, 172–3; in Hyde Park 223, 226; origins 170–2; Paxton's 185–6; and pollution 176, 185–6; in Victoria Park 162–3
Bhutan 116–17
Bicton, Devon: arboretum 46
Bilton Grange, Rugby 218
Birkenhead Park 151
Birmingham: allotments *270*
Birmingham, Botanical Gardens 279, 155–7, *156*; garden for disabled 231
Black Act (1723) 34–5
Blackwell, Elizabeth *200*
Blatchford, Robert 283
Blenheim Palace 44
Bligh, Captain 89
Blind Gardeners: Advisory Committee for 233
Boccaccio: *Decameron* 10
books: on gardening 258–9 for disabled 230–1; for women 191 women as illustrators 196–8
botanic gardens 63, 93; Aztec 70–3; Calcutta 106, 107, *107*; in English cities 156; Loudon's design for 147, *147*; Pisa 71, *72*; Rio de Janeiro 107, *108*; style of 122; world-wide 93, 112, *see also* Chelsea Physic Garden; Kew
botanical theory: Arabist 73; Hellenic 73–4
botanists *see* plant collectors
botany: and colonialism 93–5; development of 236–7; economic 3, 101–3, 112, 121–2, 291; and medicine 236–7
bothy system of accommodation 48–9
Boughton, Northants 33
Bounty: HMS 87, 89, *90*
Brailsford, Mary Ann 201

Bramley, Matthew (Bramley apple) 201
Brazil 84; rubber from 120, 121; tea introduced 107
'Bread and Roses' slogan 21
breadfruit 87, *89*
Bridgeman, Charles 39
broadcasting: women in 202–3
Brown, Lancelot ('Capability') 24, 40, 43–4, *43*; redesigned Kew 122; removal of villages 36
Budding, Edwin Beard 220
Buddle, Rev Adam (buddleia) 255
Bugg, Mistress: of Battersea 199
Bunhill Fields cemetery 132–3
Bunyan, John 20; and ownership of land 265
Burial Ground Act (1884) 139
Burton, Decimus 179, 181
Butler, Eleanor 3, 10–12

cacao 75
cactus *74*, *76*, 77, 78
Calcutta: botanic gardens 93, 106, 107, *107*, 115
Camerarius, Rudolf Jakob 249
Camley Street Natural Park, London 279
Canons Park, Middx 46
carnations 52, *276*
Caroline, wife of George II 31, 41–2, 165
carpet bedding *see* bedding-out system
castor oil plant 249, *250*
Catherine II, Empress of Russia 93
Caversham estate 34
cemeteries 3, 130–40, 224, 281–2; Abney Park, Stoke Newington 134; Constantinople 136–7, *136*; early 132–3; Glasgow 136; Highgate 136; Kensal Green 134, 137, 138, *138*; Liverpool *133*; Loudon's campaign for 134–7, 138–9; ownership of 139–40; pauper burial grounds 137–8; Père Lachaise, Paris 134, *134*; preservation of 139–40; Southampton 135; used as public parks 8, 281–2
cemetery companies 137–40, 133
charities for gardeners 48
Charles I, King of England 31, 247
Charles II, King of England 10
Charterhouse monastery 31
Chartism: land colonies 285

Chartist demonstrations: in Hyde Park 165–6; Kensal Green cemetery 138; in Victoria Park 163
Chatsworth, Derbys 36–7, 44, *45*, 46; bedding-out schemes 185–6; Great Conservatory 179–81, *181*; women employed at 199
Chaucer, Geoffrey 61
Chelsea Physic Garden 47, 55, *238*; botanical medicine 237–8
China: Chinese people 100–1; economic exploitation of 97–9, 109; gardening tradition 9; hybridisation in 251; Kubla Khan's gardens 24, 28–9; plant collecting in 94; Robert Fortune's plant collecting in 96–109; roses from 251; tea from 93; Wu Ti's royal park 29
Chippenham, Cambs 35–6
cinchona (quinine) *118*; transfer 117–20
cities: botanic gardens in 156; contrasted with country 8–9, 280; development of public gardens 173; gardens in 4, 62–4, 280; need for open spaces 130–1, 144, 148
Civil War: and development of medicine 241–3; gardening during 18–20
Clare, John 1, *2*
class distinction and flowers 257
class factor in public parks 150, 152, 154, 155, 156–7, 160–1, 165–6
Clean Air Acts (1956 and 1968) 278
Clousden Hill colony, Newcastle 285–6
Coats, Alice 198, 201
Cobbett, William 14–15, *15*, 122, 273–4, 276; gardening for health 17; herbaceous borders 217
Cobham, Viscount (of Stowe) 34–5
Collier, Mary 42
Colombia 3
colonialism 3, 55–8; Banks and 80, 86–7; and botany 93–5, 109; exploitation of raw materials 121, 140–1; trade and garden style 122
Colonna, Fabio 249
Commons Preservation Society 139
Compton, Henry, Bishop of London 255
conservation: bulbs from the wild 280
Constantinople: Topkapi Palace 66
Cook, Captain James 82–6
Cookson, Mrs James 198

cooperation among gardeners 268–9
Corn Law (1814) 92–3
Cortés, Hernando 67, 70
costs of private gardening 219–20
cottage gardens 52, *214*, 215–16; Gertrude Jekyll inspired by 225–6; influence on morality 16; Mexican plants in 77–8
cotton 55, *56*
Cottrell-Dormer, Charles 37
Cowley, Abraham 7, 8
Crabbe, George 42
Cran, Marion 203
Cromwell, Oliver 19, 242
Cromwell, Thomas 31
Crusades: influence on gardening 65
Crystal Palace: in Hyde Park 52, 175, 182–4, *184*; moved to Sydenham 179
Cuba: gardening in schools 272
Culpeper Community Garden 277
Culpeper, Nicholas 239, 241, 246–9, *247*
Cuper's Gardens, London 146
currant, flowering *197*
Curtiss, Samuel 160, 161
cypress: 'funereal' 104–5, *104*

dahlia 75, 77, *292*
Damer, Joseph, Earl of Dorchester 36
dandelion *200*
Daniel, Henry 63
Darwin, Charles 127–9, 257
David, Father Armand (clematis armandii) 255
de Morley, Daniel 64
Dee, John 248
deer parks 28–9, 33
Defoe, Daniel 215
Delaney, Mary 197
Dell, William 272
Derby Arboretum 148–50, *148, 149*, 151; pollution 175
Derbyshire: pansies raised in 52
Devonshire, William: 4th Duke of 36; 6th Duke of 102, 179, 185–6
Diaz del Castillo, Bernal 67, 68, 69
Dickens, Charles: gardening as means of reform 16–17; gardening in prison 13
Diggers, the 18, 32
digitalis (foxglove) 240, *240*
disabled: gardening and the 230–4, *231, 232*

Disabled Living Foundation 230
disease: in cities 131–2, 158; in
    Colombian flower industry 3
Disraeli, Benjamin 271
Domesday Book 29, 215
dovecotes 263
Drayton Green 195, *195*, 220
Drayton, Michael 263–4
Duck, Stephen 40–2
Durham: pinks raised in 52
Dutch East India Company 120

East India Company: and tea transfer
    93; trade with China 97, 101, 251
ecology: growth of 279
economic botany 3, 101–3, 112, 291;
    role of Kew in 121–2
Eden: Garden of 25–7, *25*, *61*, 188–9,
    268
Edensor, Derbys 36
Edgeworth, Maria 201
Edinburgh: public parks 151, 152;
    Royal Botanic Garden 123, 183,
    198
education 5, 247, 256–60; gardening
    in schools 260–1; horticultural
    colleges 203–4, 209; Joseph Hooker
    on 129
Edward, Thomas 257
Egypt: royal gardens in 27, *27*
Eleanor of Castile, wife of Edward I
    64–5
Eliot, George: *Silas Marner* 268
Ellis, John 82–3
Elvaston Castle, Derbys 46
Ely, Bishops of 63
Ely monastery 59
enclosure 1, 32–4; Black Act (1723)
    34–5; of common land 24;
    emparking 35–8; of fens 80–1; for
    gardens 29; opposition to 31–2, 38;
    royal 29–31
Enclosure Act (1845) 269
Endeavour: HMS 82, 83
Engels, Frederick 131–2, 137–8;
    gardens in cities 282; pollution 174
Epping Forest 288
Ermenonville, France 10
Eve 188–9
Evelyn, John 133, 236, 243; gardens
    for London 173, 280–1
eviction 5, 24, 34, 35–7
evolution: theory of 128–9
Ewing, Juliana Horatia 201

explorers *see* plant collectors
Eythrope, Bucks 78

Fairchild, Thomas 281; hybridisation
    251
Fairfax, General Thomas 18, 19
farming *see* agriculture
Farr, William 158
fertilisers 140–1; bone manure 140;
    guano 141, *142*
Fiennes, Celia 194, 249, 275–6
First World War: allotments in 271;
    prisoners' gardens in 13
Fitzherbert, Anthony 189–90
FitzStephen, William 62
Flemish refugees from Netherlands
    65
florists' clubs 52
flowers: exports from Colombia 3;
    florists' 257; introduced by refugees
    and crusaders 65; in medieval
    gardens 59–61; raised by factory
    workers 52–3, 273
Fonthill Abbey 47
Forrest, George (pieris forrestii) 255
Fortune, Robert 96–109; brings tea
    from China 97, 101, 103, 106–9;
    life of 99–101; plant hunting in
    China 3, 100–1, 103–6, 103
foxglove (*digitalis*) 240
France: early gardening in 64; enclo-
    sure in 37, *see also* Paris;
    Montpellier; Ermenonville;
    Versailles
French Revolution 92
fruit trees: Ralph Austen's scheme
    243, *244*, 245
Fuchs, Leonhart 246
Fulke, William 247–8

Galen (Claudius Galenus) Greek
    physician 74–5
Galton, Francis 129
garden: origins of word 1
garden cemetery movement 132–4
garden cities 280–5; Howard's plans
    for *284*; Letchworth 283
Gardener, Jon 60
Gardeners' Benevolent Institution 48
gardening: academic study of 5, 272–3;
    combination of use and beauty
    275–7; as expression of power 263;
    meaning of 8–10, 292; work and
    leisure 273–4

gardening style: Dutch 249; effect of plant collecting on 94–5; French 94, 248; Kew gardens and 122; Manchester public parks 153; modern 214, 218, 228–30; picturesque 12; Vita Sackville-West 208, *see also* bedding-out system; cottage gardens; landscape gardens; 'natural' gardening

gardens: for the disabled 230–4, *231, 232*; earliest 188; functions of 7–8; myth and reality 24; Tudor *66, 67, see also* botanic gardens

Gavin, Hector 158

Gent, E.W. 264

George III, King of England 122

Gerard, John: *Herbal* 199, 241, *241*

Germany: botany in 246, 249

Gilbert, William 238

Gilpin, William 12

Girardin, Marquis de 10

Glasgow: pinks raised in 52

glass: conditions of manufacture 183–4; development of 173, 178, 163; greenhouses 178–9, *181*; Wardian case 176–9, *177*

Goldsmith, Oliver: 'The Deserted Village' 36, 38–9

golf courses 219

Googe, Barnabe 190–1

graffiti as pollution in public parks 279

Gravetye Manor, Sussex 222, *222*, 223

Great Exhibition (1851) 183

Greater London Council 282

Greek: in plant names 256

Greeks: botanical theory 73–4; as gardeners 49, 128, 253

green belts 148; Loudon's plans for 227, 282

greenhouses 178–9

Greenwich park 29

Gresham College 247, 252

Grew, Nehemiah 249

guano 141, *142*

Gutteridge, Joseph 256–7

ha-ha 34, 39–40, *39*

Hakluyt, Richard 239

Hampstead Heath: attempts to enclose 32, 148, 139

Hampton Court 30, 50, 174; weeding women 194

Harcourt, Lord 36

Hardy, Thomas: *Return of the Native* 272

Hartlib, Samuel 92, 244, 252

Harvey, William 247

health: gardening for 17; public 131, 148, 150, 158

hedges for enclosure 38

Henry I, King of England 29

Henry II, King of England 29

Henry VII, King of England 30

Henry VIII, King of England 30–1, 164

herb women 80, 239–41

herbaceous borders 216–17, *217*

herbals 241–2

Herbert, William 251

Hereman, Samuel 178–9, *180*

hermits in landscaped gardens 40

Hernandez, Francisco 73

Hibberd, Shirley: editor *Amateur Gardening* 219; herbaceous borders 216–17; on hybridisation 251

Hildegard, Abbess of Bingen 199

Hill, Octavia 139, 148

Himalayas: Hooker's expedition to 114–17

Hindu concept of heaven 27

Hobson, Paul 20

Holborn, London: gardens in 62–3

Holland: Flemish refugees from 65; Leyden University Botanic Garden 126, 241; school gardens 261

Hooker, Joseph 113–14, *126*; and Charles Darwin 127–9; Director of Kew 3, 113, 127; expedition to Himalayas 114–17; and public access to Kew 124

Hooker, William 119; Director of Kew 111–12; opens Kew to public 123; Palm House at Kew 181; use of Wardian case 178

Horner, Francis 273

horse and ponies used for lawn-mowing 46, 220, 221

horticultural colleges 203–4, 209

horticultural societies 230

Horticultural Society: Chiswick 2

Horticultural Therapy 231

hothouses *see* glass, greenhouses

Houghton Hall, Norfolk 36

hours of work 47, 49

housing: for gardeners 48–9; urban 131–2, 283

Howard, Ebenezer: and garden cities 283, *284*

Huaxtepec: Aztec royal garden 69–70, 73
Huguenots 65
Hunt, James Leigh 13–14
Huxley, T.H. 128
Hyams, Edward 283
hybridisation 251–2; attacked 250–1
Hyde Park 164–8, 223, 226; enclosure of 31; the Serpentine 165, 168
Hyll, Thomas 247, 258, 259
hypericum perforatum: importance of accurate classification 254

Ibn Bassal 63–4
Ibn Wafid 63
Impressionism 227
Incas: gardens 28
India: cinchona transfer to 119–20; development of tea industry 93, 106–9; plant collecting in 94, 115
Indian Mutiny (1857) 119
Industrial Revolution 3–4
Iran see Persia
Ireland: gardeners from 3
Irnham Hall, Lincs: strike 46
irrigation of hanging gardens 28
Islam: paradise in 26
Islington: Culpeper Community Garden 277; Spa gardens 145
Iztapalapan: Aztec gardens 71

James I, King of England 32, 164
Japan: plant collecting in 98
Java 259; cinchona in 120
Jekyll, Gertrude 52, 187; influence on modern gardening 214, 224–6, 225; influence on Vita Sackville-West 208
Jews: and spread of horticultural knowledge 64–5
Jiardinier François ... : Le 191
Johnson, George 16
Josselyn, John 56
Juvenal 8

Kalm, Peter 237
Kamel, Georg Joseph (camellia) 255
Kedleston, Derbys 36
Keiga, Kawaha 196
Keller, Helen 234
Kensal Green Cemetery 133–4, 137, 281–2, 281
Kent, William 24, 41–2; at Rousham 39; designed Kew 122

Kerr, William 94, 255
Kett, Robert: Rebellion 32
Kew, Royal Botanic Gardens 125; heating of glasshouses 179–80; as microcosm of politics 290–1; Museum of Economic Botany 112; Palm House 181; public access to 122–7, 129; regulations 124–7; role in economy of Empire 121–2, 129; suffragettes attack 209–12; under Banks 93–5; under Joseph Hooker 127; under William Hooker 111–12, 112; women gardeners at 203, 204; women illustrators for 197–8
Knight, Richard Payne 12
Knole, Kent 206
knot gardens 172, 172
Kropotkin, Prince Peter 285
Kubla Khan 24, 28–9

labour: casual 40, 42, 50; conditions of employment 11, 47–9; division of 2–3, 26, 41; and alienation 51–3; between sexes 192–4, Table 10.1; mental and manual 24, 207–8, 272–3; workers and owners 24 in emparking 37; employment statistics 50–1; and glass manufacture 183–4; on landscaped estates 40, 44–7; seasonal 46–7, 47; significance of in garden history 291
Labouring Poor: 1843 Report of Parliamentary Committee on 270, 271
Lambert, General John 13, 242
Lambert, Rev Brook 159–60
Lancashire: weavers as horticulturalists 52, 257
land nationalisation: proposed by miners 269
land ownership: as barrier to utopia 263–5; common 265–8, 269
landscape gardens: 18th-century 5, 24, 38–40, 95; 'Capability' Brown and 43–4; and colonialism 55, 94–5; design of 36–7; golf courses 219
language: development of scientific 252
Latin: in plant classification 252–3; in plant names 256
Lawes, John Bennet 141
lawns and lawn-mowing 17, 17, 46, 220–1, 221
Lawrence, D.H. 257–8

Lawson, William 191, 192, 274, *275*
Le Notre, André 37, 94
Leasowes, The: becomes golf course 219
Ledger, Charles 120
Lee, James 199
Leeds Botanical Gardens 151
Levellers, the 18
Liebig, Baron 140–1
Lincoln, Earl of 62
Linnaeus, Carl: and plant classification 250, 253–5; use of Latin 252
literacy and gardening expertise 259
Liverpool garden cemetery 133, *133*
Llangollen, Ladies of 3, 10–12
Locke, John 252
Loddiges' Botanical Nursery Garden: Hackney 147
Loddiges, George 178
London 157–8; cemeteries 132–3; gardens in 62, 280, 288–9; market gardens in 199; medieval gardens in 62–3; pleasure gardens in 62, 145–6; pollution 173–4, 174–6, 177–8, 278; public squares 146, 147
London Wildlife Trust 279
lotus: sacred 253, *254*
Loudon, Jane 187, *205*, 219, 220; writer on gardening 204–5, *206*
Loudon, John Claudius 2–3, *135*, 204–5, 256; calls for better pay 48; campaigns for public gardens 146–8, 281; on 'Capability' Brown 43–4; on Chatsworth conservatory 180; on cottage gardens 215; and Derby Arboretum 148–50; on education for gardeners 259, 276; educational experiment 276; and garden cemeteries 134–7, 138–9; invented curved sash bar 182; plans for Hyde Park 165; on pollution 174, 175; on prison gardens 13, 15–16; use and beauty of farming 275
Luxborough, Lady 51
Luxemburg, Rosa 13
Lyttleton, Lord 34

Macclary, John 39
Macclesfield public park 151
Mack, Maynard 8
Madrid: Royal Gardens 75, 77
magazines: no women editors 202
Magnus, Albertus 128

Major, Joshua: designer of Manchester parks 153
malaria 117–19
Malaya: rubber plantations 121
Manchester: gooseberries raised in 52; housing conditions 131; pollution 174, 176, 278–9; public parks 48, 131, 152–5, *153*, *154*
manual labour 272
Marco Polo 28–9
market gardens: Huguenot 65; in London 62, 199
Markham, Gervase 192, 274
Marvell, Andrew 18–19, 20
Marx, Karl 272; gardens in cities 282; and Hyde Park 165–6; and theory of evolution 128–9
medical practitioners 238–41; herb women 80, 239–41
medicinal gardening 117–18, 236; Aztec 70–1; in monasteries 58, 60–1
medicine: botany and 236–7; Culpeper's influence on 248
medieval gardening 58–61, 189–90; botany and medicine 236; herbaceous borders 217; inspiration for pre-Raphaelites 228
medieval hunting parks 29
Meen, Margaret 196–7
Mendel, Gregor 251
mentally handicapped: gardening for 231–2
Merlin's Cave, Richmond 41–2, *41*
Merryweather, Henry 201
Mexico: importance in garden history 291; plants from 75–8, 170, *see also* Aztecs
Milton Abbas, Dorset 36
Milton, John 218; *Paradise Lost* 188–9
Mlokosewitch: Polish botanical explorer 16
modern gardening: statistics of 228–30
Monardes, Nicolas 71
monasteries: casual labour in 50; pleasure gardens in 58–61
Montezuma: Aztec emperor 70, 75
Montpellier medical school: France 64
morality: gardening and 16–17
More, Thomas: *Utopia* 264–5
Morison, Robert 248
Morris, William 163, *167*, *287*; on bedding- out 170; *Dream of John Ball 25*; and Gertrude Jekyll 224–5; ideas of utopia 267, 286–9;

influence on Clousden Hill 285, 286; on labour 45; *News from Nowhere* 286–8; on pollution 174
Munich 'Englischer Garten' 150
municipal corporations: cemeteries 139–40; gardens for disabled 230; increased spending 172; and public parks 149, 150
Municipal Reform Act (1835) 150, 158
Munn, Rev H.: and allotments 269
Munstead Wood, Surrey 52, *217*
Murray, Andrew 77

National Society of Allotment and Leisure Gardeners 271
National Union of Horticultural Workers 49
National Union of Public Employees 50
'natural' gardening 218–20; Robinson's style of 221–4
Neckham, Alexander: Abbot of Cirencester 60, 62
Nelson, David 87, 89
Nepal 116
Nesfield, William Andrews 171–2
Netherlands *see* Holland
New Forest 29
New Guinea 188
New Zealand 85–6, 254; Maoris 85–6, *85*
Newcastle upon Tyne: Clousden Hill colony 285–6
Newton, Isaac 248
Nicolson, Sir Harold 207–8
Nonsuch Palace *30*, 31
Normans: influence of 3, 61
North, Marianne 198
Northumberland: pinks raised in 52
Northwood Common, south London 32
Norwich: carnations raised in 52; medicinal herb garden 64
Nunappleton House 18, *18*, 19, 20
Nuneham Courtenay, Oxon 36

oaks for ships' timbers 243
Offer, George 159
opium trade 97
Opium War 93, 97
Orta, Garcia de 73, 74
Oxford University 243

Padua 236, 241
Pain's Hill, Surrey 40

Paisley: pinks raised in 52, 174, 227
Pancras Wells gardens, London 146
Pankhurst, Adela 211
Pankhurst, Christabel 209
Pankhurst, Sylvia 210–11
Paradise 26–7, 263–5, *266*
Paradise Lost (Milton) 188–9
Paris: Jardin Royal des Plantes Médicinales 236, 238; Père Lachaise cemetery 134, *134*
Parish, Robert 199
Parkinson, John 173, 241, 275; *Paradisi in Sole* 266
Paxton, Joseph 111; at Chatsworth 36, 179; and bedding-out schemes 185–6; designs Crystal Palace 51–2, 182; and development of glass 178, 179–84, *180*
Pennethorne, James: designer of Victoria Park 160–1
Penney, Thomas 245
Pepys, Samuel 5
Persia 67
Peru: guano from 141; Inca gardens 28
Peruvian bark *see* cinchona
pesticides 278
petal: origin of word 249–50
Pettigrew, W.W. 176
Petworth: bananas grown under glass 181–2
Philips, Mark 152
Phillip, Captain Arthur 86
picturesque style of gardening 12
Piercy, Marge 276–7
pinks 52, *276*
Pisa: botanic garden 71, *72*, 237
plane trees: resistance to pollution 175
plant classification 253–5
plant collectors 29, 55, 93–5, 98, 290, 291; and plant names 255–6; Veitch & Sons 173, *see also* Joseph Banks; Joseph Hooker; Robert Fortune
plant names: origin of 255–6
Plantin, Christophe 196
plants: availability of 219; exchanged between neighbours 268–9; introduced 65, 94–5
Plas Newydd 11–12
pleasure gardens: in London 62, 145–6; medieval 59–60

political demonstrations: in parks
  163–4, 165–7
politics: combined with gardening
  18–22; of gardening 2, 5–6, 236,
  290–1; incompatible with gardens 9
pollution: by lead 278; by pesticides
  278; effect on urban gardening 4,
  173–6, 278–80, *278*; in London
  158, 174–5, 184; in public parks
  278–9
Polo, Marco 28–9
polyanthus: development of 257
Ponsonby, Sarah 3, 10–12
Poole, Dorset: Victoria School garden
  for disabled 230
Poor Law Commission (1834) 271
Pope, Alexander 20
Prescott, William 68, 69, 71, 73, 75
Price, Uvedale 12
prison: gardening in 13–16
privet: resistance to pollution 175
public access: to Birmingham
  Botanical Gardens 156–7; to Derby
  Arboretum 149; to estates 33–4; to
  Kew Gardens 122–7; to parks
  150–1, 142–3
public health: and need for public
  parks 131, 148, 158
Public Health Act (1848) 150
public parks and gardens 3, 7–8, 131;
  Birmingham Botanical Gardens
  155–7; Derby Arboretum 148–50;
  development of 142–3, 144–68; and
  the disabled 233; economic arguments for 151–2; Hyde Park 164–8;
  Loudon's campaigns for 142–3,
  146–8; Manchester and Salford
  152–5, *153*, *154*; medieval 62;
  moral rationale for 150–1; regulations 154–5; Victoria Park 157–64,
  see also bedding-out system
Pückler-Muskau, Prince 34
puritanism: and gardening 19–20
Puritans: as horticulturalists 242–6

quinine *see* cinchona
Quintilian, Marcus Fabius 8

racism: in Australia 90; of colonialism
  3, 58; Hooker's 116–17; plant
  collectors and 85–6, 100–1, 109
railways 174
Ranelagh Gardens, Chelsea 145–6
Ray, John: and plant sexuality 249, 250

Reading Gaol garden 15–16
Regent's Park, London 147, 151, 222
religion: compared with gardening
  19–20; gardening utopias in 263
Repton, Humphrey 24
Revesby Abbey, Lincs 80–1, *81*
rhododendrons 113–14, *113*; resistance to pollution 175, 176
Richard III (as Duke of Gloucester) 63
Richmond Park 31
Rio de Janeiro 84; botanic gardens
  107, *108*
Robinson, William 3, 144, 170, 226,
  253; influence on modern
  gardening 214, 218, 221–4; influence on Vita Sackville-West 208
Rohde, Eleanour Sinclair 4–5, *4*,
  258–9; on 'Capability' Brown 43;
  on cottage gardens 215–16
Rollisson, William: hybridisation 251
Rome: influence of 3; Nero's gardens
  29
roses: hybridisation 251
Rousham, Oxon 37, 39, 44
Rousseau, Jean-Jacques 10
royal gardens 27–9; Aztec 69–70
Royal Horticultural Society: few
  women in 202; garden for disabled
  230; and hybridisation 251; and
  Kew 112; and prisoners in Germany
  13; and Robert Fortune 98, 100,
  101, 102
royal hunting parks 28–9
Royal National Institute for the Blind
  233–4
royal parks: Hyde Park 164
Royal Society, The 92–3, 252
Royal Society for Nature Conservation
  234
rubber: transfer 120–1
Ruskin, John: gardens in cities 282;
  and Gertrude Jekyll 224, 227; influence on modern gardening 227–8;
  on plant sexuality 250, 253
Russell, Edward: Earl of Orford 35–6
Russia (USSR) 57, 93, 230

Sackville-West, Vita 18, 187–8, *207*,
  259–60; at Sissinghurst 206–9;
  gardening and politics 20–1
Sadler's Wells gardens 145
Sahugun, Bernardino de 73
St Gall monastery, Switzerland 60
St George's Hill, Surrey 32

St Paul's Cathedral 59
Salford, Peel Park *51*, 153, 155
Salter, Alfred: campaigns for gardens in cities 280
Schinz, Salomon 196
schools: gardening in 260–1, 277
scientific independence: myth of 117
Scotland: gardeners from 2
seaside resorts: bedding-out schemes at 186
Second World War: allotments in 271, 285
Sedding, John 228
seeds: collection of 105; development of trade 64, 173; exchanged between neighbours 268–9
Selborne, Hants 195–6
sexism *see* women
sexuality of plants 249–51
Shanghai 98–9
Shanks, Alexander 220
sheep: merino 81
Sheffield: cemetery used as public park 282, *282*; polyanthus raised in 52
sheltered employment: gardening as 232–3
Shenstone, William 12, 219
shepherds in landscaped gardens 36
Sicily: Arab gardens in 61
Siegesbock, Johann 251
Sikkim 115–16
silk: brought from China 102
Sion House 10
Sissinghurst, Kent 206–8
slave labour 107
slave trade 55, 122, 183
smoke *see* pollution
Smoke Nuisance Act (1853) 174
socialism: and gardening 21–2, 282–3
Solander, Dr 82, 84, 91
Soochow, China: 'Garden of the Unsuccessful Politician' 9
South Africa 95, 170
Southampton cemetery 136
Spa Fields Pantheon 146
Spain: Arab gardens in 63–5; *conquistadores* in Mexico 67–9
speakers' corners: in public parks 155
Spitalfields: auriculas and pinks in 52
sports facilities: in public parks 153–4, 157, 161–2, 168
Sri Lanka (Ceylon): Peradeniya Botanic Garden 121, 122
Stearn, William 249, 254

Stepney: gardens in 63
Stockport: pollution 174
Storer, Tom: tulip grower 53
Stourhead, Wilts 45
Stow, John 31
Stowe, Bucks 34–5, *35*, 95
Strawberry Hill 40
strikes: at Irnham 46
Strutt, Joseph 148–9
Studley Women's Horticultural College 204
suburbs: gardens in 218–19; growth of 144
suffragettes: attack on Kew Gardens 209–12; demonstrations 163–4, 166–7
Sunday opening: of public gardens 123
Sunday Trading Act (1855) 165
Suter, Rev 161
Sutton and Sons, Reading 173
Swanley Horticultural College 203–4
Sydenham gardens 185
Syon Park: garden for disabled 230

Tahiti 84–5, 87
T'ao Ch'ien 9
Taverner, John 245
tea: brought from China 97, 101, 103, 106–9; introduced in India 93, 106–9
tea plants *109*
Temple, Sir William 192
Tew Lodge Farm 275, 276
Texcotzingo: Hanging Gardens of 28, 49–50
Theophrastus of Athens 49, 128, 249, 253
therapy: gardening as 231, 234
Thiselton-Dyer, W.T. 111
Thompson, Flora 192–3
Thompson and Morgan, Ipswich 173
Tierra del Fuego 84
Tipping, H. Avray 44
tobacco plant *70*
Tower Hill: market gardens at 62
towns *see* cities
trade unions 49, 50
Tradescant, John (father and son) 57–8, *57*
training: for disabled 233; for women 203–4
transport: of plants and trees for landscaped gardens 44; of plants in Wardian cases 178

trees: planted in landscaped estates 44
Tuggie, Mistress: of Westminster 199
tulips 52, 53; mania 252
Tull, Jethro 40
Turkey: garden cemeteries 136–7, *136*;
    gardening in 65–7; wild bulb
    exports 280
Tusser, Thomas 192, 268
Tyburn Tree, Hyde Park 164–5

United States of America *see* America
use and beauty 275–7
USSR (Russia) 57, 93, 230
Utopia 263–5; William Morris's 286–9

Vauxhall Gardens *145*, 146
Veitch and Sons 46, 173
Versailles, France 37
Victoria Park, London *160*, *162*;
    construction 159–61; demand for
    157–9; horticulture 162–3; public
    demonstrations 163–4; sports in
    161–2; wildlife in 279
villages: lost to emparking 35–7, 38
Virginia, USA 57–8; as Paradise 264
vistas: avenues 32–3; landscaped
    39–40
Voltaire: *Candide* 9–10
Vries, Hugo de 251

wages 2, 11, 48–51; Stephen Duck's 41
Walpole, Horace 40, 122, 165
Walpole, Robert 34, 36
Wang Chin Tsz 9
Ward, Nathaniel Bagshaw 176–7
Wardian case 176–9, *177*
Warley Place, Essex 52
water-lily, gigantic (*victoria regia*) 180,
    182
weavers 52, 227, 257, 273
weeding women 194–6

wells, pleasure gardens around in
    London 62, 145
West Indies 87
Wherwell nunnery, Hants 59
Whig Ascendancy 79–80
White, Gilbert 17, 82, 195–6
Wickham, Henry 120–1
wild gardening *see* 'natural' gardening
wildlife reserves: in London 279
William I, The Conqueror 29
William III, King 173–4
Willisel, Thomas 242–3
Willmott, Ellen 52
Wilson, Sir Spencer Maryon 148
Winstanley, Gerrard 246–7, 249; and
    land ownership 263, 265, 267, 268
witches 239–40, *239*
Withers, Augusta *197*, 198
Woburn, Beds 194
women: in agriculture 42, 188, 191;
    and division of labour 192–4, *194*;
    in early gardening 189–91, *190*; as
    gardeners 4–5, *190*; as illustrators
    196–8; 'invisible' 198–202; knowl-
    edge of plant lore 80, 201–2,
    239–41; lawn 46; as professional
    gardeners 209, 226; and sexism in
    gardening 4–5, 187–8, 202–4, 212;
    wages 51; weeding 194–6; as writers
    187, 199–200, 204–5, 208–9
Women's Farm and Garden
    Association 204
woodlands: in London 288
Woods, Richard 46
Woodstock, Oxon 29, 260
Wordsworth, William 272
work and leisure 273–4
working conditions 11, 47, *47*
Wye College, London University 283

Young, George Frederick 158